THE PHANTOM CISO

Time to step out of the shadow

Mishaal Khan | Hisham Zahid

The Phantom CISO:
Time to step out of the shadow

Copyright © 2023 by Mishaal Khan & Hisham Zahid.
All rights reserved.

ISBN: 979-8-218-19894-7

For more details, visit: https://www.PhantomCISO.com

Chief Editors: Mishaal Khan, Hisham Zahid
Cover Design: Mishaal Khan
Formatting template inspired by "This Book Was Self-Published"

No part of this book and publication may be reproduced, distributed, or transmitted in any form or by any electronic or mechanical means and methods, including information storage and retrieval systems, without the authors' prior written permission. The content of this book is protected under copyright law and may not be distributed in any form or offered as an electronic download without permission from the authors except as noted below.

The information contained in this book is intended for educational purposes only and is not intended as legal, financial, or professional advice. The authors make no representations or warranties of any kind, express or implied, about the completeness, accuracy, reliability, suitability, or availability with respect to the book or the information, products, services, or related graphics contained in the book for any purpose. Therefore, any reliance on such information is strictly at your own risk.

First Published: March 2023

The information in this book is distributed on an "As Is" basis, without warranty. The author has taken great care in preparing this book but assumes no responsibility for errors or omissions. No liability is assumed for incidental or consequential damages in connection with or arising from the use of the information or programs contained herein.

Rather than use a trademark symbol with every occurrence of a trademarked name, this book uses the names only in an editorial fashion and to the benefit of the trademark owner, with no intention of trademark infringement.

The authors have chosen to display the American rule of punctuation inside of quotes.

All technology references in this book were confirmed accurate as of March 2023. Readers may find slight discrepancies within the methods as technology changes.

"My Lord! Increase me in knowledge" [20:114]

ABOUT THE AUTHORS

MISHAAL KHAN

Mishaal is a highly experienced cybersecurity professional with a technical background across multiple technology areas. As an ethical hacker, he gained deep insights into the tactics and techniques used by malicious actors, which has helped him better protect the organizations he works with. He has also honed his skills in implementing various security controls at his startup, where he gained hands-on experience deploying and managing security technologies. With his ability to translate technical jargon into business-relevant needs, and his forthright, results-driven approach, he is committed to acting as a catalyst for change.

His international exposure and diversity of client types have given him a unique perspective on the issues that organizations face, particularly regarding their culture and technology leadership.

HISHAM ZAHID

Hisham's professional background consists of technical and leadership roles within the cybersecurity industry. He launched his career as a proficient network and system administrator, where he gained mastery in implementing different security measures for the organization. Over the years, Hisham has held several positions in engineering, risk management, compliance, and audit, thus developing a comprehensive understanding of security challenges organizations face.

Hisham's passion for creating connections and improving an organization's security posture is evident in his ability to foster robust relationships with stakeholders and provide awareness of security risks. With his vast knowledge and expertise, Hisham is committed to ensuring organizations are well-equipped to navigate the ever-evolving security landscape.

Note: This book is a creative collection of 20 years of experience and advice, written by 2 authors, compiled in 2 years, consisting of 200+ pages, and capable of being consumed in 2 hours. This book is a culmination and collaboration of thoughts and experiences between 2 authors; therefore, the pronouns will interchange between I, us, and we.

CONTENTS

1. INTRODUCTION 1
2. THE BIGGER PICTURE 7
3. ROLE 11
4. RESPONSIBILITIES 19
5. NOT A CISO 39
6. GRC 45
7. POWER 59
8. PATHS 65
9. TYPES 71
10. SOFT SKILLS 79
11. TECHNICAL SKILLS 97
12. ATTITUDE 105
13. HUMAN NETWORK 109
14. PHANTOM CISO 119
15. IMPOSTER SYNDROME 125
16. INSECURITY 135
17. SUPPLY & DEMAND 165
18. COMPENSATION 171
19. SELF PROMOTION 183
20. CAREER PLANNING 191
21. YOU MADE IT 199
22. PREDICTIONS 221
23. CONCLUSION 231

The Phantom CISO manages cybersecurity risk and programs without the official title of a CISO.

Preface

We started this journey by having many long discussions around how to collaborate better within our community to provide people the platform they deserve to express themselves better and progress in the field of cybersecurity. Through multiple online meetings every Sunday between Mishaal Khan, Hisham Zahid, and Salim Scafuto, together we came up with the code name Project Spiderweb. This project was to be a collaboration of like-minded individuals in the field of security that would set up networking and training events. The goal was to provide a launching pad for those who had the skills and passion in their field but lacked the network and social skills to get noticed and avail the opportunities in front of them. Unfortunately, setting up a collaborative in-person group like that during the pandemic years proved challenging.

We saw great potential in people, and their skills, yet noticed a big void in them getting the right opportunities by not meeting the right people. These are individuals in every community that are inspired, interested, and influenced by technology and are looking to be represented, recognized, and appreciated amongst their peers.

As we looked through the notes of our meetings with the various ideas and advice we had compiled, it became clear that this needed to be organized, documented, and shared with others. Mishaal and Hisham took this initiative further and decided to compile a practical book on leadership that focused on overcoming the hurdles in career progression in the complex field of cybersecurity. We had plenty of stories to share and a lot of content to write. This is how this book materialized.

Through collaboration, discovery, and discussion, we addressed the void and coined the term "Phantom CISO." We will dive deep into various topics and perspectives so you can benefit and continue these discussions with your peers or with us. Everything we do is a learning opportunity, and we hope to empower you. Know that you are not alone in building your career and making a safer future.

As cybersecurity professionals, we are the unsung heroes behind the scenes, working diligently to combat cyber threats. We are the cyber heroes in disguise. It's time for the world to know who is behind the mask.

Time to step out of the shadow.

1. INTRODUCTION

The CISO in you

As Simon Sinek famously said, "Start with why."

The "Why" will help motivate you toward your goal.

One of the key questions one should ask themselves when embarking on their higher purpose is "Why?" Unfortunately, we don't learn this concept early in life when we are required to make critical career decisions that begin from high school and influence the subsequent decades of our life. Instead, we accept and explore the career options that our parents, guardians, and friends present to us, such as a doctor or engineer, and we blindly embark on a journey until an exciting role model crosses our path. Sometimes we pick a career to mirror our role model and realize that isn't our reality, so we learn from our mistakes. We continue to operate in trial and error; we fail fast and learn quickly. The authors, us, were explicitly influenced by a culture where education was prominent but thinking outside the box was not. We had to do what was told to us, and there was no other way. Not everyone faces this reality, as there are always exceptions to the rule, but the majority do face this way of life, and for some, there is still some trauma left behind.

On my visit to the university where I applied for early admission, my dad asked me, "Why do you want to attend this university?" I replied, "I will learn more about technology, and their co-op program will give me experience." I loved technology from a young age, so it was natural that my passion was in technology. Regarding the co-op program, there is nothing better than experience coupled with the knowledge from books I already had. The experience would help me think outside the box, and I wouldn't have obtained this experience without pursuing my passion and dreams.

This book is intended to be creative, opinionated, and open-ended, allowing you to think outside the box. It is not meant to be perfect but to be thought-provoking and lead to the path of exploration, leadership, and endless yearning for experience.

The ultimate fact is that we may not know the future of our success, and we were never fully ready when we started our careers. Yet, we still ended up where we are, victorious. So, as you read this book, embrace this quote by Mel Robbins as you pursue your path to becoming a Chief Information Security Officer (CISO):

"Start before you're ready. Don't prepare, begin."

I wish this book had been available when I was starting in my professional field to lay out a growth plan, but I have no regrets. The journey that led me here was fun and full of great learning experiences. The trial and error not only made me emotionally stronger but also wiser and humbler. There is no right or wrong way, no hard and fast rule regarding success. I hope you will take this book as a guide, not an instruction manual, and learn some techniques for being a successful cybersecurity leader.

> **Fun fact:** Steve Katz is widely regarded as the first CISO, appointed by Citicorp in 1994 after cybercriminals hacked them.

Let's segway into our next topic, "Why A CISO."

WHY A CISO

Your Journey

Think about the time, early in your career, when you started making decisions about your future and what you wanted to do. That time could be right now. Ask yourself: Why did you enroll as a Computer Science major in college? Maybe because all your friends were taking it? Did you switch majors after six months? Why did you take your first job? Why did you become a security engineer or a programmer? The answer may be, "I don't know," and that's okay. On the other hand, for some people, the goal was set early in their career, and every job, certification, or project was built upon that goal. However, if you did not have defined goals early on, it's not too late, as many paths lead to becoming a cybersecurity leader.

You should ask yourself, "Why do I want to become a CISO?" Your answer may be "I don't" or "I'm not ready yet." Also consider another scenario where you may not yet know you want to be a CISO. I certainly didn't when I started my cyber journey. It only became apparent halfway through when I realized I was a Phantom CISO.

Whatever your situation, you can learn from the advice and struggles of those who have reached the top of the security leadership ladder and incorporate some of that advice into your journey.

Next Best Thing

If you're anything like me, striving for continuous growth by challenging yourself, this book was made for you. One common trend I've noticed with many individuals in cybersecurity is that they can't stay put. Take my example; when I became comfortable at a particular job, I was already aiming for the next best thing, trying to excel further. As I moved up the ladder with every job, I stopped midway to reassess my situation as I was growing fast, but I didn't know where I was going. So, I have a straightforward question, what does the peak look like? In the cybersecurity field, the role with the highest responsibility is the Chief Information Security Officer or CISO. It can also be the highest-paying one. The more significant reason for becoming a CISO is to be in an influential position and make a meaningful and secure difference. A security analyst or pentester desperately wants to see change and secure systems but seldom has control over what happens after the managers read their reports. A CISO has more decision-making power to see those changes through. The best part of the role is the respect that comes with it. People listen and take action, well, most of the time.

The goal now was a no-brainer. So, I began focusing on getting to that role by filling in the gaps and working my way backward. This started the journey of discovering the gaps and planning the next steps.

Launching Pad

You may think it's a long journey and you missed the train, but you don't need to start from the bottom. When I mentor individuals trying to get into cybersecurity, I tell them to start with where they came from and use that as a launching pad. There's no need to create what others began. There are plenty of skills that are common across professions. Security touches almost every field. If you start in the medical field, go into healthcare security risk assessments; if you are a coder, dive into DevSecOps; if you have an MBA or a project management background, be a security operations manager or a team lead; if you're in sales, go into security product sales. The list goes on. There is a misconception by many that cybersecurity requires technical skills or programming. That is far from the truth. Security professionals come from all backgrounds; we need them in every industry and level.

So, as we wrote this book, we kept the transition neutral. As a result, we all can enter this field from many different professional backgrounds, and we can all aim to be a leader by following the framework we have laid out throughout the chapters of this book.

Who this book is for

This book is for the aspiring cybersecurity leader, an information technology professional, or someone new to cybersecurity. Reading this book should open opportunities and give you the confidence you need to achieve anything with the proper time and guidance. Simply put, it is a collection of advice we wish we had when entering this field decades ago.

There are countless ways to succeed in this field, and this book will outline some of them. In addition, you may have ideas on how to better protect the data, which is our new currency, and the systems that house it. This book is for you if you feel no one is listening or your efforts are falling on deaf ears. The techniques discussed will give you what you need to break through those barriers.

Breaches of our personal lives or the organizations whose security we are entrusted with are inevitable. Time is of the essence, and the adversaries are not waiting for you to be ready. This book will help you climb the corporate ladder faster and help you become more effective in securing your workforce.

As cybercrime continues to rise and companies get hacked, the demand for qualified individuals goes through the roof. There couldn't be a better time to enter this field. This book will help you fine-tune your skills to take advantage of the tremendous opportunities that await you. This book is intended not only for the next aspiring cybersecurity leader but also for current IT and security professionals who wish to realign their skills and priorities for optimal outcomes.

While everyone can benefit from this book in their careers, being a CISO is not for everyone. We all have our passions and areas of interest. It would help if you sacrificed something to get to your goals. It would be best to reach outside of your comfort zone. Being a CISO also means taking risks, taking time away from family, taking on additional stress and responsibility, and being more dynamic in your career. The advice spread across this book will help you in your journey with your professional dealings no matter what destination you set. You will get a better understanding of how security operates across the organization and the struggles of a CISO. If being a CISO is not your goal, I still encourage you to read this book, as you may be closer than you think. You may already be a Phantom CISO.

THE NEED

We all read about the skills gap in cybersecurity. Yes, we know that the demand for skilled professionals far outnumbers the supply. We often hear that the unemployment rate in cybersecurity has been 0% for a while.

While these are exciting statistics, we also don't see the skills gap closing as fast as it should with the tremendous amount of free resources available. Therefore, this book also tries to address the harsh reality of this situation, narrow the gap, and provide actionable steps for those willing to take advantage of this great time to be in security.

Even though we tell everyone that cybersecurity is the responsibility of everyone, the reality is that there is a hierarchy of duties. At the top of that pyramid lies the Chief Information Security Officer, or the CISO.

> **Common CISO pronunciations:** See-Sow, Sisso, or Sai-So

Like the skills gap, the path to becoming a CISO is also not well defined, and people will often fall into imposter syndrome or get lousy career advice. This is where we felt an immediate need for this book to provide an honest perspective of the ground reality. It tackles the challenge of navigating the rough waters of professional career progression in an old-school environment where change is not well embraced.

As you read this book, you will quickly realize that most people will be comfortable in their roles, thinking they have reached their potential. They may be stuck doing mundane tasks that no longer excite them or build stress as time passes. A career change may be around the corner. All they need is a little guidance. On the other hand, your responsibilities may be piling up, and your role may be so fluid that you may already be a CISO and not know it!

A GUIDE

This book is not intended to be a tutorial or a technical reference to the various technologies, roles, frameworks, or architectures mentioned throughout this book. It is meant to guide anyone, including mentors, trying to progress in this field, and present the most optimal routes to a successful security leader. Your starting point may be different. Your set of skills and background will be different. It is not possible to cover every single scenario. Therefore, we present a loose structure so that anyone can fit in the right place and navigate to the top. Many options are given, but they are not meant to be a checklist of things to do. They are options and alternatives to broaden your mindset so that you may get inspired by a few ideas.

Disclaimer

The contents of this book are provided for informational purposes only and should not be taken as legal or professional advice. The authors are not lawyers and do not offer any legal advice. We offer our personal experiences and opinions solely to share our professional development journey. Any views or opinions expressed in this book do not reflect those of our current or past employers.

The names of products, services, and companies mentioned in this book may be trademarks of their respective owners. The authors and publisher do not claim any ownership of these trademarks and do not endorse any specific product or service mentioned in this book. Therefore, seeking professional legal or other advice for specific questions or concerns about your situation is essential.

2. THE BIGGER PICTURE

Defining the Undefined

Looking at the bigger picture before diving into its elements is essential. An individual tasked with securing an organization from online threats needs to zoom out and put things into perspective before judging the situation and deciding what to do. They require a broad set of skills, knowledge, and experience to do it effectively. Understanding the elements discussed in this chapter identifies your areas of strengths and weaknesses while opening opportunities to fill those gaps. It also allows you to delegate responsibilities and define paths to success. We have briefly categorized the areas of interest as depicted in the following mind map. We will dive deeper into these core principles in subsequent chapters.

Review this mind map and reflect on the scope of the role of a security leader. You might find some elements that make a successful CISO that you did not realize before. Then, identify your blind spots and create a plan of action to address them.

Mind Map

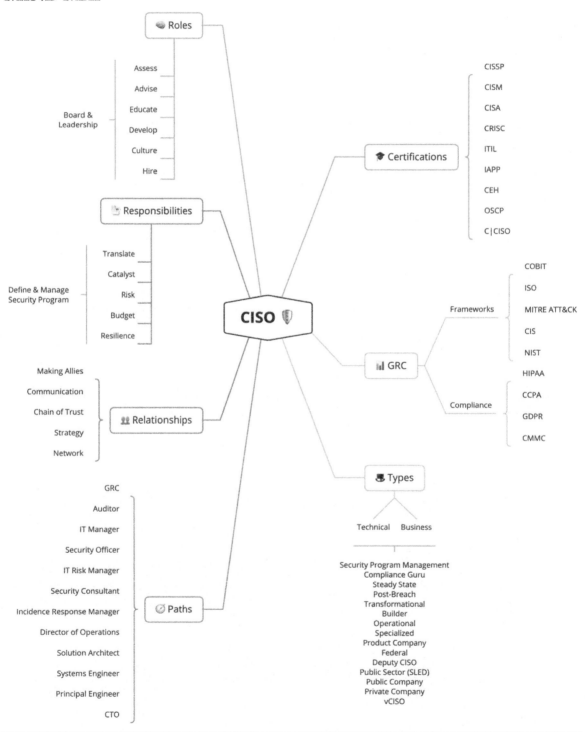

Planning

When beginning a new journey, we must start with small steps. Sometimes we plan these steps, and sometimes we go with the flow. Take the example of GPS navigation. Before we start driving, we input our destination. Then, we get to pick from 1-3 options on how to get there, and once we select an option, the GPS software provides us with turn-by-turn directions every step of the way to get to our destination using the most efficient route.

Getting to the position of a CISO is our goal. If we work backward from our destination, we are in a much better position to get there faster and not miss any crucial milestones. With the field of cybersecurity changing so frequently, it is not easy to pave that path, especially when the bigger picture is blurry. In our careers, we've seen many leaders switch fields, take jobs they regretted, or be misguided. Our goal is to provide clarity in the process and provide multiple options so that you can confidently navigate your way up the ladder as you embark on the CISO journey.

Most people are visual thinkers. So, we created a high-level mind map to illustrate the bigger picture of becoming a CISO. It helps visualize the goal and allows us to see different paths and identify gaps.

We will provide a reality check on each topic, present skills that will help better relationships, and advise on different stages of the journey. By reading through alternative perspectives on the different focus areas in this book, you will be in a better position to conduct your research and form your conclusions. As with everything, you may agree or disagree with the opinions. Nonetheless, this text will help you think outside the box.

As you progress through the book, refer to the mind map. The bigger picture will begin to take color as the individual pieces come together.

Options

If you're looking at the mind map and thinking that you must check all those boxes to be a CISO, this is not the case. The perfectionists reading this would want to accomplish all the options to be well-rounded. It may trigger feelings of imposter syndrome in those with less experience or self-confidence. You should not feel overwhelmed when looking at the bigger picture. This is not a checklist of everything you should do but rather a large repository of options from which to choose your adventure.

TAKEAWAY

Multiple paths, skills, and backgrounds can lead you to your goals. You do not need to have all the skills or all the responsibilities in the diagram. You will not fit all the types of CISOs either. However, by looking at the various options, you can place yourself in at least a few spots while reading through all the other areas that may not apply to you. This will give you a better understanding of your path and may invoke some ideas for your improvement.

3. ROLE

The Security Champion

The CISO is considered the "security champion" of the organization. The CISO is passionate and knowledgeable about everything encompassing security and advocates for it in every process. While we cannot ignore that almost every function in an organization touches security, the role of the CISO is to develop, educate, assess, and advise all the other functions to intertwine with the fabric of security.

One of the biggest and ongoing challenges the CISO needs to overcome is bridging the gap between cyber threats and business functions while helping the board and leadership to make better decisions. This is where non-technical, business, and communication skills will help. Some examples to develop these skills include cross-functionally working with various teams, having risk brainstorming sessions, understanding risk across industries and markets, attending conferences, and, most importantly, listening to people's concerns. While these aren't the only examples, this effort will broaden perspective and enhance the role. With this approach, a CISO becomes the champion of the sought-after "Security First Culture" that adversaries dread.

To succeed as the security champion, the CISO identifies and fills the appropriate roles to build and grow the security clan. That makes the CISO valuable in the eyes of the business owners as talent is identified quickly and qualified people are mapped to the right roles to fulfill the goals of the security program.

We must remember that while the CISO can provide business and security solutions, they may not have all the answers immediately based on the complexity of the organization. It is okay to be a fish out of water as this feeling will not be the first. As you read this book, hone your ability to cope with the feeling of ambiguity, as it will be part of the role. With a structure of defined roles in place, the process will become easier. As a security professional, expecting the unexpected is the mindset to keep.

ASSESS

To be effective in that role, a security leader will need data and put things into perspective before presenting their ideas. This will provide a level of accountability to raise the standards of security practices in the organization. Security risk assessments create the foundation to have that conversation. Assessments collect raw data and highlight potential security risks. The goal of the assessment is to help identify gaps based on security control frameworks. Once gaps are identified, you need to determine the appropriate remediation based on the organization's risk appetite It's important to list gaps in order of risk priority and to consider the cost, time, and resources required for remediation. All this is then communicated to the stakeholders with quantifiable and measurable metrics.

> **Security Control:** A measure to prevent, detect or mitigate a security threat in an information system and helps manage security risk. (e.g., antivirus, encryption, endpoint security, multifactor authentication, firewall, Security Incident and Event Management (SIEM), user access, vulnerability scanners, segmentation, password managers)

You can start with a self-assessment using some of the tools and templates provided online by popular security frameworks discussed further in Chapter 6 - GRC.

Process Hacking

Auditors assess the design and effectiveness of controls by understanding processes, controls within the processes and identifying control gaps, essentially "hacking" them. I call this Process Hacking.

Process Hacking builds upon the assessment phase and fine-tunes it. The control design may have gaps, or its implementation may be ineffective. Let's elaborate with an example of a typical security control like Vulnerability Management. As part of the design for this control, you will have a vulnerability scanner that scans the entire network because the policy will state that a scan is scheduled to run once a month. Once the scan is complete, for the purpose of the control effectiveness, all high and critical vulnerabilities must be addressed by opening a ticket and to ensure the remediation is complete. As you evaluate this process, you take a sample of last month's scan. The control may be appropriately designed as the scans were performed, and the reports were generated. Still, you notice a few high-severity vulnerabilities from last month's scan that did not have remediation tickets open. Now you've discovered a gap in the effectiveness of this process.

From your responsibilities as a Phantom CISO, you may have played the role of an auditor and performed some process hacking. In that role, you have probably assessed processes, interviewed stakeholders, and even helped to build process maps for business areas (security or non-security related) to:

1. Baseline and identify the current operating model
2. Identify existing controls
3. Identify process efficiencies and deficiencies
4. Determine if controls need to be optimized
5. Highlight gaps
6. Provide recommendations

You've ensured that the policy documentation aligns with the stakeholders' interviews. Moreover, you also find yourself reverse engineering processes and connecting the dots by comparing inquiries about one process with different people to understand if it also aligns.

It is important to note if a control is not designed appropriately, you cannot perform effectiveness testing, and it is reported as a control failure. Testing the design of a particular security control should be completed in its entirety before assessing its effectiveness. For example, if security awareness training is not fully rolled out to all employees using a centralized learning and tracking platform, it fails at the design stage. Most often, controls that fail at design and are not remediated can lead to breaches and long-term repercussions.

Once you've dissected, fully understood, and evaluated a critical process and control in the environment, you can move on to the next. This is a continuous cycle of improvement.

The process hacking exercise is an excellent way to improve the organization's security maturity and can be implemented through process mapping.

ADVISE

The leaders in the organization rely on the CISO's knowledge and expertise to improve the organization's security posture. In addition, the CISO entertains questions and plays an advisory role in reducing the risk of being breached.

The security issues engineers, developers, and administrators share with the CISO are brought to the forefront of board meetings and stakeholders. A CISO is a representative of the security group and advises vertically and horizontally across the organization. Since security affects all areas of the organization, the CISO must be dynamic and be able to communicate with different stakeholders, leaders, and the boots on the ground in the organization. The better you can build bridges across various domains, the more respected you will be.

This way, you earn the rank of a trusted advisor. Don't be afraid to talk to different departments and listen to their concerns. They will all be expecting advice from you, so take your time to evaluate before you provide your suggestions.

EDUCATE

Awareness

One of the most challenging jobs of a CISO is to educate and bring cybersecurity awareness to the organization. This is particularly challenging as various roles in the organization have different concerns and perspectives on security. For some, it's a hindrance. For others, it's something they've wanted forever.

Education comes in many forms, from formal security awareness training that takes the form of video-on-demand courses to demonstrations to simply telling a story. As you grow into this role, you will notice that people will only care if they can envision a personal loss. This could be a loss of their hard work, time, embarrassment if they are a targeted victim of a scam, ransomware or phishing attack, or leakage of personal information.

Education should not be taken lightly as you become a CISO. You quickly realize that no one cares about the video assignments or reporting an internal phishing exercise. You also realize that executives are better targets for attackers and that training should be tailored accordingly. Once upper management is on-board and recognizes the value of what you are doing, then everything else becomes more manageable.

To develop this skill, you must be better at listening, telling stories, and being a people person. Wait for the right opportunities in board meetings to insert your views about security threats. Be subtle, and don't overdo it. Starting with a simple story about a personal incident and what you learned from it will resonate with your audience.

Process

For a CISO to educate, the CISO must continuously learn and keep up-to-date on various cybersecurity domains. Education is internal as you also need to educate yourself on the processes in place. You will do this during the assessment phase. More importantly, you need to understand why these processes exist and if they are required. Security vendors and advisors often look at existing systems and quickly critique them without understanding why they were put in place. It could be because there is no other choice. I've recently seen a Windows XP machine in a factory because the costly machine (used for precision wood cutting) could only take commands from custom software that ran on Windows XP. It was business-critical to keep things this way, and the company would not profit without it. In situations like this, if your only answer is to upgrade and get rid of everything that's not patched and updated, you will lose support very quickly, as people will think that you do not understand nor care about the processes in place.

In the example above, compensating controls can be put into place to minimize the risk of a highly vulnerable system. Compensating controls are alternative controls put in place temporarily for a security measure that cannot be implemented at present. One such solution for this example can be to isolate the systems using the concept of micro-segmentation. This can keep critical systems separate from other systems in the network. If a hacker gets access to one segment of the network, they would not be able to move around the environment freely. Other compensating controls can be installing end-point protection, hardening the operating system, or implementing application allow-lists. Many other layers of security can be placed to compensate for the inability to patch or upgrade. There is always more than one way to handle risk.

DEVELOP

Understand before being understood. Develop a plan after understanding how and why things are currently implemented. Once you understand the process flows within the organization, you are better positioned to create a security program and customize those policies.

A security program is developed over time and goes through a maturity cycle. During its lifetime, milestones are set, budgets are assigned, work is delegated, and systems are continuously tested.

The heart of the security program is the information security policy documentation. It is your master plan, documented in many sub-sections. This document is developed through security risk assessments and matures with system audits and continuous testing. A thorough information security policy document may have the following sections. These are referenced from the SANS Institute (SysAdmin, Audit, Network, and Security) templates for policy documentation and grouped according to the National Institute of Standards and Technology (NIST) controls. These documents are not technical and talk about high-level policies. Think of these as chapters in your master information security (MIS) document. You can use the following list to develop each section of your information security policy.

1. Protect
    - Remote Access Policy
    - Network Security Policy
    - Server Security Policy
    - Technology Equipment Disposal Policy
    - Backup and Restore Policy and Procedures
    - Password Protection Policy
    - Acceptable Use Policy
    - Device Security Policy
    - Web Application Security Policy
    - Device Configuration Policy and Hardening Standards
2. Detect
    - Event Logging and Auditing Policy
    - Vulnerability Management Policy
3. Respond
    - Security Incident Response Plan (IRP) Policy
    - Data Breach Response Policy
    - Pandemic Response Planning Policy
4. Recover
    - Disaster Recovery Plan Policy
5. General
    - Ethics Policy
    - Bring Your Own Device (BYOD) Policy
    - Email and Electronic Messaging policy
    - Software Installation Policy
    - Security Awareness Training Policy
    - Asset Management Policy and Procedure

These sections can be anywhere from half a page to five pages. The purpose is to keep the plan at a high level as the details will frequently change with technology. Other teams will create specific detailed procedures or configuration guides based on this policy document.

You can expect a great security program with proper policy documentation, enforcement, delegation, reviews, training, testing, and fine-tuning controls.

Hire

A CISO cannot do it all. They may have the vision, but they need help in executing it. The stakeholders usually do not understand security risk as well as the CISO, and that's why they hire one. They also do not know how to hire security professionals for the job. As a result, many jobs are not fulfilled because the stakeholders don't know whom to hire to build a team.

Filling the resource gap is where they look for help from the CISO. Coming from a technology and security culture, the CISO knows whom to hire and where to look for suitable candidates. Hiring the right people to do the job is of great value to the organization. Part of the role of a CISO is to help build the team that will execute the security vision. As you prepare for this role, keep your network strong, as you will need to tap into it every so often.

Security Culture

Every organization has a security culture. It may be different from the ideal expectations. However, assessing, understanding, and developing a security plan paves the way for a new security culture.

We want to be in a place where all users, no matter what their roles are, understand and appreciate security. Everyone plays a role in security, from the janitor to the Chief Executive Officer (CEO). Once people realize how security affects everyone, from physical, cyber, working from home to even collecting documents from trash, they feel a sense of responsibility that creates that culture.

Companies with a strong security culture are much harder to breach. The proof is based on my testing. I've been contracted to perform social engineering campaigns that involved vishing (calls) and phishing (email) attacks. One client of mine would not fall for either. No matter whom I impersonated, they would call me out on my bluff. I tried impersonating employees on vacation, interns, delivery persons, marketing agencies, and existing partners. Security awareness was so well ingrained in their workflow that they all presented various dead-ends to my attempts. I later found out that what contributed to this culture was that they had frequent company gatherings, and the management was always talking with their employees in person. They also had an open seating plan and were not confined to rooms. They were a very close-knit group. Their IT and security team consisted of two to three individuals, and they knew members of other teams by name. They took the opportunity to conduct periodic security briefings at informal company lunches or events. Furthermore, they offered rewards for aligning with the "Security First Culture" and reporting phishing attempts. This created a fantastic security-aware environment.

The security culture of a company is transformed over a period of time, sometimes years. It is the longest security endeavor to achieve but likely the most robust defense. Even employee turnover can create challenges so work on the culture strategically from day one and keep it fun.

Takeaway

People will look at you as their savior and the force for change. Your role will bring them hope. With a systematic approach and a plan in place, you will keep them excited while building a "Security First Culture". This is your opportunity to demonstrate value to the organization and the units within them in a unique way.

4. RESPONSIBILITIES

Myth: A CISO is responsible for security

A company gets hacked with ransomware, and the hackers hold the data for ransom. They expose the data when they don't get paid, and the company faces reputational damage through the media and stacks up legal fees. Who is the first person they question for this breach? Not surprisingly, the CISO is the first to bear the brunt of the executives, investors, and media. They want a statement from the CISO. Is the CISO responsible?

You will often hear the saying that "security is everyone's responsibility." We just mentioned it in the previous chapter as well. Then again, the onus still somehow falls on the CISO. While a CISO may not be solely responsible for security, they are accountable. A CISO needs to protect themselves from being the subject of finger-pointing. The CISO needs to set expectations early on. Part of the responsibility of the CISO is to bring to light the risks currently present in the organization to the board. They need to understand how it impacts the organization and what should be done to minimize it.

A CISO is not solely responsible for a company's security. There, I said it. It's a shared responsibility that spreads equally across the organization. Think of all the situations where executives get spear phished, a receptionist is socially engineered, or a janitor who knows little about cybersecurity allows someone through the doors in the after-hours. Without executive buy-in, security controls are not implemented, and without awareness, employees do not adhere to the policies. The CISO will help facilitate available resources for employees to be security-aware.

The CISO is an enabler and responsible for defining and managing the security program. In addition, the CISO is a strategist and provides the tactical teams with guidance.

THE TRANSLATOR

A CISO translates cybersecurity threats to business impact for the organization. Having a good grasp of technology on the tactical side and knowing how it affects the strategic side of the business makes you a great asset to the organization.

Translating cybersecurity to business impact brings together multiple skills. First, it requires you to be business savvy and understand what affects the bottom line. In addition, you must align with the CEO, the Chief Financial Officer (CFO), and the board of directors to discuss priorities that would enhance the organization's growth and future. Finally, you must identify and match the organization's security investment with the board's appetite for risk. Only then can you connect at their wavelength and explain how specific cyber threats may impact their goals.

On the more technical side, a CISO needs a clear understanding of vulnerabilities and cyber threats to guide the remediation and maintain the organization's risk appetite. The synergy between those two worlds will allow you to move the needle in the right direction. The various business functions that a CISO translates between are depicted in the following diagram.

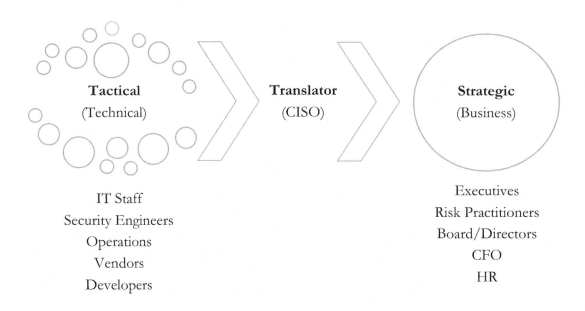

VALUE

While referring to the previous point on being a good translator, a CISO should highlight the importance of security in the context of the organization's mission and values. How many organizations confidently say that security is part of their core values? Those that specifically define protecting their clients' information and privacy as part of their fabric attract confidence. If a CISO can help demonstrate it, then the company looks at the role of a CISO as directly contributing to company values.

Some of the ways a CISO can highlight value is to focus on security risks that directly and indirectly affect the organization. They provide recommendations on addressing these risks to maintain core values. Traditionally, the business impact is seen in terms of something tangible such as monetary loss due to a cyber attack caused by ransomware, as an example. A CISO should still highlight all the other indirect losses that may occur as well like:

- Fines
- Lawsuits
- Legal Fees
- Identity Theft
- Remediation Costs
- Insurance Premium
- Business Disruption
- Loss of Business or Customers
- Loss of Intellectual Property (IP)
- Damage to Credibility, Brand, and Reputation

Sometimes you will need to focus on these value statements to attract confidence from the board of directors. The company's vision and outlook should also align with values that support security and privacy initiatives to strengthen its stance. Everyone looks at the CISO for answers in case of a cybersecurity breach that compromises the organization.

SECURITY PROGRAM

An ounce of prevention is better than a pound of cure. While detection mechanisms and processes are still important, a good security strategy will focus on preventing breaches. All companies need someone knowledgeable to create and run a security program. They look for a security leader to lead from experience. The CISO manages the security program.

To proactively manage threats, a thorough security program needs to be put in place. This program must have broad coverage. It needs to cover aspects like assessments, policies, training, adoption, systems, internal and external threats, supply chain, vendors, third-party access, incident response, and security testing, to name a few.

We can divide a security program into two sections based on these responsibilities: the creation process and technology implementation.

Process

Companies look up to a CISO to create a plan to address current and future security concerns. Therefore, a CISO must take a forward-thinking consultative approach. This includes assessing the current situation, advising on necessary changes, defining the details of the program, educating stakeholders, developing processes and policies around information security, liaising with third-parties regarding security policies, and managing cybersecurity risk. Once a solid plan has been defined, we can then implement the technologies that put it into action.

Technology

The implementation of the plan is not the responsibility of a CISO. Instead, they will watch over it to see their plan to fruition. That will usually come from a combination of resources like in-house engineering, partners, system integrators, and third-party vendors. A managed security services provider may perform regular monitoring and maintenance tasks like patching and upgrading. Partners may handle product selection, design, integration, and documentation. In-house resources may enforce policies and minor configuration changes categorized as moves, adds, changes, and deletions (MACDs). Finally, third-party vendors may provide security testing and recommendations.

Together, all these parties form a symbiotic relationship where without the other, security is incomplete. It is truly a team effort led by the vision and foresight of the CISO. However, in organizations that still need a mature security program, the onus is on one or two individuals to handle and manage security risks. These individuals are your Phantom CISOs.

When working as a vCISO for clients, the roles and responsibilities are better defined between the two parties as the CISO is now an external resource and working towards a common goal. The following diagram depicts this separation of roles and responsibilities better when a CISO is an external entity. This can also apply to an internal CISO where the synergy may be better.

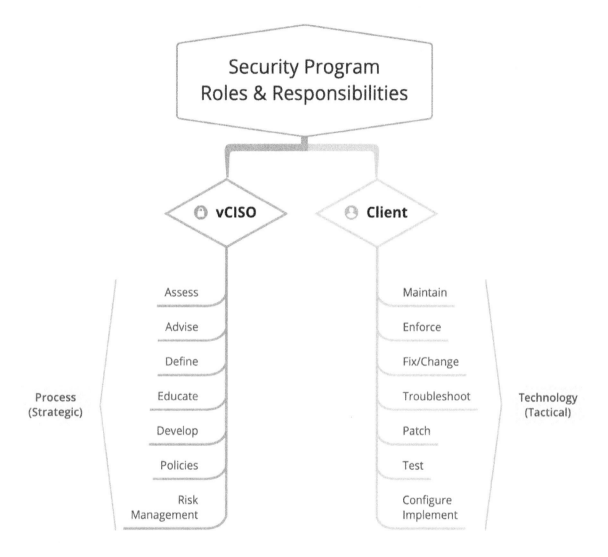

In larger organizations, you will often see resources on both sides of this diagram. The CISO will own the process side, whereas the internal IT Director will manage the technology implementation and maintenance pieces. Parts of both the process and technology side may also be outsourced to managed services partners and vendors to fill skills or knowledge gaps.

It is almost inevitable to get pushback from either upper management or end-users when you introduce new security controls that involve even the slightest participation from the user. Users won't like video training; they will rarely report a phishing attempt, whether legitimate or an internal campaign, and they will continue to try and evade any security controls that come their way. It is human nature to take the path of least resistance. They do this for one of two reasons. They either don't understand the value of security controls, or they don't care. The former is dealt with education, and the latter with stricter controls. Let's take an example of each.

Education

"Tell me, I may listen, show me and I may look, involve me and I will understand." – Unknown.

When people don't understand the value of something, they ignore it. Suddenly adding MFA (multifactor authentication) to the login process and requiring users to use an authenticator app for push notifications or entering six-digit codes becomes an annoyance. They will often say, "Why do we have to do this? We never got hacked before. How much difference will this make?"

I used to conduct in-person security awareness training for company groups where I presented most of the threats live and involved people from the audience. I used to send them a phishing email, ask them to click on it, and share my screen to allow them to see firsthand what a hacker would see. On my phishing dashboard, I showed them their IP address, who clicked it, and their Operating System or phone model. Then I asked them to enter any random fake credentials on that phishing page. We could all see their passwords live on the screen as soon as they did. I could then use that to log into their real accounts. As a result of this live demonstration, everyone understood the simplicity and severity of that attack as they were involved in the process.

You are only as strong as your weakest link, which is why baselining is essential to evaluate the level of security awareness. When you involve people, they never forget. No one likes to sit through long power point slides, screenshots, lectures, or video training. Most adoption objections are addressed by helping to understand security controls to protect them and the company. On the other hand, there will always be a subset of people, usually a small number, who will not care and continue to ignore the advice. For such a subset of individuals, a different approach is needed.

Stricter Controls

During regular phishing simulations, a few people always fall for the phish. They may have their reasons. For example, they could be on a mobile device, driving while clicking, multitasking, or not noticing the signs of phishing. From my experience, it's not hard to notice that some employees will become repeat offenders in phishing exercises, and repeat offenders become the weak link in the chain. Often the user does not care. They will tell you they understand the education and the attack but need more convincing on why they should do anything to contribute to security. They feel they have nothing to gain or lose by ignoring the problem. Reasonable persons exercise care to avoid harm to the organization from a cyber attack. This care includes following through with security awareness training, reporting threats, and following the security policies. Repeat offenders who aren't educated on due diligence can become self-centered and pose a weakness to the security program. They need to understand that security is a collective responsibility.

I'm not a fan of assigning more training to top offenders. Everyone should get the same amount of training. More training does not help because it only frustrates the individual further. I'm also against publicly calling out individuals who fall for a phishing attempt or penalizing them financially or emotionally. For example, I met a CEO who had a "fun" way of dealing with employees who clicked the most on internal phishing campaigns. He made them wear a clown hat for a week in the office. He said they all enjoyed it. I'm sure there will be a few people that will not appreciate the unwanted attention. This may also negatively affect disgruntled employees that become insider threats.

The proper first step in addressing this situation is to have a candid conversation and explain to them why the program exists and why it's essential to be vigilant. Then, if the trend continues, stricter security controls should be introduced for those repeat offenders until their numbers improve. Putting more layers of security around such users quarantines them from threats and incentivizes them to pay more attention to security policies.

Let's take the example of someone who repeatedly fails on a phishing campaign. Once you've exhausted all other methods, you can tighten their password policy and MFA settings. You can reset their password and set their minimum password lengths to be higher, like twenty instead of twelve. Unlike for other users, you can set their MFA to prompt them at every login instead of once a month. Additionally, you can tighten their remote access by only allowing their home IP address to use the Virtual Private Network (VPN) software and blocking all other IPs. This way, they can't have remote access into the organization from a coffee shop or airport and would need to call IT if their home IP changes.

These are just some small examples that can quickly be baked into your policy documents. You can take any security control and make stricter modifications, such as tightening the security perimeter around users that refuse to comply. Based on my experience, system administrators have disabled a user's account entirely when detecting an unauthorized remote login attempt after the user clicked on an actual email phishing link. They get management approval before doing this as part of their security training program for problematic users. Some may feel these are extreme measures, but they are used for exceptional cases. When the user's work routine is affected, they are now involved and have much higher chances of understanding a real threat and being vigilant the next time.

Use the techniques most appropriate to your situation. These stricter controls are usually adopted over extended periods after understating the security culture and the maturity of controls in place.

Trust the process and follow a progressive approach. I am not a fan of skipping security education and going straight to enforcement. I've met IT Directors who've told me, "I'm not their babysitter," "It's not my problem," and "I don't have time to educate people on the basics." To them, enforcement of stricter controls leads to the same security posture but without wasting time. While there may be some truth in that, it's not what you do; it's how you do it. Doing it the right way leads to better adoption and creating more allies. Somewhere down the line, you will need the support of individual users. So having them support your initiatives is always in your best long-term interest. The last thing we need is disgruntled employees who are always looking to bypass the system and become a bigger problem.

Keep a balance on how strict your controls are and if they are effective and enforceable. For example, in one of my previous jobs, the company network had blocked access to all social media websites so that people would only work in the office and not get distracted. Most people found a way around it. Some connected to a portable hotspot while others created a wireless hotspot on their phones and used the cellular connection for unrestricted internet access. I connected to a guest WiFi, one of many in the building. I did not need local printer access, and my resources were cloud-based. Now I could access my social media and take multiple short mental breaks.

This entire process of educating, training, objection handling, and tweaking various security controls should be defined in the security awareness training program.

THE CATALYST

A CISO can also be defined as a catalyst for change. The elements of the security controls you put in place cause a reaction in the organization and result in a more robust security posture. The CISO is the catalyst for that reaction. They ensure things happen at the right time and the right resources are in place. This gradual change provides value to everyone, from the end user to the business owners, but this can be challenging. Sometimes, the voices of internal security resources are not heard. I am often hired as a virtual CISO to move the needle within an organization. When an external party (a vCISO) is involved, they are not in touch with internal politics, individual relationships, biases, or policies. This can be a good thing as it helps move things forward. The CISO will find new and creative ways to navigate roadblocks to continue with their roadmap.

Risk Analysis

Before you can implement any change, you must observe and analyze it. The first step is to talk to different business units and listen to their top concerns about security threats. Then we need to analyze the current security situation, typically termed as the security posture.

A cybersecurity risk assessment needs to take place to establish that baseline. While you may use a custom model or questionnaire to perform the internal assessment, the ideal method is to use industry-standard frameworks (discussed later in Chapter 6 - GRC).

A Mathematical Approach

Before we move further, it is important to remind ourselves of the elements of risk using a basic definition. Risk is the combination of three things: **Vulnerabilities**, **Threats**, and **Impact**. We can define risk in one sentence using these three terms as follow: A system vulnerability exploited by a threat that causes a business impact produces risk.

Along with its definition, let's take a mathematical approach that will help logically define risk.

$$Risk = (Vulnerability) \times (Threat) \times (Impact)$$

According to the rules of multiplication, if either of the three variables in this equation is zero, then the risk is zero. So, we don't always have to concentrate on all three to reduce risk. With this logic, any of these elements approaching zero is enough to control risk. Let's see a real-world example of how either one can be reduced to zero to minimize or eliminate risk. In reality, there is always some risk, never zero risk.

Zero Threats

Needless to say, "old and unpatched," I've seen a Windows XP desktop computer used for the occasional label printing, but it was not connected to the network. Although highly vulnerable, the system was not exposed to any real threats, and no one would benefit from compromising that PC. Because of this, it would also have no impact on the business if it were to go down. So, in this case, the risk to the organization was zero, and the upgrade to that system moves to the bottom of the priority list.

Zero Vulnerabilities

A few years ago, I was contracted to perform a penetration test on a single public IP address of an organization. There was one firewall behind it. They had hardened it well. Only ports that were needed were open, and only the specific source IP addresses were allowed to connect to. They had updated the firmware to the latest version just days before. I did not find vulnerabilities that I could exploit from a scan, and I could not find a way to bypass the firewall. They also had redundant hardware and proxies configured in case I flooded their interface with requests to mimic a Denial of Service (DoS) attack. They had their controls implemented well.

All internet-facing devices have a fair number of threats from hackers and bots as they are in the public domain. There were still no known vulnerabilities found on their devices. Therefore, the impact of the firewall going down was minimal. If you refer to the risk equation, the vulnerability was approaching zero. So, the firewall posed a minimal risk.

We avoid saying zero or no risk because there are unknown factors and zero-day vulnerabilities that the vendor still needs to learn. With enough time, effort, and resources, anything can be compromised.

Zero Impact

In my past technical roles, my job was to highlight the need for patching vulnerable systems or advising to put in security controls to protect against threats. The business owners would always ask me a simple question: "How does this impact our business?" Embarrassingly enough, my answer wasn't always convincing to them. The reality is that fixing certain security issues won't always have a direct business impact that you can effectively articulate. We are trained to think that every little thing helps. However, security in-depth or having a layered approach has enormous effects on overall security. That is what should be highlighted instead of individual controls.

The last variable in the equation is business impact. To demonstrate this with an example, I once consulted for a marketing company that collected client articles and contact information. All that information was either already public knowledge or would be in the public after a few days of review. Like most organizations, they had external threats like competitors or ransomware groups. They had some vulnerabilities due to the lack of regular patching and basic controls like multifactor authentication or micro-segmentation. However, they had great backups. Their workforce was all remote, and they also didn't rely on many systems or software. So, with high vulnerability and regular threat levels, the impact of a breach was close to zero as they didn't hold important data nor relied on specific systems to perform work. They could also recover very fast with their offline backup and restore policies. Because the business impact is low to zero for certain systems, the risk becomes almost zero. The company then shifted its priorities to internal risks related to process and business continuity if it fell victim to an attack.

Assessment

To avoid any gaps, we must analyze the three elements of risk in an organized manner. An assessment will examine the risk level in each security domain based on the framework being used. It will then prioritize the security controls based on the assigned level of risk. This analysis allows you, as a CISO, to create a roadmap of actionable items. You now have multiple projects and tasks to oversee for the next six to twelve months before you re-assess your security posture. This is a gap analysis for security.

Without a thorough assessment, you will waste valuable time and go in the wrong direction. I have seen many companies implementing various security products and configurations without ever performing a security assessment. For example, I once talked with the IT Director of a company that had spent a fortune trying to implement a NAC (Network Access Control) solution when the organization did not even have MFA (Multifactor Authentication) implemented. A pentest clearly highlighted the importance of MFA and a few other security controls over NAC. Again, it's about prioritizing risk.

When presented with a prioritized plan, companies often realize what a waste of time and effort their team was undertaking with items that presented a low risk. They could have finished high-risk tasks in a fraction of that time and budget. A security risk assessment, performed early on, saves them from this trouble.

Financial Risk

Sometimes the only way to understand risk is in terms of monetary loss. Most organizations are in the business of making profit. So, it is easy to show loss. Presenting risk in terms of how it affects their bottom line is the most powerful way to engage the CFO. When dealing with profit and loss, the CFO has the most leverage in decision-making in most organizations.

Besides just assessing the organization's cybersecurity posture, you need to add two things to make it real and for the company to take action on it:

1. Financial impact per area of risk
2. Remediation Costs per identified risk

Financial Impact

A financial impact analysis is necessary to show why a certain security control is important and why it should be in place. As an example, if you inform the CFO of a potential DDoS attack that may cause your e-commerce website to be down for a few hours, it's important to also communicate the potential impact. In addition to frustrated customers who may publicly express their discontent on social media and seek out alternative options, there is a significant financial cost to the business. For every hour the website is inaccessible, the company stands to lose one million dollars in revenue, as well as potential damage to its reputation and loss of existing customers. You can project another one million dollars to that loss estimate with these additional intangible costs. Now you have their undivided attention.

Remediation Cost

After the financial impact is presented, the immediate question is, "How much will it cost to remove this threat and be proactive?" This is where you will need to be prepared to analyze the remediation costs of different solutions that fill those gaps to reduce the overall risk of each threat presented. In the example above, the answer could be the implementation of a web proxy, the cost of hardware, software, licenses, and implementation labor.

With the costs put into perspective, now the CFO sees the complete picture in a language they understand. From the example above, the cost of plugging a security hole may come out to be $200,000, while the cost of doing nothing and potentially being subject to a breach may be $2,000,000. This is obviously an oversimplified example, but you get the idea. If you don't make it simple, you lose their attention.

Non-Profits

What if the company has no profits? Like a non-profit organization running on donations or a government entity running on taxpayer money. Nonetheless, these organizations may have millions of dollars in budget. If you use the same tactics as previously mentioned, they will not understand the financial impact of profit, loss, or remediation cost as they don't have profits and usually have subsidies or grants to spend on solutions. For them, financial risk resonates in the form of loss of trust, support, reputation, or lawsuits. They care about their service, vision, or goals. Helping them understand how their purpose can be affected by a security incident will help them in their cybersecurity journey.

If a non-profit cannot fulfill its mission because of a breach, they have no reason to exist. If the list of their top donors contains politicians or influential business owners that would like to remain anonymous, it would harm their reputation if that list were leaked to the public. People would think twice before donating.

Hackers breach millions of records from government entities every year. These entities lose billions of dollars yearly, and it's getting worse. The financial loss argument falls on deaf ears as government agencies are rarely fined. In my internet search, I found a handful of incidences where local counties or schools had to settle based on a class action lawsuit that came from taxpayers' pockets. Without stricter regulations, their situation will not change. So, in dealing with school districts, counties, states, or other local government entities, the focus needs to be on business continuity, efficiencies, fraud prevention, and avoiding lawsuits.

BUDGET

Once the people in charge of money understand the risks, defining a cybersecurity budget becomes a reality. One of the main bottlenecks in implementing security measures is the need for more funding. I often see cybersecurity budgets at insufficient numbers. When asked about how they got to these numbers, it's usually an estimate provided by the IT Director based on a few small security projects on their wish list. This is a flawed approach to calculating any budget. One of your duties as a CISO is to redefine it in terms of risk. A prerequisite to that is to perform a security risk assessment. Based on that, you can define budgetary numbers for each gap identified and each control that needs to be implemented. The CFO also needs to understand that the total budgetary numbers you present don't have to be spent all at once. They must spend it over time in a prioritized fashion. Those budgetary numbers are also not an all-or-nothing; you don't have to spend all of it at once. You can spend a bit at a time and pick and choose a few security controls to start with. There will be numbers comprising the purchase of products or implementation of services. There will also be monthly recurring costs of services, subscriptions, or licenses. It is important to sit with the CFO or anyone else who plays the role of a CFO to help them understand the variable costs, the spread, and the prioritization of spending that makes up the overall cybersecurity budget.

Here's a sample table to help you visualize what efforts should be put into each security control and convert it into a budgetary number. The table should also be arranged according to priority. In this case, prioritization is based on multiple factors, not just risk. The cost of the solution, ease of implementation, and resource availability are also considered when putting together a prioritized list. For example, implementing a backup solution may be critical and more important than email security, but implementing email security controls may cost a fraction of that and may be done in a few days rather than a few months with in-house resources. So, email security takes priority.

Have a look at this sample budgetary list that you should create out of a risk assessment and present to a CFO. A conversation around timelines and when to expect the actual spending should supplement the discussion to put things into perspective.

Priority	Solution	Min Cost	Max Cost	Resources
1	Vulnerability Assessments	$4,000	$6,000	Third-party
2	Email Security	$5,000	$7,000	In-house
3	Multifactor Authentication Licenses	$8,000	$10,000	Vendor
4	Incident Response Policy Document	$2,000	$3,000	Internal
5	Security Awareness Training	$8,000	$10,000	Third-party
6	Network Hardening	$9,000	$11,000	In-house
7	DNS Filtering	$3,000	$5,000	Vendor
8	Logging Solution	$15,000	$20,000	External
9	SIEM/SOC/MDR	$80,000	$120,000	Third-party

Time Is Money

You may wonder why projects with internal or in-house resources have a cost associated with them. Even though the organization is not paying an outside party to help implement a solution, every company has an internal hourly cost assigned to their employees. Time is money, and in some cases, it is cheaper to have an outside party implement the solution than spend a lot more time and internal costs to do it yourself. So, when management sees that it's costing their employees a lot of time (and money) to implement a project, they may turn to their systems integrators or third-party vendors to see if outsourcing is more cost-effective. This strategy also allows employees to focus on more productive things within the organization. That's why I like to put a number to everything. It is wrong to consider using internal resources as a no-cost option.

Steady Progress

The first year that you provide your security pitch, people will listen. Consider this is the education stage. Once people understand why they need security controls, it will be easier to justify spending. On the other hand, budgets are not available immediately. They will only increase or take into effect for the following budget cycle. This could be the beginning of a calendar year, like January 1st, or the beginning of a school semester, like summer in the US school system.

The whole model collapses when there is a cyber attack. So, depending on how convincing your argument is, it will take anywhere from six months to a year to get budgetary approval for your multiple security initiatives. So, stay persistent; it is a long-term process.

You are selling security internally. Add sales to your required skill sets.

Cyber Insurance

Only some risks can be dealt with directly (through risk reduction and risk acceptance). Otherwise, risk needs to be addressed by either discontinuing certain actions that would give rise to the risk or by transferring the risk to insurance providers. The former is known as risk avoidance; the latter is known as risk transference.

When exploring options, understand what cyber insurance can provide to your organization. Some policies will cover the cost of an attack in terms of ransom payout, while others will only cover remediation or incident response costs using their pre-approved partners. Don't forget about premiums and deductibles. If your data is held ransom for $100,000 and your insurance premium is $250,000, do you even contact insurance when you know they won't pay but instead risk raising your renewal cost because you've just had a breach? Talk to your insurance provider about this in advance, as it may be a legal requirement to report.

It is also essential to read the fine print. Most insurance providers will require you to have certain minimum protections in place. In our experience in talking with many insurance providers, they will take a subset of a popular security framework like Critical Security Controls (CSC) developed by The Center for Internet Security (CIS) and provide a questionnaire that will ensure you have a decent security posture before offering you with any insurance. So, following a well-known cybersecurity framework prepares you for the application process.

Make sure you also address unknown costs. One such example is breach notification. If you are part of the healthcare industry and need to comply with HIPAA (Health Insurance Portability and Accountability Act), you will need to send out a letter to each affected patient that may have been affected by the breach. If the postage cost of one letter is 20 cents and the affected records are 10 million, you now need to spend two million dollars just for postal mail. Will your insurance provider cover such costs? Other typical costs may include the cost of rebuilding systems, putting in better security controls, regulatory fines, legal fees, lawsuit coverage, or incident response. Notice we haven't even talked about the cost of ransomware here.

Use your experience to run through different scenarios with the insurance provider. Ask "what if" questions. No one has time to review the fine print, and not everything will be mentioned. Remember, you are never tied down to one or two providers. A cyber insurance broker can help narrow your options at no cost.

You may also be required to obtain a certain minimum amount of cyber insurance to do business with your partners or vendors. For example, a partner may require your company to have at least five million dollars of cyber insurance coverage to do business with you. Again, ensure you're asking the right questions and exploring all options.

In your efforts to mitigate risk, remember the option to transfer risk. Your organization may already have agreements with its insurance providers, and cyber insurance may be more affordable than implementing a control to mitigate a particular risk. For example, consider a small business with limited resources operating a website that collects sensitive customer information. Hiring a full-time cybersecurity expert to manage website security is expensive, so the business considers purchasing cyber insurance instead. By doing so, the business can transfer the financial risk of a potential data breach to an insurance company while still implementing other security controls like multifactor authentication, encryption, and firewalls to mitigate the risk.

VENDORS

Along the journey to secure the organization, part of your responsibilities will include interfacing with cybersecurity vendors. You will come across many vendors that will help you close some of the gaps. Feel free to explore new options as product portfolios change and people come and go. Sometimes the products and vendors in place lose their passion, which was evident in the first year they were introduced but started dropping the ball. Other times there are better options out there. As a security leader, staying abreast of the company's third-party vendor onboarding program and continuously monitoring their activities will help secure the organization. Competition keeps everyone performing at their best.

Part of this responsibility is fulfilled by attending security conferences, talking to new vendors, seeing their demos, and understanding how they can solve existing challenges you have.

You must create a balance here with limited time and creeping deadlines. Security product vendors are notorious for having pushy salespersons. Most of their new sales staff are young, energetic, and focused on the sales commission. You need to be aware of this; otherwise, it will take away your precious time and energy. Over the past few years dealing with hundreds of security vendors, we have found that if you set a few ground rules, you can make the most of them. Here are some things that may help you in dealing with the plethora of vendors that will reach out to you:

- **Short calls**: Only take a short call with them if you think they have the potential to solve an existing problem. Your initial purpose is to qualify them. If you start taking multiple calls or attending their workshops, it will quickly fill up your calendar. If they start sending unsolicited calendar invites, reject them and call them out politely. This bad habit needs to stop, and they need to be informed. Setting realistic expectations with them on the first call benefits both you and the vendors. Do not commit to future calls or demos if you do not think they will work.

- **Control**: Always remain in the driving seat. Remember, vendors are coming to you as a sales team, even if you are the one who reached out to them. It would help if you controlled the entire communications from the initial call to any follow-up, referrals, or closure. If you don't, it can quickly slip away with great sales influencing tactics. Before you know it, you are answering to the schedules of multiple vendors and sitting on calls thinking about how you got there.

- **Swag:** Over the years, I've collected tons of t-shirts, stickers, gadgets, and useless toys from vendor stalls. At the same time, I've also rejected gifts during meetings when sales representatives (reps) request my t-shirt size or shipping address. It was inappropriate and would dilute the conversation's legitimacy, especially when I wanted to set up a call to learn more about them. While there's no harm in accepting their swag or merchandise in return for a call, you must have a legitimate use case to present to them. More importantly, check your company policy on receiving gifts, as it sometimes feels like a bribe. The safest and guilt-free way to accept gifts is when there are no conditions. Keep a balance. $50 worth of some fancy gadget is not worth your time or reputation. People will see right through it. You don't want to look greedy. Be picky in your meetings and in a public display of vendor logos, as you also don't want to promote a product you don't believe in inadvertently.

- **Food:** The same policy applies here as with gifts. Going out for food or drinks takes up even more time and puts you in a spot where you may feel obliged to reciprocate. That is the whole point of taking a client out.

- **Ask Questions:** Always ask them challenging questions during a demo. Interrupt them politely with questions, keep it interactive, and educate yourself. Remember that this time is for you. If you don't keep it conversational, it usually ends up being death by PowerPoint, and you may as well watch a YouTube video about their product instead of a live one-on-one presentation. Vendors appreciate it when you ask questions.

- **Expectations:** Set the expectations in the introduction of the call. Tell them the challenges you are trying to overcome. Vendor products usually have ten or more features, only three of which may apply to you. Ask them to focus on only those; it will save everyone time. Then transition into a demo and talk about pricing. Try to cover everything in one call rather than scheduling three calls over three weeks. Otherwise, it will only add to stress.

- **Follow-Ups:** Vendor representatives are trained to ask and schedule follow-ups. If you are impressed and think you could have a buy-in to the product, schedule a follow-up with a specific purpose. That agenda should be pricing, partnership details, or a further deep dive with your technical team.

- **Invite:** Invite the appropriate people from your team on the call. No one on the call should ask themselves, "why am I needed on the call." As a pre-sales engineer, I used to hate being on five vendor calls weekly where no one introduced me or asked me a single question. Don't be that person. Remember you are here to create better relationships within your team and with external resources, like vendors and partners. Wasting someone's precious time by thinking it may be helpful in the future only worsens it. Also, don't forget to invite the right people from your team on the call. Suppose they're not available; re-schedule the meeting to when they are available because you value their opinion. Otherwise, you'll have to sit through the same product pitch again.

- **Rejection:** Be honest with yourself. If you do not view the relationship as a good fit, end it there. There are ways to do it respectfully. I will often tell them great things about their product, repeat the value as I understand it, and get their validation. At the same time, I will say that we are content with our current solution, and we do not see significant added value in the differentiators discussed. If they push for a follow-up call in a month, ask them to email you for an update since they need something to show their sales leadership. If all else fails, blame it on the budget. Be honest and say, "I do not want to waste your time, this was very educational, let's keep in touch. I have your contact information, if anything changes, I will be sure to get in touch with you." They will value your honesty. If they insist, start being blunt and repeat yourself.

We need partners and vendors to fulfill a lot of the cybersecurity requirements. Security is a team effort that extends beyond the boundaries of your organization. The preceding tips should not be misunderstood as warnings against sales calls. In this book, we are looking at this topic through the lens of a CISO and how they can take advantage of the vendor resources while at the same time being efficient and managing their limited schedules.

Cyber Resiliency

The saying goes, "it's not if but when." Cyber-attacks are inevitable, and businesses must continue during and after them. How quickly can your organization anticipate, recover, adapt to new threats, or defend against them? That is known as cyber resilience.

As a CISO, you will often be asked about your cyber resilience strategy. You must be prepared to answer that. This strategy builds as the practice matures. As threat vectors evolve, so should the CISO.

At one point, credit card data was the most critical data to protect. Confidentiality-related attacks were the core focus of security, and we have spent a lot of time in the industry improving confidentiality, such as encryption (data at rest, data in transit, data in use). Today, we have ransomware that has not been biased toward any person or industry. As a result, cyber insurance companies have started paying attention to ransomware because it costs money. Availability of data has been the new focus just as much as confidentiality. For example, the health industry has taken a significant toll on availability-related attacks, and ransomware has become a crippling threat due to the unavailability of critical systems. Because of our increased reliance on third-parties to drive our business, supply-chain and ransomware attacks are disrupting businesses locally and globally.

When it comes to confidentiality, integrity, and availability (the CIA triad), what is our organization's risk appetite? The same question should be asked for prevention and detection capabilities. We may only be able to prevent some attacks, but we can detect and minimize risk through layers of defense-in-depth. Since we are talking about availability, how are our backups? Have we tested to see that our backups are restorable? How is our network segmented? What is our detection, containment, and response mechanisms? The answers to these fundamental questions assess our resilience.

CISOs must consider and make huge decisions when facing attacks like ransomware. If the data is compromised, will human life be affected? What will the organization do when there is information leakage? From a supply-chain perspective, have you evaluated the third-party's view on security? What is the third-party's footprint on your business if they are affected? Does it align with your policies, especially regarding business continuity and disaster recovery plans? Has there been an annual refresh on the policy documentation to include responding to attacks in a pandemic? How else have you introduced risk into your business by attempting to improve the security posture? While logs are being collected for every network device, how do you determine which log is critical? Will a cloud compromise affect your on-premise environment or vice-versa? Will you use automation to scale and move fast amid a breach?

These are a lot of questions that need answers. Over time, you will have answers to them all. Regular incident response exercises will also help you answer them quickly and allow you to prioritize them to take action. These exercises can be performed with technical teams, vendors, or business stakeholders.

Panic Management

As you can see, many of the security domains are connected when it comes to resiliency. The best way to prepare is to learn from the past and expect the unexpected. Breaches are in the news every day. Study them and stay connected with your leadership network to determine how best to respond in your organization. Not all solutions fit every organization, but it is essential to listen to ideas when companies are affected by the same type of breaches with disruption to the business. An excellent way to involve the board is to perform annual incident response tabletop exercises. Walk them through a mock scenario. Keep it brief and non-technical but very realistic by referencing recent examples. Invoke responses and hold back your opinions until they've had a chance to absorb the problem. They will appreciate your advice after that. I call this Panic Management. This exercise prepares them for a worst-case scenario and minimizes panic to allow rational thinking when a situation like that occurs.

TAKEAWAY

One of the goals of the CISO is to help the employees secure the organization as a team. In addition, to spread awareness to the decision-makers, provide suitable options based on prioritization of risk and ensure everyone understands what's at stake. Due diligence is what will save a CISOs reputation when panic strikes. If done right, there will be a plan of action every step of the way.

5. NOT A CISO

Expectations: Super Human

People expect far too much from a CISO. Any issue from IT to cybersecurity is thrown at them in hopes they will take care of it. When someone asks a company about its security posture, they answer, "We're fine; we have a CISO," as if that automatically equates to security. This section should provide you with some solid distinctions between the role of a CISO and what some people expect them to do.

In the previous chapters, we defined what CISOs are in terms of their primary roles and responsibilities. In this chapter, we will talk about things outside the role's scope. We have included this section because it clarifies the CISO's role. There are high expectations of a CISO, and assigning too many responsibilities relating to risk, security, and privacy gives the impression that a CISO is responsible for everything under the sun.

A CISO will start very enthusiastic and want to be involved in everything during the discovery phase. They can be go-getters and are usually very opinionated. A CISO is highly involved with their team, other teams, and third-parties. While they may be able to think and work like them, they must stick to only understanding them and focus on the actionable responsibilities of a CISO. Because once the lines get blurred, it's hard to change that thinking and reset expectations.

Sometimes CISOs will take on too much and later realize that they can't do everything. This may reflect in their performance and their ability to be effective. If you want to be good at something, it is better to be hyper-focused than to do many things at once.

Now is the right time to determine your focus so that you are not absent from your responsibilities when you take on the CISO role. As a Phantom CISO, you are doing a bit of everything today. We want you to be fully present and recognized as the current or future CISO. So, let's draw some hard lines and make that distinction. Once we understand them, let's communicate with the stakeholders to set better expectations.

A CISO IS NOT

A CISO is not a **glorified security engineer**. They can be technical in their role, but they will have technical and engineering resources at their disposal. If they start digging into configuration changes, they will have no time for their core responsibilities. Sometimes it is tempting to do things yourself as you may be able to do it twice as fast as delegating it to someone else, but you need to stick to the role. Otherwise, people will not only take this ability for granted but also expect it next time.

A CISO is not a **project manager**. They may choose to oversee and manage aspects of a security project, but a dedicated Project Manager is usually assigned with the right tools and training. If you take that initiative, thinking you are on top of each project, you will quickly find yourself running after people and micro-managing each phase.

A CISO is not a **security researcher**. They may be passionate about security and research all the time, but it's not their job. They will likely seek advice from professionals in those areas to make better decisions. If you start researching every technical issue that comes your way, it will consume your entire week. It will take you down many rabbit holes, and you will wonder where all your time went.

A CISO is not a **pentester**. I come from an ethical hacking background and am often involved with in-house or third-party pentest engagements. That is only because I have a keen interest in it and love to stay updated on the latest hacker techniques. It defines my personality and previous roles. However, it is certainly not what a CISO requires. As time passes, it becomes impossible to keep up-to-date with all the new tools and techniques used by hackers and pentesters. To sharpen your skills, it takes hundreds of hours to dabble with tools, servers, specialized hacking operating systems like Kali Linux, or online challenges. Being a good pentester in a particular focus area is more than a full-time job. Work with security testers closely, don't do it yourself.

A CISO is not an **auditor** or **compliance** officer. Knowing the details of the many security frameworks and local regulations requires a lot of reading. Knowing how to verify their implementation requires a lot more time and experience. Moreover, report writing is an art that most technical people have not mastered. While this is a great background to have, it should remain in the background. You should build from this experience to make better, faster business decisions and not get into the weeds of lengthy questionnaires and checking boxes for compliance. There will be phases in your CISO role where this may be required. Take a practical approach and get assistance from other team members who may benefit from this exercise. A third-party's perspective on security audits and assessments is also valuable as you see the organization from a different angle.

A CISO is certainly not a security **analyst**, tech **support**, security **architect**, or any other dependent function. There are dedicated functions for these roles. Background and experience in these roles benefit the CISO by being the eyes and ears of the field.

It is harmful to a CISO to perform duties that impede their goals. Therefore, they should focus on their core responsibilities to be successful. Other people often take advantage of the supplementary skills a CISO has. For example, they will pull in the CISO to participate in design or implementation projects. They will also expect a CISO to troubleshoot technical problems, open cases with vendors, research, and follow up on technical issues that don't concern them. Recognize the goals and requirements, so you don't remain a Phantom CISO overloaded with out-of-scope work.

If this happens to you, correct this notion as a CISO is part of the executive leadership team.

A CISO IS

A CISO is responsible for being involved in processes for creating, maintaining, and setting the direction of the security program. It starts with assessing the current situation, identifying gaps, defining better policies, educating the board, developing those processes to maturity, and minimizing the security risks due to internal or external threats. Then, everything else trickles down to the various teams to see the projects to completion.

In simple terms, a CISO's primary role is cyber risk management. It is a long-term process that requires vision, an understanding of security controls, and what it entails to remediate risk.

Planner

A CISO is responsible for prioritizing security goals. Prioritization is a skill that makes the best use of your expertise and your teammates under time constraints. It prevents wasting your time and progresses you faster towards your security goals. Prioritization of tasks based on risk is complex. Everyone's definition and risk appetite will vary. Many prioritization principles are available, like the priority matrix from Steven Covey's book "7 Habits of Highly Effective People." He defines putting tasks in a quadrant according to urgency and importance. While this is great for planning your daily tasks, cybersecurity initiatives have many more variables, and everything seems important and urgent to someone. So, we must use other variables to create our priority list. These variables include risk level, time to remediate, resource availability, and cost.

Prioritization techniques are discussed in detail in Chapter 6 - GRC.

Team Player

A CISO is a team player. Developing a robust security program also has many facets to it. It is a shared responsibility and requires support from upper management and various teams within the organization. The CISO builds those synergies into the role. This will include cooperation from internal engineering, the software development team, partners, vendors, and managed services providers like a NOC (Network Operations Center) or a SOC (Security Operations Center). In addition, someone will have to take care of all the system-level changes that need to be implemented as an outcome of the security assessment recommendations. These include regular maintenance or configuration changes through MACDs (Moves, Adds, Changes, Deletions) and patch management. A CISO gels the team together by moving the needle, delegating tasks, and providing direction.

Outcome Driven

A CISO is responsible for the outcomes based on the implementation of technology. Therefore, a CISO needs to explain and convince all the parties involved why a certain change needs to happen based on risk. Assumptions can be made that changes enforced by a CISO make an end user's job much harder, but the CISO will have usability and security in mind.

Some software engineers assume they are undervalued or become defensive when they are directed to implement security features in their code. They think their job is only to implement the functionality. When a vulnerability scan of their code results in security gaps, they must put in more time to fix the code. This may be an area they are not comfortable with and need training. Your job will enable them with tools and "Shift Left" training that they need. You show them the benefits of secure coding so that hackers cannot exploit the applications. Your efforts in establishing the value of shifting left in their work will result in more productive hours and appreciation for the engineers.

> **Shift Left:** Refers to the efforts of the development team to introduce security at the earliest stages of the development cycle along with operational testing. This collaboration is also known as DevSecOps.

Additionally, you may experience users complaining about security controls that slow their ability to complete their work. There are user adoption issues for security controls such as multifactor authentication (MFA) apps, blocking or delaying certain emails through filters, blocking links, or complaints about mandatory video training consuming five additional minutes of their week. If we can turn these hurdles into opportunities to educate and show the users how they can contribute to a security culture, they will feel less frustrated to go through with it. Compare it to how putting on a seatbelt in a car is second nature because we adopted it in our driving culture for safety. Similarly, security culture will evolve as well.

Enabler

Finally, a CISO is an enabler in the realm of security. Unfortunately, some executive team members are unaware of the arduous process of maintaining and sustaining a secure environment. They may not have the time or patience to understand it either. It will become your task to bridge that knowledge gap and enable your team to progress in their goals.

Having the right contacts, experience, knowledge of the process, and people skills, all enable a steady path for change. Nothing happens magically. Some things require shortcuts based on past experience, while others require a lengthy process of vetting technology, solution providers, comparing costs, and ROI (Return On Investment). A CISO also must navigate through internal company politics and the hierarchical structure of processes for change approvals that make up the company bureaucracy. A CISO shields his teams from all of this and enables them to move forward with the security initiates, providing them with everything they need to get the job done.

Takeaway

The roles and responsibilities of a CISO are often confusing for senior management and CISOs alike. While there are many flavors of CISOs, create a platform by being outgoing and sharing information about your role, expectations, and what you plan to achieve. Set clear boundaries for your role and how you plan to interact with different functions of the organization. This will make your job easier, as the organization will support and respect your work.

6. GRC

Know the rules, and then break some

A CISO guides the implementation of security "best practices." The CISO accomplishes this by working with the three lines of defense. As a Phantom CISO, it is useful to understand the Three Lines of Defense model. This model includes the Security Operations team, the Governance, Risk, and Compliance (GRC) team, and Internal Audit. The diagram below is a CISOs perspective of this model.

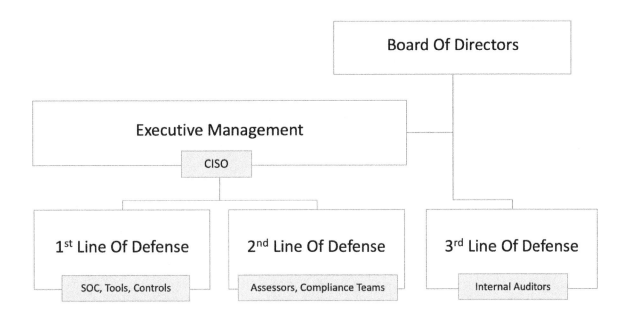

First line of defense: This line consists of the security operations teams, usually headed by the CISO. These are also business operating units for different areas of the company, and the leaders of these units are known as risk or control owners. The organization depends on these teams to identify and assess new risks, implement controls, identify control weaknesses based on self-assessments, and enhance business processes. These business units report to the executive management of the company, in this case, the security operations team reports to the CISO.

Second line of defense: This line consists of the GRC teams in most organizations. Depending on the organization, they may report to the CISO but not always. This team helps to monitor, record, and report the compliance and appropriateness of processes for the first line of defense. There are exceptions where GRC can also be within the first line of defense.

Third line of defense: This line consists of the company's Internal Audit and assurance team. The Institute of Internal Auditors provides standards for the Internal Audit profession. Internal Audit performs independent and objective monitoring assessments of all business operating units in the company. The Internal Audit team reports to the executive management team, but to remain objective, they also report to the board of directors and risk committees.

BASELINING

Once we understand the lines of defense, we must create baselines for measuring progress. In almost every architecture and design, one must follow a certain set of principles and guidelines to get optimum results. This applies to building structures, software code, and hardware alike. Without an agreed-upon structure, things would fall apart. It's no different for security. Fortunately, we don't have to reinvent the wheel. Instead, we have hard-working groups of individuals that have put together general guidelines that allow you to measure a baseline of your security posture.

Policies, procedures, and guidelines provide a structured approach to accomplishing security and non-security goals. Baselining the company's landscape through established frameworks allows for measuring risk and the current security posture. The business owners are presented with these risks and decide whether to act on them.

GRC takes the guessing out of implementing an initial baseline risk assessment.

While GRC provides compliance harmony for the organization, let's discuss an environment without GRC. This approach will help you better understand and value it.

Learning From Breaches

Any time a breach happens, we should ask ourselves, "How did they catch us sleeping?" Unfortunately, there's a significant rise in breaches because we have poor security hygiene. Negligence, poor configuration practices, patch delays, ineffective backup strategy, inadequate testing, supply chain attacks, and intentional and unintentional insider threats will keep us trailing the threat actors and prevent us from staying ahead.

Some of the largest hacks have happened due to poor implementation of the most straightforward security controls. It can be attributed to inadequate due diligence in practicing the policy, standards, best practices, and guidelines. Moreover, these may also be ineffective. Some companies only go through a security assessment to "check a box."

The following are a few real-world examples to highlight this point. While these are just examples, it is a reminder that a breach does not discriminate against any person or company. The point is to learn from these high-profile breaches, and real-world examples resonate better than hypothetical scenarios. Each incident demonstrates that the lack of even one essential security control can result in a breach.

Equifax: The lack of patching a known vulnerability on their consumer complaint web portal led to the initial compromise of Equifax, one of the three main credit bureaus in the USA. The hacker breached the network due to the lack of segmentation. To make matters worse, the company stored passwords in clear text. The breach exposed sensitive data for close to half the population of the US, including the credit data of citizens of the UK and Canada.

We all take our creditworthiness seriously as it is weaved into our society through financial institutions that determine our ability to make purchases. Without it, we become hard to trust with money. To believe a credit reporting agency is vulnerable can be shocking to many but not to security experts. This example of pure negligence could easily have been prevented if basic security checks were in place. Unfortunately, this breach's impact is still high today as it provides the right data for identity thieves.

T-Mobile: In one of the many T-Mobile breaches, I lost count after six; the hacker claims to have breached through a misconfigured gateway used for testing. The hacker shared screenshots of an SSH login to an Oracle server. As a result, personally identifiable information (PII) like social security numbers, home addresses, IMEI numbers, and driver's licenses of 100 million users were breached. The company could have avoided this breach if basic security controls had been in place for separating development, testing, and production environments. This could have been achieved with network segmentation, which is part of all security frameworks. Instead, now they are dealing with class action lawsuits.

The Dow Jones: The parent of the Wall Street Journal leaked a watchlist of 2.2 million records on government officials and politicians that were considered high financial risk. The records contained sensitive information like alleged criminal histories, possible terrorist links, and individuals who could embezzle money, accept bribes, or launder funds. How? 4.4 GB of data was sitting on a publicly accessible Amazon Web Service (AWS) S3 storage bucket. A security researcher stumbled upon it with a simple public search on an IoT search engine. Unfortunately, a simple cloud misconfiguration resulted in a sensitive data leak. Popular security frameworks recommend classifying confidential data and applying the appropriate controls, especially if stored in the public cloud. Continuously monitoring internal and external access and configurations to third-party vendors, a standard best practice, would have raised the alarm bells immediately.

Advocate Health Care: One of Illinois' largest healthcare providers, Advocate Health Care, was fined $5.5 million for not taking patient privacy and security seriously. They had at least three incidents that exposed millions of patients' sensitive medical records.
- The first incident involved four desktop computers stolen from the office, demonstrating poor physical security controls.
- The second breach was indirect as it involved their billing services company Blackhawk. It allowed unauthorized access to the healthcare provider's network. Why would a third-party provider have access to health care? This shows poor oversight for managing third-party controls and potentially not complying with business associate agreements (BAA) in accordance with HIPAA compliance.
- A few months later, they had a third-breach. Someone stole a laptop from an employee's vehicle. The laptop drive was unencrypted; therefore, anyone can access the data directly from the drive. Every major framework recommends full disk encryption, in many cases, the configuration to enable full disk encryption literally requires "checking a box."

Deep Root: A voter analytics firm left an Amazon S3 storage server insecure, making it publicly accessible. The breach included the personal data for 198 million American voters, including analytics data about who a person is likely to vote for and why. A basic check on cloud security, API, or user access credentials would have identified this gap earlier.

Being proactive in your approach to cybersecurity will reduce the impact of breaches in your organization and will save you the embarrassment when the details get out. The purpose of frameworks, audits, and compliance is to ensure the organization evaluates and manages risk to fit the organization's risk appetite.

Layered Approach

The core advantage of implementing security controls strategically comes from the layered approach model or defense-in-depth. If one layer is breached, the adversary encounters additional layers of security. For example, if an adversary obtained your account password to log into your network remotely using VPN, they should be presented with multifactor authentication (MFA). If they manage to bypass MFA, additional controls should be enforced, such as denying administrative privileges to the account, also known as the concept of least privilege. In this manner, multiple hurdles are presented to the attacker which makes the attack very expensive in terms of time, resources, and cost.

There are additional layers and controls that could be implemented based on risk and the technological environment. It would be helpful to build a "Top 10" list of security controls for your organization.

Prioritization

Tackling every security layer in a framework is not only time-consuming but not practical. A security risk assessment aims to provide a prioritized roadmap of remediation steps. This priority is established by considering the threat level, risk, cost, time to implement, and complexity of the proposed solution. A CISO must handle all these factors well to build a plan of action. You can only prioritize tasks once you have the data in front of you by performing a risk assessment.

For example, fixing your DNS records for email (like SPF and DKIM) will take a few minutes compared to implementing MFA, which may be more critical and disruptive to users. In contrast, implementing MFA may be easier and faster than deploying a new Security Information and Event Management (SIEM) solution that may give better visibility and be required by compliance but could prove very costly. The decisions you make are all comparative.

To effectively prioritize cybersecurity controls, you must consider multiple factors. The formula below outlines those factors: risk level, time to remediate, resource availability, and cost. To do this efficiently, you will have to assign arbitrary weight to multiple aspects. Think of it like a simple formula:

$$\text{Priority} = \left(\frac{\text{Time x Cost}}{\text{Risk x Resources}} \right)$$

Let's brush up on our math skills. For this formula, we assign the number 1 as high priority and 10 as low priority.

1. **High Priority:** For a task to be close to number 1 on our list, the time and cost associated with the project need to be very small, like a simple configuration change. On the other hand, the denominator (Risk and Resources) needs to be high for this number to be small. A high-risk item like blocking an insecure protocol such as telnet with readily available network engineering resources meets this criterion and puts the task high on our priority scale.

2. **Low Priority:** The opposite is true for low-priority tasks. For example, implementing a Mobile Device Management (MDM) solution will take time and money (increasing the numerator). Moreover, it is also a low-risk item with little in-house resources to configure it (decreasing the denominator). This puts the task low on our priority list, like a number 9 or 10 on our top-10 list.

This new priority list helps to take care of the "low-hanging fruit" or simpler tasks first. As a result, it will show more progress and be motivating. Tasks that require a lot of investment (high cost) and third-party expertise (low resource availability) may go lower on that priority list, even though they may be higher in risk than a few tasks in your top three. This is normal as some hurdles like budgeting, vetting the right partners, and finding the right product or solution, need to be resolved first. This is especially true for Security Operations Center (SOC), Managed Detection and Response (MDR), or Incident Response (IR) services which take more time to finalize.

Sometimes, things will get thrown out of the priority list for various reasons, such as a smaller budget or having low risk in some areas. Moreover, you may accept risks in certain areas and introduce additional temporary solutions called compensating controls. You may also find products that combine multiple controls in one solution. An example can be a single product that handles MFA, but also have built-in capabilities of geo-blocking IPs, Single Sign-On (SSO), and mobile device compliance. Altogether, you will figure out how to tackle the challenges based on informed decisions and calculate the priority and risk.

Due Diligence

During every one of the security assessments I have performed, the client and I have always learned something new. There are always great discussions, from basic technological concepts to why certain security controls need to be in place. If you cannot elaborate on the importance of a security control, the organization will be less inclined to remedy it. Therefore, putting it in the proper perspective based on the client's environment becomes a skill.

After implementing some or most of the security controls, if a company gets breached, due diligence and implementing multiple layers of security minimizes impact. You will be better positioned to answer your superiors or clients. There will be no finger-pointing by upper management because we all played our part in following the process and leaving no stone unturned.

We have also seen this in the media. People start to analyze and comment on their security controls when a company breach becomes public. Companies that openly apologize and demonstrate their efforts to implement security measures but still experience a breach tend to receive less criticism than those who failed to meet basic security standards and suffered a hack. However, the latter companies often face significant negative attention for their lack of due diligence in implementing adequate security measures.

Compliance

The "C" in GRC stands for Compliance. Frameworks and compliance are terms that can be used interchangeably, but there is a fine difference. Frameworks are guides and may require compliance depending on the environment. For example, NIST is a framework and a compliance requirement for the United States Federal Government and its contractors. If you want to do business with the US government, you must show you have undergone a security risk assessment using NIST or the Cybersecurity Maturity Model Certification (CMMC). NIST and CIS can also be used as guides in private businesses, but there is no compliance requirement.

Fines

The California Consumer Privacy Act (CCPA) is a legal requirement that businesses must comply with to secure privacy rights for California consumers. Similarly, General Data Protection Regulation (GDPR) is a privacy-based compliance for data collection for EU residents. If you've ever been to a hospital in the US, you've signed a HIPAA form. Health Insurance Portability and Accountability Act (HIPAA) and Clarifying Lawful Overseas Use of Data (CLOUD Act) are also legal requirements administered and enforced by the US Federal Government. Organizations pay hefty fines when they become non-compliant. A simple online search will reveal the millions of dollars worth of lawsuits companies had to pay in fines for violating HIPAA or GDPR. They couldn't protect their user's data well enough and paid fines for it.

The largest health data breach in the United States exposed the sensitive personal information of 79 million people, including their social security numbers, addresses, medical history, and employment information. The governing body fined the healthcare provider $16 million, the US Department of Health and Human Services (HHS) Office for Civil Rights (OCR). They had failed to implement the most basic security controls and had yet to perform a risk assessment. They ended up paying an additional $115 million in class action lawsuits.

Fines, customer loyalty, and reputational risk should motivate organizations to perform security risk assessments. Usually, the first question I ask an organization before performing a risk assessment is why they want one. Is it for compliance, or is it for security? Because very often, compliance-driven assessments end up being "check the box" exercises with no risk discussion involved. Compliance does not equal security.

FRAMEWORKS

As the name implies, frameworks build the foundation for GRC. Understanding the scope of cybersecurity is fundamental to the role of a CISO. Putting together a roadmap, action items, and remediation steps is a necessary skill required.

Consider frameworks like a structured list of security controls that, if implemented, could strengthen your overall security. Depending on the framework, it could consist of fifty to over one thousand checklist items, known as security controls. While all controls may not apply, you will score yourself based on the implementation of that control. Then, once you go through them all, you have an overall score and a plan to improve it.

At an early level, you should read through and implement a few different industry-standard frameworks that will help you understand their differences, where they apply, and how they help in quantifying and prioritizing risk. Once you come to terms with the fact that an organization cannot eliminate all risks but rather minimize them, you will have the mindset of a consultant with a vision of a better security posture.

It is essential to know that frameworks can be mapped to each other and you are not bound to one. Begin with one that fits your requirements and transition to another framework as conditions change. This will allow you to work with the CISO to manage risk and monitor the controls to ensure they are working appropriately.

Examples

You've probably come across multiple security frameworks. Depending on which vertical you work in, these could be anything from the National Institute of Standards and Technology (NIST), Center for Internet Security (CIS), International Organization for Standardization (ISO), and The MITRE Corporation, to name a few. Security professionals create and maintain these based on discussions, experience from the field, and some common sense.

Frameworks have different purposes and are used in various assessments and audits. They can also be used in the design process. For example, suppose you try incorporating security by design in your web applications. In that case, you may study the OWASP (Open Web Application Security Project) Framework that discusses the top ten web application vulnerabilities. Frameworks help organizations establish and maintain a minimum security baseline.

Frameworks can be used for point-in-time assessments and as a reference for implementing controls. They are a great way to start and guide you in your security journey.

Implement

To familiarize yourself with these frameworks, perform self-assessments using the available tools and templates provided by the organizations mentioned on their websites. As you review the controls in these documents, evaluate the level of implementation and take detailed notes on where it stands or what needs to be done to fulfill this requirement. At the end of the exercise, you will have created a list of action items that you can prioritize based on your understanding of risk in the organization.

Going through the CIS Critical Security Controls is a great place to start. It is updated more frequently than others and applies to almost every company irrespective of size or industry.

Mapping

With regulatory scrutiny continuously underway across the industry, adhering to policies and various regulatory and legal frameworks takes center stage. Sometimes you are required to adhere to multiple frameworks. For example, an organization may adopt a single framework but shifting to utilize another framework may be required. This is where the mapping of various frameworks becomes beneficial.

For example, imagine an organization familiar with CIS Controls is using the CIS benchmarks documents as a guide. It takes on a project with a client like the Department of Defense (DoD). The DoD will require them to use NIST Special Publication 800-53 or CMMC as a controls benchmark and to show their level of compliance. You may think you must now redo your security assessment based on NIST to test compliance.

As a result, mapping frameworks came into play. Mapping CIS to NIST 800-53 will be beneficial for the organization to understand its client's needs. You will not have to redo your lengthy analysis. Controls overlap with various frameworks. Mapping tools and documents exist online that demonstrate, for example, that MFA satisfies CIS control 6.3, which maps to NIST control IA-2(1).

Another use case where mapping frameworks can be essential is when a merger occurs between two companies. These companies may be following two different frameworks and may want to know if they are on the same page regarding the depth of security compliance. Again, knowing and understanding how the frameworks are mapped will demonstrate a firm handle on controls and their implementation across the two organizations.

While working in the Federal environment, I found that NIST Special Publication 800-53 was the standard framework to rely on when implementing and assessing security controls. After joining the private sector, the heightened focus on preparing for regulatory audits led companies to map CIS, ISO/IEC 27001, or other frameworks to NIST 800-53 to ensure they had coverage of the organization's risks and controls and to ensure we managed risks appropriately. Taking the time to read and study each framework will make it easy to connect or map them. In addition, it will allow for enhanced conversation with individuals in multiple security roles and an understanding of the direction of the industry. For example, MITRE ATT&CK Framework (Adversarial Tactics, Techniques, and Common Knowledge) is relevant and not limited to the Red Team operations. The Red Team is responsible for taking an adversarial approach to attack an organization with its written permission. If I wanted to discuss a specific control from NIST 800-53 with a Red Team professional, I would link it to the MITRE ATT&CK Framework to speak their language. This will allow for better communication and the point to get across in the conversation.

Certified Information Systems Security Professional (CISSP) is a certification developed by ISC[2] that focuses on security domains within these frameworks. Studying these security domains is an added value to applying these frameworks to an organization.

While frameworks are a great guide, they may only cover some of your bases.

ASSESSMENTS

Compliance checklists only identify gaps. Frameworks provide the guidelines. A risk assessment highlights the risk associated with the gaps while providing remediation guidance.

Some organizations or consultants don't always know how to define a security assessment. They may not know the difference between a risk assessment, vulnerability assessment, network assessment, IT assessment, or even a pentest. I've read security assessment reports that were the output of an automated network vulnerability scan. This type of scan covers a tiny subset of the overall vulnerabilities present in the organization. I often see insurance companies provide "security testing" or even "pentests," but all they do is run an external vulnerability scan on your website to provide you with a security score. That scan only looks at an even smaller footprint – web-based vulnerabilities. They do not even scan other public infrastructure that you may have, like firewalls or cloud services. It misses 90% of the elements that make up an overarching cybersecurity risk assessment.

As someone who comes from an IT and Networking background, the differences between the bubbles below are obvious. However, for someone who doesn't come from a technical background, it is important to know the overlap and how each assessment differs from one another because you need to be looking at the right things to make the right decisions. The following diagram depicts the overlap between different types of assessments.

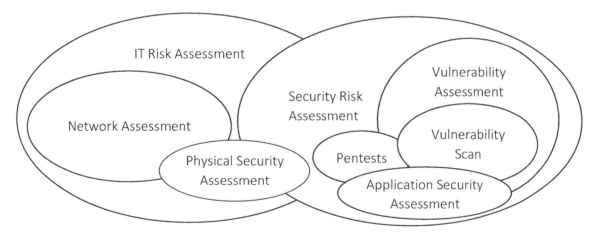

An assessment is a broad term, and below are the different types.

- **Vulnerability Scan:** A vulnerability scan is conducted by running a tool that scans the network and checks against a database of known and published security vulnerabilities or misconfigurations. It categorizes them as critical, high, medium, or low.

- **Vulnerability Assessment:** A vulnerability assessment builds on the scan and adds business value by providing a high-level summary of all connected assets, prioritizing the vulnerabilities discovered based on actual risk, aligning recommendations, and eliminating false positives.

- **Security Risk Assessment:** A security risk assessment looks at things from a much broader view. It considers technical and non-technical gaps in security. For example, a vulnerability scan may also be part of a security risk assessment to add value, but it is a separate project. The frameworks mentioned previously are used to conduct Security Risk Assessments.

- **Network Assessment:** Network assessments focus on the design of the infrastructure and may have a component of security like the redundancy of firewalls, VLAN segmentation, secure protocols in use, and access controls. Risks pertaining to system availability and network security best practices are managed as part of this assessment.

- **IT Risk Assessment:** An overall IT risk assessment focuses on assets and procedures. It may include a review of suppliers, vendors, inventory tracking, spares, backups, disaster recovery sites, or policy and procedure documentation.

- A **physical security assessment** has value for physical breaches that use social engineering tactics. Suppose an intruder can walk through the front door by tailgating an employee, enter the server room by lock picking the door, plug in a device in a USB port or an ethernet jack, or simply walk out with a laptop unnoticed. In that case, there is no need for them to utilize remote hacking techniques. A Physical security assessment looks for areas that an intruder would target to gain unauthorized entry. These include the evaluation of entry and exit doors, turnstiles, reception desk, sign-in process, locks, sensors, alarms, response time, RFID badge cloning, access to dumpsters, sensitive documents in trash bins, surveillance cameras, access to the IT equipment room (IDF/MDF), and even wireless signals to name a few.

- **Application Security Assessment:** If the organization develops applications and writes code, then application security assessments are a must. This assessment can evaluate applications against the Secure Software Development Lifecycle (S-SDLC) and highlight the need for static or dynamic code testing, business logic testing, removing sensitive data or comments from code, review error handling, and securing the software supply chain.

- **Pentest:** A pentest (a.k.a penetration test, ethical hacking, red teaming, adversary emulation) looks at the vulnerabilities and tries to exploit them. The goal of a pentest is to test the defenses and demonstrate a breach. It is best conducted by a third-party to ensure independence. This scope is agreed upon and signed by both parties. There are many different types of pentests like wireless, internal, external, social engineering, web application, API (Application Programming Interface), or phishing. The techniques used are documented in the report, along with any exploits that were successful. Recommendations of this report are reviewed by the team to patch or remediate the identified gaps. It is important to note that a pentest does not test or highlight every single vulnerability that exists. The pentester will find the fastest or most effective way in and use that to compromise the organization. Frequent pentests on different systems with varying scopes are considered best practices to stay ahead of the latest attacker techniques.

All these assessments are essential in gauging your current state security posture. Knowing the differences and overlap between multiple types of assessments is important. This becomes the basis for consulting an organization on its cybersecurity risk. A quick way to learn them is to look at actual or sample reports.

One of the significant benefits of performing security assessments is that you may hit "three birds with one stone":

1. Establish a baseline and create a roadmap
2. Fulfill compliance requirements
3. Be ready for cyber insurance requirements

INSURANCE REQUIREMENTS

Cyber insurance can fulfill the transfer of risk when required. As previously mentioned, with the rapid increase in breaches, insurance providers now require certain minimum requirements even to offer cyber insurance to their clients. The checklist they provide is often taken from popular security frameworks like the CIS or NIST. Keeping up with one of these frameworks also ensures that you will comply with insurance provider demands. Without the implementation of these controls, insurance providers are simply rejecting clients as it is too much of a risk for them because they will end up paying the ransom and incident response costs. In some instances, meeting all their requirements should also allow your organization to decrease the insurance premiums, which will gel well with the CFO.

Takeaway

If there's one thing you can take away from this chapter, no one knows everything, and there is no such thing as absolute security. However, a mature security practitioner will keep everyone motivated by implementing proven strategies of a defense-in-depth security approach to make it difficult for attackers to succeed.

The art of the assessment process is to assure the custodians of security that they are doing their due diligence and are fully utilizing the resources they have while at the same time making enough small changes over time to strengthen their security posture.

7. POWER

With great power comes great accountability

A CISO strives to maintain a defense-in-depth strategy for the organization and ensure controls are working. With the CISO's ability to manage people and understand what it takes to manage cybersecurity in an organization, the CISO becomes the owner and controller of security. With this power comes great "accountability." We say accountability because security has become everyone's responsibility as it's a collective effort from all organization members. It takes a combination of a few techniques to juggle relationship building, strategic growth, vision, and influence to grow and keep that power. A CISO can also empower others to take steps in their respective domains to contribute to the overall security culture. As a result, the CISO becomes accountable.

One of the biggest reasons one would strive to be in the position of a CISO is to influence the stakeholders on security initiatives. Unlike other roles in cybersecurity, a CISO has a direct channel to the final decision-makers. You must use this access carefully, as it can either move your cause forward or undermine it. Developing this power of influence requires some work upfront. It works best when you create the proper relationships within the organizations. When people trust you, they are less likely to question your judgment because you've proven yourself to them through your decision-making. You will also need to utilize the chain of trust to get referrals and delegate work to save time. The stakeholders usually ask for other people's opinions in their circle of trust which can also be their peers in other companies. You will need allies outside the organization to validate your decisions further.

Overall, your cyber strategy should align with the company's strategic vision. A lot of the time, we make the mistake of focusing on tactical issues of implementing security measures. Leaders think strategically. They leave the tactical side to the technical or project team leads and keep their relations closer to the stakeholders to strengthen their power over influence.

Avoid things that will weaken your power and influence. Your attitude and how you deal with people will make the difference. Ignoring opposing opinions, not showing empathy, making threats, and putting people in a difficult spot by manipulating the situation will cause your eventual downfall.

Let's break down some elements that bring a CISO this power.

RELATIONSHIPS

The CISO is a hybrid role consisting of management and technical skills. The CISO operates in the boardroom with executives and on the operations floor with the security teams bringing them confidence and motivation. It is a position that brings stability, confidence, and positive organizational change by heightening the security posture. The CISO must effectively communicate the company's security posture internally and externally in an appropriate fashion. Building relationships is fundamental to this process.

Trust

All relationships are built on trust. Trust is developed with your experiences and how you deal with people over time. It revolves around building rapport with individuals. It requires you to have empathy and to help others unconditionally. As you build relationships, some people will betray your trust. It only makes you stronger, which improves your ability to recognize deceit.

Remember that you will not come into this role alone, and you won't be starting from scratch. Through your past roles, you will have existing relationships with colleagues and vendors that you will utilize in your CISO role. Building trust is a continuous process. It allows you to do business with others without the worry of micromanagement and things going wrong. As a CISO, every minute is precious. You will leave a lot of decisions up to others to save time. You will make that call based on your level of trust with that person. That is the secret of getting more things done in your limited time.

If you don't have established trust with your team members, a quick way to develop it is to take smaller risks and entrust others with duties. If they follow through, they've gained your trust. Now you can go bigger and assign more responsibilities to them, knowing they will not disappoint you. Sometimes the smallest things can establish great rapport, like taking your team out to eat, getting to know them better, listening to their concerns, and asking for their opinion.

Chain of trust

Let's look at a real scenario we're all faced with when trying to select vendors. Let's say I need a SOC service. As you might know, there are hundreds of vendors. They all have similar capabilities on paper, but I only have enough time to sit through a presentation and demo for a few of them.

They're all new to me, and I don't have any form of trust established with them. I've been burned in the past by choosing the wrong vendor. How do I maximize my chances of finding the right vendor for the job? Either inquire within my peer network or ask one of my existing security partners whom I trust to provide me with recommendations. They may provide me with contact details of one or two vendors they have worked with and trust. Now you develop trust through a proxy and shorten your selection process.

We do not have enough time in our lives to develop trust with everyone, let alone every potential vendor or client. That's why we must embrace the concept of the chain of trust. Just like a chain, if the recommendation provided to you fails, the other links in the chain get affected as well. That's why people are hesitant to recommend someone for fear of breaking the chain of trust. However, when recommendations do come through, they are usually solid. Hiring managers also use the strength of this chain to elicit internal recommendations for open positions in a company. Someone coming through the chain of trust is less likely to be a fraud. Most positions are filled through internal referrals without needing to advertise.

Regulators

The CISO must also be able to hold relationships with the regulators to understand the company's responsibilities to law and regulations. These requirements are often presented to the organization in vague legal documents. The CISO needs to decipher these requirements from the regulators' perspective to ensure they are all on the same page. Depending on which person you talk to, their understanding will depend on compliance and technical details. Creating a good rapport with the regulators will help cut through the back-and-forth emails or meetings and shorten the cycle.

I was once asked to perform a NIST assessment for a client. They were doing it to be compliant with a regulator's request. They also wanted it completed immediately. Since they had yet to do such an assessment in the past, it presented a hurdle as it would take a lot of time and cost money. When I finally had a chance to speak with the regulator directly, he only wanted a vulnerability scan presented, and we had plenty of those to show. It seemed that the original request was lost in translation. Because of experiences like this, I'm always a proponent of simply picking up the phone and calling people to clarify requirements.

STRATEGY AND TACTICS

A CISO should have the authority to make informed decisions that improve the company's security posture and reduce risk, but they don't always have that power. They must convince the stakeholders with numbers and metrics before getting approval.

A good way to attain some of the power of making reliable decisions is to establish a strategy that aligns with the company's vision. If every decision you present aligns with the company vision, approvals become a formality. You want the stakeholders to know and hear that your solution forwards their vision to gain their approval and support.

How do you develop that power? By thinking strategically instead of tactically. As a CISO, you should create a strategy based on the company goals, vision, threats, budget, and appetite for risk. This strategy trickles down to the IT Directors, Operations Managers, or Project Managers to implement. Your implementation guidelines will be tactical based on the project and its priority. These two approaches go hand in hand.

> "Strategy without tactics is the slowest route to victory. Tactics without strategy is the noise before defeat." Sun Tzu.

For example, you will often see companies implementing many security controls without any strategic leadership. They will be great tactically but lose efficiency and productivity. They end up opening themselves to many security gaps. We also see the opposite where great security leadership has a plan of action based on a thorough security assessment, but they fail to follow through with the plan by not putting in the necessary security controls due to the lack of resources, budget, or technical know-how.

This synergy is a group effort. You need both approaches to be successful. Learning how to collaborate with the team to achieve this common goal will aid in your success.

MAKING ALLIES

CISOs can be placed under multiple categories, discussed further in Chapter 9. The broadest ones are Technical CISOs and Strategic (operational) CISOs. Each type has its strengths and areas where they need assistance. Newly established companies frequently seek the Unicorn CISO - an individual who possesses all the desirable qualities and lacks any deficiencies. However, it is important to acknowledge that such an individual does not exist. A Technical CISO should be well supported by a strategic leader, while a Strategic CISO should be well supported by a technical leader. This supporting role could be the Deputy CISO or other peers in the organization. Nonetheless, a CISO needs buy-in when building or managing a security program, from the CEO to Human Resources to Legal, and even the janitor! (Think physical security).

A CISO's number one goal is to collaborate, persuade and influence. There will be a lot of security issues that make you tick, but how would you implement them organizational-wide if you don't have the support or backing of other leaders? Additionally, good rapport with the folks on the ground and in the field can go a long way to achieving your objectives. Many CISOs make the mistake of implementing policies or trying to implement controls based on a compliance framework first. It's common that people don't read policies, and the job of the CISO is not to perform compliance activities.

Experiences with people matter the most when being a CISO. Paying attention to every interaction you have while developing allies will make you a strong CISO. As a CISO, you will need to justify your existence, navigate territory wars, address prior decisions, understand the culture, and think outside the box. Highlighting all the issues with security will not make you friends, especially within the security teams.

An aspiring CISO (and current CISO) should be able to (but not limited to):

- Give presentations to technical and strategic teams
- Contribute to the overall information security community
- Explain the "Why" and "How" for implementing their vision
- Be flexible, not rigid, to achieve their objectives
- Have an opinion backed with facts
- Be humble and open to learning from others

The above describes a Human CISO with the ability to influence others. You are likely already doing this in your current role.

Finally, don't be afraid if you struggle with relationship building. CISOs come from all walks of life with various experiences, especially non-security related. Relationships require time. Instead of jumping head-first, walk into the role to do your best job.

KRYPTONITE

To become a competent CISO, it's crucial to concentrate on constructing a robust foundation. However, you must also be attentive to actions that can diminish your abilities, tarnish your standing, and potentially terminate your career. Like Superman, your vulnerability, kryptonite, lies in external interactions and behaviors such as manipulation, intimidation, professional coercion, and exploiting your authority to overrule or reject decisions. Although some of these behaviors may appear apparent to steer clear of, they can unconsciously creep in amidst the stress and pressure of any job.

Manipulation

Getting a person to do something they don't want to do is manipulation. You will leave them feeling used. They will feel uncomfortable around you and start despising you. Avoid this at all costs. Instead, make them part of the process so that they want to help. Manipulation tactics are often used by people who are very impatient and do not have much empathy. You do not want to be labelled as self-centered.

Threats

You will find yourself in situations where people don't listen or follow your instructions. I have often heard toxic jokes in the workplace, like "if we could only take people out of the equation, they are so stupid." Don't get frustrated. This is part of the job. It is easy to use your position as a senior executive and resort to threats. I have heard managers coercing their engineers to finish tasks through the night, including ones that are not part of their duties. They are threatened by denying bonuses, being demoted, or being fired. No one should be subject to such behavior. No one benefits from threats. In fact, the person giving the threats has time against their side and will eventually get replaced. There is always a better solution than resorting to threats. Instead, use motivational tactics, incentivizing with bonuses or even treating them with gifts or lunch. It only costs you your patience.

Veto

Make sure you are not abusing the executive powers you have. You may be right about certain decisions, but part of your job is to bring everyone on board with your thought process. If you are unable to convince others of the security risks or your tactics, then you should try other tactics and approach them from a different angle until you succeed or are convinced otherwise. Overriding the decisions of others just because you have the authority to do so makes people feel powerless. Don't flex your CISO muscles at others. Humility will take effect in the long run.

Instead of going against other people's suggestions because you are right, spend time demonstrating your thought process. Don't tell people they are wrong or stupid for not agreeing with you. Instead, listen and help them understand your perspective. Realize that people come from different backgrounds and see things from their point of view. Failing to see it from their point of view will make you fall deeper into the abyss and fail at understanding others. You can still get your way without using your veto powers. You must learn to convince others and how to disagree respectfully.

TAKEAWAY

Cultivating your CISO powers takes a lot of patience. The struggles help you grow into a leadership role and prepare you to drive change with your powers. There is little room for error. Making others feel wanted and respected enhances your powers and solidifies your position.

8. PATHS

Myth: You need an Ivy League degree to be a CISO

As you advance in your professional journey, it's crucial to be aware of the routes that lead to the position of a CISO. While beginning as a junior or mid-level IT security expert, there may be various pathways that lead to other rewarding career advancements. However, if our objective is to attain the role of a CISO, it's essential to avoid the routes that don't align with our aspirations.

The roles that are "one hop away" from a CISO include those with a mix of technical and managerial responsibilities. These can consist of a Chief Information Officer (CIO), Chief Technology Officer (CTO), IT Risk Manager, IT Director, Auditor, Director of Operations, Incident Response Manager, Solutions Architect, Security Practice Lead, and other similar designations. By no means is this an exhaustive list, as there are exceptions as well. For example, I've heard of CISOs with medical degrees. Nonetheless, certain roles should be in mind with a promotion or new job offer if you want to pave a shorter path to a CISO.

> **Gatekeepers:** People with influence within a company who define the entry into the field. More in Chapter 16

I often hear from "gatekeepers" that you need either a management degree or a computer engineering degree as a minimum requirement with twenty years of experience to even think about a role in cybersecurity. This could not be further from the truth. So as a response, I ask these simple questions:

1. Whom are we trying to defend against?
2. Do the most skillful and organized cyber criminals and masterminds meet those minimum requirements?

We are primarily trying to defend against hackers. The typical profile of one of these criminals would likely not meet the standard job requirements for a cybersecurity role. While a lot of attacks are carried out by organized cyber gangs, the reality is that most organizations become victims to "script kiddies" – people who are merely testing their newfound skills on organizations that are not yet taking security seriously.

ENTRY

Many of you may have noticed that new college graduates face difficulty obtaining cybersecurity jobs. Unfortunately, some job descriptions state entry-level and require five years of experience, which can be confusing. Indeed, certain cybersecurity roles need to be more entry-level. At the same time, there are also many cybersecurity roles that require basic IT or management skills and some level of knowledge or experience to understand basic cybersecurity concepts. In addition, there are junior security analyst roles and internships that can get you in the field early. Some folks also contribute to social media, write blogs, and build a brand around themselves to become attractive to employers. Finally, I've noticed many folks in cybersecurity with past degrees in biology, journalism, or finance proving that it's possible to get into cybersecurity based on your motivation and passions. Consider these to be stepping stones to your career.

Once you have gained a few years of experience, you are ready to focus on mid-career roles that will help you become a CISO.

How do you transition into a cybersecurity leadership role like a CISO? There are job roles that overlap based on a fundamental understanding of technology and management concepts that meet the prerequisite skills needed to succeed. For example, if you are in a technology, sales, management, programming, or engineering role, you can easily pivot into a CISO role. There are also lateral paths by being a CIO or CTO. While these aren't a complete list, some of the common roles that can directly transition into a CISO are:

- GRC Auditors
- Security Consultant
- IT Risk Manager
- Incident Response Manager
- CTO/CIO
- Director of Operations
- Solutions Architect
- Systems Engineer
- Principal Engineer/Architect

If you aim to be a CISO one day but don't know if you're next job will get you closer or further away from the target, then consider aiming for the roles mentioned above as a guide. The next chapter discusses the skills in depth for these roles.

Education

In the 90s, we saw a boom in IT certifications and a focus on security. At the time, security was very rudimentary and undefined in terms of concepts, standards, and technology. Now, dedicated fields in college focus on various aspects of cybersecurity. There are also crash courses and bootcamps that get you up to speed very quickly without the need for a four-year degree. This begs the question, what level of education is required to perform your duties in a cybersecurity role?

The path to cybersecurity does not require a formal educational degree. While cybersecurity degrees are maturing, they still do not reflect the daily responsibilities of the jobs that are being offered in the field. A degree helps you stay structured and organized, but at the same time, any competent, motivated individual can customize their own learning program based on their interest and market needs.

It will make no difference whether you have a college degree or not. What matters is your skill sets. The more relevant skills you have, the better you will be at your job. Most of these skills require a few weeks to a few months to acquire, and they could very well come from a college program. These skill sets range from hands-on technical labs, public speaking, presentation, documentation, understanding the business, product knowledge, and the technology that makes up the infrastructure you will eventually deal with. Companies will teach you these soft and technical skills, which will bring you closer to a CISO role. What companies can't teach you and what you need to bring to the table is your willingness to learn, passion, and attitude.

Experience

Once you've successfully made your entry into the right field and attained the necessary education to be successful, you need to get experience. Most roles require experience, but to gain experience, you need a job. If you are faced with this catch-22, realize that you don't always need a job in cybersecurity to fulfill experience requirements. Instead, you need experience in any relevant field that utilizes your skills in cybersecurity.

What jobs will provide you the experience to transition from a Phantom CISO to a CISO? One approach can be to focus on a cybersecurity domain and master its associated skills. For example, if you want to attain experience in the risk management domain, apply to a GRC or auditor role. A better approach would be to become a jack of all trades and understand each cybersecurity domain over time. For example, you can transition within various security roles in a company, such as threat intelligence and incident response.

In time you will naturally levitate to one or a few areas of expertise. However, your value as a CISO will always come from knowing a bit of everything. As a result, you won't miss the forest for the trees (Review Chapter 2 - The Bigger Picture.)

Titles

Should you care about Titles? The politically correct answer is No. But the reality is YES! This book is called "The Phantom CISO" for a reason. Authority, power, and access come from titles, not your experience or skill sets, unfortunately. We're not advocating title abuse. Maintain your professional credibility, but also don't take all the responsibility with no authority. Setting yourself up for success or failure is often tied to the titles we have.

As a Phantom CISO, we do not have the title of a CISO. On the path to attaining the title of a CISO, we care about the subsequent tiles that help us reach our goal. The examples presented in the 'Entry' section of this chapter help us get closer to our goals.

An important exception is that there are disruptors in our industry who title themselves creatively, like a Chief Security Strategist, Chief Ethical Hacker, Chief Chaos Officer, Chief Human Hacker, or Chief Hacking Officer. They can do this because they stand out from the rest of the pack based on their experiences and reputation.

Outliers

There are plenty of folks that have gained experience through hands-on learning. They have spent their time teaching online, learning practical skills, participating in Capture The Flag (CTF) tournaments, public speaking, and consulting for non-profits. These are the outliers that do not follow the conventional degree path. Again, we are not undermining the degree and certification collectors, but these alone don't qualify you as a cybersecurity professional.

Mentorship

A mentor can guide you towards gaining the right experience, help you where you get stuck, and keep you motivated on the right path. To get the most out of a mentor, the mentee should drive the conversation and agenda to truly learn. While it may take time to find the right mentor, it will be a worthy investment of your time as you will learn some good shortcuts.

Reputation

Once you put in the hours and feel you have the skills, confidence, and experience it takes to apply for a CISO position, your reputation is the cherry on top. Experience and reputation go hand in hand. Without a good reputation, you may struggle to get recognition. For all the paths that lead to a CISO, your professional reputation will play a significant role in determining whether you get the position. Remember that the higher the role in an organization, the more they focus on responsibility. Trust and reputation are the pillars of responsibility. Therefore, you must be cognizant of keeping your image positive or, at the very least, neutral. Companies are looking for people they can rely on, especially for senior roles. So, if you don't have a reputation, start building one.

If you are not sure what others think about you, ask some of your close friends candidly if they would hire you as a CISO if put in that position. Again, talk to a few people who will give you some constructive feedback, and you may uncover some gaps that you need to work on in gaining public trust. If the answer is "yes, I don't see why not," then you are ready to take the leap.

TAKEAWAY

While formal education is important, it does not define you as a cybersecurity professional. Hands-on experience is education in and of itself. There are multiple ways to attain a CISO role. Attaining relevant experience and developing a good reputation in the professional community will pave your path to a CISO.

9. TYPES

Myth: There can only be one

With the multitude of paths available to become a CISO and the variety of skills required, you will naturally see many types of CISOs emerge. This field has become so mature and in-depth that no one CISO is like the other. Depending on the sector or role, you will see a significant variance in skill sets, backgrounds, and personalities.

If I could broadly divide CISOs into two categories based on their background, it would be **technical** and **business**. This equates to **tactical** and **strategic**, respectively. Every CISO has a mix of both, but the proportions vary significantly. Having a healthy ratio of technical and business skillsets is ideal and is influenced by your background experience. I started with 80% technical and 20% business-focused skills, slowly growing towards the side I had less experience in; strategic planning. Eventually, I see myself settling at a 60-40 ratio of technical-business focus.

Variation and diversity are not only healthy in this profession but are required as all environments have different needs. The various types of CISOs exist because of the wants of different organizations. For example, technology companies that deal in software or products will want a CISO who speaks their language and understands their process. In such an environment, a Technical CISO will blend in well. On the other hand, a bank, financial institution, investment firm, or law firm will want to talk to a strategic or business CISO. Finally, sales organizations will love a Product CISO with experience in pre-sales and marketing.

Rising to be a CISO has different challenges today. The industry has matured into many verticals and technology-focused fields. It calls for security leaders across various backgrounds, industry knowledge, soft and hard skills, education, culture, or relationships. With all these variables, it is natural to have a variety of skill sets, backgrounds, and industry experience, giving rise to many different types of CISOs. It is essential to mention the types as it highlights that not every CISO is comfortable or even fit to work in every environment.

Technical

You may have noticed that many transition paths to a CISO come from technical roles like IT Directors, Auditors, Solution Architects, and other Subject Matter Experts (SMEs). It is primarily because the role of anyone in IT or Security is considered technical by default. Almost everything a CISO will deal with will have a baseline element of technology. For example, technical security controls may need to be implemented to protect technology or processes. Implementing the control will come naturally to a technical individual educated in applying various controls. In most cases, a Technical CISO will devise such a solution effortlessly based on their background. This is their tactical side.

If a CISO is not well versed in the nuances of the technology they are trying to introduce, they may struggle to communicate the value it provides upstream. They will require assistance from their technical staff and third-party solution providers or spend time brushing up on it themselves. They will spend more time on technological research to vet the right solutions. Finally, they will need to get comfortable with technology as almost everything they touch will revolve around some technical security controls.

The true power of a technical CISO is when they are required to articulate the solution for a current security gap to their stakeholders. A CISO will use their skills like an educator to help bridge the knowledge gap and get everyone on the same page. However, they also require a lot of soft skills to influence the stakeholders, which is where the Business CISO has an advantage.

Business

The first question I always ask my clients is: "What are you trying to protect?" The answer could be their sensitive data, trade secrets, or reputation. Then the discussion leads to a deeper conversation about what is worth protecting and what is not. You may have heard the saying: "you don't protect a $100 bill with a $1,000 safe." In my experience with clients, they often want to implement a security solution worth more than the assets they're protecting. For example, I may ask them if their data is worth more than the $100,000 SIEM solution they want to purchase. Conversations like this allude to the concept of acceptable risk. Once we have an answer to these fundamental questions, it becomes our epicenter, and we focus our security initiatives towards it.

I've greatly simplified the process here to help understand the point. The challenge is to equate value to what needs protection. This is an area where individuals from a technical background may struggle if they remain in their comfort zone. The answer to this question is not tangible. In other words, an asset can have different value depending on who you talk to. The CFO may value business units that create more revenue and profit. The CEO may value their sales and marketing team, which allows them to cast a wider net on the market. The COO will value things that provide more process efficiency. The IT Director will value the availability of their systems. The founder will value visionaries and anything that promotes the initial cause. Therefore, it becomes imperative to spend some time understanding the business to know what to protect before we even dive into how to protect it.

Can you secure a business without understanding the business? Business CISOs are very successful at understanding and articulating business impact. If you are not presenting arguments that appeal to business impact, your efforts will be futile. You must "sell" your security services internally and show the business owners why your role is essential; otherwise, they look at you as a cost center. Traditionally, individuals with a business background transition to a CISO quite comfortably because the stakeholders need someone who thinks like them. In addition, Business CISOs naturally have the soft skills required to succeed in this role by having a business background.

Most Business CISOs come from roles requiring them to manage people or processes, like a CIO, Operations Manager, or IT Director. They may also have a strong background in finance with an MBA and auditing experience. A Business CISO may also be termed a BISO.

OTHER TYPES

Besides the two broad categorizations above, a CISO can be categorized based on other backgrounds or whom they serve. This could be based on verticals that give rise to Public Companies, Public Sector, Private Companies, or Federal CISOs. CISOs can also be grouped by the type of industry they belong to. For example, they could be focused on Product, Program Management, or Consulting.

There are a lot of other factors that bring about the variations you see below in the types of CISOs. These include temperament, skills, specialty, or need.

Not everyone ends up in this role based on career progression or even intent. Many "accidental" CISOs transition amongst the ranks simply because they were in the right place at the right time, knew the right people, or the company couldn't find anyone else to fill the role.

The following is a non-exhaustive list of theme-based CISOs:

- **Product Company**
  These are typically roles at vendors of security products. They are public advocates of security, and their products support the gaps they identify. You will often meet them at conferences as sponsors. They may give talks on security and position their products. Their primary role is to get everyone excited about security and attract more product and services business to the vendor.

- **Private Company**
  These are the most common types of CISOs at private enterprises that usually don't like to advertise their security program and are heavily focused on business impact and company profits.

- **Public Company**
  Publicly traded companies have CISOs with high visibility, as every incident affects their shareholders and makes the news. This is a very volatile position as the focus of security is to protect the company's reputation. News of a breach usually result in the CISO leaving.

- **Public Sector**
  Using public funds and creating the right allies in State and Local governments takes work. A lack of profitability also makes the "business impact" discussion difficult. A CISO in this position needs to have a lot of good relationships and a knack for navigating a lot of red tape. You will often see a Deputy CISO in this sector.

- **Federal**
  Like the Public Sector CISOs, challenges in the Federal government are similar in terms of bureaucratic red tape. There are more stringent policies on spending, approvals, and adhering to standards like NIST. Federal CISOs may feel powerless as things take a lot of time to get done.

- **Security Program Manager**
  Companies with many employees and a global presence will have the challenges of maintaining a security culture. Building a security program is one of the goals of a CISO. Those with a project management background excel in this role. In many situations, companies label a CISO a security program manager.

- **Steady state**
  Establishing a security program is only half the battle. A CISO that keeps pushing for impactful changes, sticking to the roadmap, continuously hitting milestones, and validating each step is an asset. A steady state CISO will come into an organization with a well-developed foundation and be tasked with continuing their growth in security initiatives.

- **Builder**
  If you need to start a security roadmap from scratch, a Builder CISO is up for the challenge. Non-tech companies or startups needing a security roadmap usually look for such a CISO. The CISOs in this space have experience as entrepreneurs with startups and building companies from the ground up.

- **Transformational**
  These are CISOs of companies undergoing significant digital change, such as migrating to the cloud, switching some major baseline technology, shifting workloads, or embracing remote work. A CISO in this role is usually great at discovering new risks with changing environments and proactively advising on closing those gaps.

- **Post-Breach**
  This type of CISO is hired after a breach happens. This high-stress and quick-action role requires a CISO to be on their toes and get things done quickly. A background in Incident Response greatly benefits this role.

- **Compliance**
  While every company follows frameworks in their security journey, a Compliance CISO will be well-versed in IT and security audits and have a well-documented and detailed approach to security controls with their GRC background. In addition, this person enjoys dotting all the i's and crossing the t's, typically with experience as an auditor.

- **Tactical**
  Sometimes an organization needs a doer to lead the team with an example and start plugging holes from day one. Coming from a technology background, a Tactical CISO will get straight to implementing controls and closing the gaps.

- **Strategic**
  A CIO or CTO transitioning to a CISO will be a planner. They will work closely with the business, get their buy-in, and approve budgets before implementing any change. They pave the path for security maturity in the long term.

- **Specialized**
  A CISO may be chosen for specialized sectors like industrial control systems (ICS), the airline industry, the stock market, blockchain, or government intelligence. Most typical CISOs will not fit this role; they are usually hand-picked.

- **Consulting**
  Unlike a conventional CISO that guides their organization, a consulting CISO provides guidance to their clients. This customer-facing role is usually found at managed service providers (MSPs). Depending on the size and scope of the organization, this engagement could be one-to-one or one-to-many clients.

From this short breakdown of the types of CISOs, you can see that while there are commonalities between them, they are quite different from each other. Yet all of them are required.

To compare the different flavors of CISO, consider the following: Everyone may not have the vision to start a security program from scratch (Builder). Some enjoy running well-established programs (Steady-state, Security Program Manager). Not everyone has the patience for delays in adoption (Federal) or to convince different departments on budget allocation (Public Sector). The anxiety of a breach is not for the faint-hearted (Post-Breach), and not everyone is ready to be dissected in the media for their security practices (Public). Some enjoy improving the gaps in frameworks (Compliance), while others like implementing it (Tactical). Others enjoy talking about technology and leveraging a partner ecosystem (Consulting).

There is yet another type of CISO that deserves its own specialized category.

vCISO

A virtual CISO, a.k.a a fractional CISO, is like a part-time CISO for an organization with specific use cases. A vCISO may also be employed as an interim CISO until the organization hires a full-time CISO. The more common use case is for mid-sized organizations developing their security program but are not quite ready to hire a full-time CISO; they take the services of a virtual CISO. A vCISO may be independent or part of a company that provides it under a Security-as-a-Service (SECaaS) contract.

A virtual CISO will likely be dividing their time between multiple organizations. There are many benefits for an organization to hire a virtual CISO instead of a full-time CISO. The following are some of the reasons that make this an attractive option.

Answering Critical Questions

How much at risk are we? What should we be doing to improve our security? These are the fundamental questions most small to mid-sized organizations need help answering. They are aware of the multiple security products out there and the third-parties that offer their services, but the options quickly get overwhelming. This is where a vCISO analyzes the security posture and creates a roadmap for remediation. A vCISO also provides product and vendor knowledge to help guide the organization, pairing controls to solutions or products that offer it. A vCISO will also help create a security budget to factor in cost.

Manageable Cost

The average CISO costs an organization $250-350K with benefits depending on which survey you look at online. A vCISO, on the other hand, is usually a monthly service with either hourly billing or a fixed monthly fee for their services. Not being full-time saves the organization the costs of a full-time CISO while getting the experience and the right amount of work from the vCISO. Cost is another great advantage, as a company spends around a third-or half of the cost of a full-time CISO. Most small to mid-sized companies will benefit significantly from a part-time CISO as they build and grow their security practice. If they no longer require the services of the vCISO, they can end the contract. This makes the vCISO a very convenient and digestible on-demand service.

Flexible Investment

Since this is an hourly or monthly service model, as the organization matures in its security posture, it can invest more time and money in the services of a vCISO. This makes it a pay-as-you-grow model, and they can scale up or down with changing demands. They can eventually either hire the vCISO as a full-time position or open a new position to fill the role.

No Turnover

An average CISO lasts 18-24 months due to burnout or lack of management buy-in. With a vCISO, the organization does not have to deal with this turnover issue. Usually, a vCISO is provided by a security consulting organization as a service to other organizations. If their vCISO leaves, they will have more on their bench. So, the client will not have to deal with the supply and demand issues and the gap of not having a CISO if the individual decides to move on to another role. The consulting company will replace them with an equivalent option with a proper knowledge transfer.

Access to Network of Experts

A CISO is not responsible for implementing security controls. It is an advisory role. A CISO will delegate security work to their team, but how does a vCISO handle this for a smaller organization with one or two IT folks? A vCISO must be a jack of all trades and have a network of resources. They know people in the industry who can jump in and provide assistance. When provided as a service, the vCISO will either have some in-house resources to address security controls or can leverage their partnerships with vendors.

Training

The expectation is that every security leader stays up-to-date with the news, the latest threats, and training. Organizations can benefit from a vCISOs expertise as they get a one-stop-shop for all their security concerns without investing time in training for in-house resources.

Challenges

With all the benefits an organization can have with a vCISO, it also comes with challenges unique to the vCISO. This person must juggle between a few different organizations. They need more time to build proper rapport with other departments as a resident CISO would. Without clear communication channels, they struggle to get the message across, and a lot may get lost in translation. It is also challenging to be focused on the organization's long-term goals by juggling between clients. It becomes even harder because companies only contract a few hours a week of their time. Even with these challenges, a vCISO is a great way to plug the gap in the industry quickly.

Deputy CISO

A great way to build yourself as a CISO is to apply for a Deputy CISO position. Although not a very common position, a Deputy CISO assists a CISO in managing risks in the organization. The CISO will groom the Deputy CISO to perform some of the responsibilities mentioned above. While the CISO will make head-on decisions and be the front-facing security representative, the Deputy CISO will share the duties. The Deputy CISO may support the CISO as a liaison to senior executives, interact with key stakeholders routinely, and run the security function when the CISO is unavailable. While there may be some exceptions, the Deputy CISO is generally considered the second in command within the information security department. For most other organizations, the person playing this role may not have the official title of a Deputy CISO; they will fit the definition of a Phantom CISO.

Takeaway

The goal is the same, yet there are various personalities. When forging your path, consider your work background to decide what type of CISO you want to be and use that as an advantage to enter the industry and gain relevance. Find your style of managing risk and then embrace it. Each type of CISO is unique and provides value to different organizations.

It's good to be well-rounded and understand your strengths and weaknesses. If you are a technical CISO, embrace it and get help on the business side. If you are Business CISO, don't worry about the technology side, plenty of support will be available. There's no shame in getting assistance and addressing your shortcomings. It will help you succeed faster and ensure confidence in difficult situations.

10. SOFT SKILLS

Hard impact

You cannot build a house with just a hammer. You must have a toolbox of versatile tools, each serving its purpose. The analogy of the house also applies to your career. You will need to incorporate many different skills over time to inch your way toward success.

When it comes to managing an organization's security risk, it takes a combination of technology skills, soft skills, and experience. This chapter focuses on the soft skills needed to make a CISO successful. Soft skills include but are not limited to communication, interpersonal skills, teamwork, decision-making, critical thinking, and leadership. The CISO's role is highly cross-functional, and a CISO with good soft skills will demonstrate an influential impact on the organization.

As you read this chapter, you will find that you gained some soft skills from previous experience, while others need fine-tuning. While you don't need every soft skill in this chapter, these skills have their purpose, and you will use them as you see fit from your toolbox. Reflect on your soft skills and decide how to enhance them or introduce them in your interactions. This chapter aims to help you become a dynamic CISO by empowering you with a broad range of skills.

PROJECT MANAGEMENT

An individual tasked with the responsibility of managing cybersecurity risks in the organization needs to have many priorities on their radar. CISOs need to have a bird's eye view of the status of security projects without really doing the work of a project manager. Some CISOs will handle this very well due to their past work, while others will want nothing to do with it and will focus more on executive buy-in and relationship-building. Whatever comfort level you have with managing projects, you will need to know the big picture, the many smaller projects that make up your strategy, and who can help you fulfill them. At some point, you will be a project coordinator or at least get regular status updates from one. At the end of the day, it is your responsibility to see them through. Understanding the structure of projects, their dependencies on other tasks, and their place in the timeline will help you build a roadmap.

The following chart is a sample that I show clients and stakeholders to help them better understand the high-level overview of multiple siloed projects that need to be executed to stay on top of the game.

Jan	Feb	Mar	Apr	May	Jun	Jul	Aug	Sept	Oct	Nov	Dec
QBR			QBR			QBR			QBR		
Security Assessment											
	Remediation Guidelines										
	Budgetary Analysis										
		Vulnerability Scans			Vulnerability Scans			Vulnerability Scans			Vulnerability Scans
			Traffic Analysis	Policy Docs		IRP					
			Solution Development					Solution Development			
		Phishing Campaign	Tracking/ Validation			Phishing Campaign	Tracking/ Validation			Phishing Campaign	Tracking/ Validation
					Security Awareness Training			Web Application Scanning			Pentesting

While each one of these tasks may be handled by separate teams, a lot of them will depend on the completion of the other. For example, performing a pentest before performing vulnerability scans and patching systems is not the correct order and will not provide you with the best results.

This project chart shows that many smaller projects run concurrently. If one does not complete a project in time, it will affect common resources and overlap with other projects. So, keeping track of project timelines is an essential skill to make progress with your security roadmap.

The prerequisite to a defined security project roadmap is a cybersecurity risk assessment. Based on the assessment, gaps are discovered, and remediation guidelines are drafted. As a result, budgets need to be updated, policy documents need to be created or revised, and incident response plans need to be solidified and rehearsed. In parallel, we will vet vendors, establish a vulnerability management program, begin phishing campaigns, build a security awareness training program, and perform security testing periodically. All of these activities need to be tracked and validated so that progress is documented. Stakeholders must also be updated regularly in quarterly business reviews (QBR). The cycle then repeats with better efficiency. While all this is occurring, you need time for strategic planning with stakeholders.

Regardless of what stage of security maturity an organization may be in, the CISO must be able to manage their initiatives efficiently and effectively. Short-term and long-term plans will need to be laid out. Depending on the organization's size, the CISO will either appoint a project manager, team leads or manage the initiatives themselves. Working closely with project managers will help you understand their process. Taking the time to plan and review with the project leads will also help enhance this skill.

People Management

Projects and people go hand in hand. If you have managed people before, you will realize everyone has a different personality and is motivated for different reasons. One of the ways to manage people is first to define and share expectations proactively. This will help make the team successful in its goals. Expectations should be clear and include an expected time to complete. Next is to schedule one-on-ones with your team to focus on their strengths and weaknesses and get to know the person better to tap into the human element. Often, managers keep one-on-ones transactional and strictly business, resulting in less impact, motivation, and productivity. Keep a balance between professional, cordial, and informal. Finally, have team building events, including personality leadership assessments, so the team can get to know each other based on their strengths and skills. As a leader, this will also allow you to place your players in positions to accentuate their strengths.

Time Management

With multiple concurrent projects to oversee, hundreds of emails to reply to in a week, dozens of people to meet, and thousands of pages to read, time management becomes a necessary skill to master. This skill requires you to change the way you work and think. A few techniques that help include the following:

Micro-Tasks

People often ask a CISO, "How do you get time to do that?" Time management skills develop over time. It starts with being organized and carving out chunks of time on your calendar to accomplish specific tasks. These are small yet important tasks to finish as they may be holding up other tasks. These small wins require discipline and can be termed as micro-tasks. These could include documenting a short process, meeting with a project lead for clarity, or even sending out a few emails to get the ball rolling. Avoid putting these things off due to procrastination. As you start accomplishing smaller tasks in a timely manner, it will have a snowball effect.

Your calendar schedules are very critical to your discipline strategies. Don't let others set your schedule. Also, don't accept meeting invites without having a clear agenda and discussing with the host why your presence is required. You should only attend meetings if you are absolutely needed.

Hyper-Focus

If you have dedicated an hour on your calendar for a particular task, you cannot afford to multitask and sneak in other smaller tasks in hopes of getting more done. It is easy to get distracted by conversations, calls, texts, or emails, but we must resist the urge. Instead, focusing on the matter at hand and getting it completed early should be the goal. A good way to stay focused is to close your email client, keep your phone in another room and work in a dedicated, distraction-free workspace. Once you learn how to hyper-focus, you will realize you can achieve much more in a day than you previously could imagine.

Realistic Expectations

Another great element of time management is knowing how much work you can get done in a day. Have a goal to get one or two high-priority tasks accomplished per day. Anything else is a bonus. Don't overwhelm yourself. It is inevitable for other things to get in the way and eat up your time. Aiming to cram too many meetings in a day or overpromising on timelines will cause you to underdeliver. So, set realistic expectations for the day. Any new tasks go into the calendar for the next available day.

Mental Breaks

Periodic breaks are healthy for the mind. It is like recharging your battery after a focused session that drains you mentally. Getting time away from the screen is also essential. You may think you're wasting time by introducing off-screen time and mini breaks in your routine, but the opposite is true. A rested brain can achieve more in an hour versus an entire day full of work, stress, and fatigue. Allow yourself to avoid burnout in the long run by taking frequent breaks.

SAYING NO

"The difference between successful people and really successful people is that really successful people say no to almost everything." – Warren Buffet

Saying no is not an easy skill to master, but it complements your time management strategies. The basic concept of this skill set is to focus your time on what you can do and say no to the rest. Say no to doing everything yourself and learn to delegate some tasks. Say no to micromanagement and learn to trust. Say no to opportunities that don't align with your goal and learn to be selective. Say no to useless networking and learn to build meaningful relationships.

While you want to be liked by your team and get more things done, saying yes, and agreeing to everyone's requests may waste your time by leading you away from your goals. Saying no is challenging. You don't want to come off as rude or non-accommodating. You also want to build better relationships and help others by doing a few favors.

How do you know when to say "no"? If someone asks you to take on new projects, lead initiatives, build contacts or explore options, evaluate if it directly promotes your cause as a CISO. If it doesn't, here are some ways to respond to such requests while not sounding rude.

- Suggest someone competent with the skills to assist. Say something like, "This would be a great opportunity to get Adam involved." This demonstrates your ability to delegate the appropriate talent and sincere humbleness to get others involved. You don't have to do everything yourself. You have a team of smart people around you. Let others help you. Provide them with an opportunity, not a burden. Don't micromanage them either. Trust and see how people can add value to your team.
- Get clarification on the initiative and evaluate it against the roadmap. It will demonstrate your openness to listen as you are not rejecting it outright. Provide proper rationale if you can be included in a limited fashion or not be involved at all.
- Involve other expertise in the conversation to solicit ideas. Ask important questions like:
    o How does it affect security?
    o How urgent is it?
    o Does it take precedence over what you are doing now?
    o What resources are we pulling from other projects and into this one?
- Be direct yet supportive. Say, "I wish I had more time to do this," instead of, "I don't have time."

COMMUNICATION

Talking to people in the language they understand is pivotal to everything you do. There are quite a few elements that make up this skill set. As you read this section, take the time to evaluate yourself. Some of the useful skills to develop to become a great communicator involve the following:

- **Confidence:** Don't confuse confidence with ego; they are not the same. Also, don't assume that you can't be humble and confident, they are not mutually exclusive, and you can be both. Think of confidence as a multitude of factors. When people encounter you and your brand, they look for confidence based on your behavior, performance, skills, attributes, and response in critical situations. As you gain experience, you will develop confidence, but you must consciously focus on how you are valued at any given moment, just like a stock price. You want people to bet on you. Confidence can be built by participating in activities outside your comfort zone with support from peers such as a local public speaking group like Toastmasters International or common interest meetup groups. A judgment-free environment ensures the opportunity to fail and improve. Also, preparing research, educating yourself, and teaching a technology concept helps immensely in learning and building confidence. Soon you will notice people confiding in you as you make good decisions.

- **Building Rapport:** "How to Win Friends and Influence People" by Dale Carnegie is a must-read. The CISO's role is not only to worry about security initiatives but also to understand the company's initiatives. It includes collaborating with other key leaders on shared initiatives that will affect security. Building relationships makes you a better listener and allows you to make a higher impact. Many CISOs fail and give up because they aren't influential. It can be due to having a poor rapport with peers and leaders in the organization. Building rapport takes time and patience. To build great rapport with colleagues, incorporate the following techniques:
    o Develop and build trust. Express your trust by listening and taking into account other considerations. Avoid micromanaging unless it is required. When people notice you trust them, they don't want to let you down.
    o Reduce formality by sharing stories and experiences.
    o Be proactive in assisting others in supporting the business and aligning on similar initiatives. Let it be natural to help each other.
    o Use active listening skills by allowing others to share their ideas. People enjoy giving their perspectives and speaking their minds if you allow them to. It will create a better bond.
    o Ask open-ended questions to solicit opinions and exchange value. It will demonstrate appreciation towards others.
    o Pick your battles and suppress the ego where appropriate. It's not about winning or losing but agreeing on doing what's right. If multiple solutions bring the same results, agree on a reasonable solution, and execute it.
    o Don't be afraid to ask for a lending hand. You'll be surprised by the number of hands raised to assist in gaining experience.
    o Provide genuine feedback and validation of work. Avoid being quick to criticize. Don't forget to complement and acknowledge hard work for encouragement.

- **Sales Acumen:** Most successful sales folks communicate well and sell confidently. You must sell the idea of security internally to everyone, from the end user who sees it as a hindrance, to the top executives who see it as a cost. Working in pre-sales roles, you develop some good technical sales tactics.
    o Focus on value and not cost
    o Talk about potential savings instead of the potential loss
    o Focus their attention on long-term benefits rather than short-term growing pains

- **Active Listening:** Be mentally engaged when someone is speaking with you. Active listening is a choice, and it takes practice. Avoid distractions in your conversations by putting away your phone, silencing it, or moving to a quieter place. Your commitment to avoid distractions can be noticed based on eye contact and body language.

- **Teaching**: Teaching is the best way to demonstrate knowledge learned through sharing. It also results in questions by your listeners or students, allowing you to research, if necessary, and dive deeper into the subject. Teaching does not have to be formal; sharing facts can occur in everyday conversation. When done in a smaller focused group, it will help develop your communication skills. Next time you read something insightful, like the latest hacking technique, make a conscious decision to share it in a meeting or over lunch.

- **Public Speaking:** This should not be surprising, and you have probably been through multiple roles to know that public speaking brings people together. It is a combination of communication bullets mentioned above, including confidence and teaching. After any talk, take advantage of the follow-up conversations with your audience. This is a time to listen to them and receive feedback. These are great conversation starters. Sign up for the next security event's "call for speakers" and seek out opportunities to build your peer network.

There are many other ways to attain and build soft skills. You can refine this powerful skill by continuously reading, socializing, and sharing.

Personality Styles

Every individual has varying personality traits when it comes to interactions. For example, your communication style can be dominant, influential, supportive, compliant, or condescending to name a few. Whatever that type may be, the purpose here is not to change it but to discover your style, identify the other person's style and adapt accordingly for effective communication. This way, you minimize conflict and have a better chance of getting the message across.

For example, if you are a loud and dominating manager and speak to a network administrator who is shy and introverted, you will make them feel very uncomfortable. Instead, meet with them in their comfort zone, adjust your tone to match theirs, and provide them time and space to allow them to express their opinion.

Conversely, if you are of the analytical and soft-spoken type, having a conversation with a fast-paced and outspoken person will create serious gaps in communication. Therefore, you will need to adjust your style and meet halfway. You must be concise, direct, cut out details, and present more impactful facts upfront.

A more formal approach is presented in the concept of DiSC profiles (www.discprofile.com). The four primary personality types of DiSC include:

1. **Dominance:** This personality type describes a bold, confident, and outspoken person who speaks their mind and is goal-oriented. They are determined and like challenges.

2. **Influence:** This type describes an open and trusting person who likes to persuade and influence others with their enthusiasm. They like the limelight that comes with victory. Entrepreneurs and risk-takers often exhibit these qualities.

3. **Steadiness:** This type describes a calm, dependable personality that promotes cooperation and collaboration. A person with this personality type likes to work in teams and is very trusting.

4. **Conscientiousness:** People of this type are very detail oriented, take their time doing the research to produce quality work, and don't like being wrong. They are also usually solo players. A lot of analysts and technical folks fall into this category.

Our personality is a blend of all four profiles to different extents, and we utilize them accordingly. However, we tend to lean towards one or two profiles more than others. Online DiSC tests help determine our dominant areas. By learning about these personality types, we can recognize them in others and leverage this understanding to achieve consensus towards a shared goal.

EMPATHY

Empathy in business is the ability to understand the needs of others, to know how they feel about your decisions, and to care about how it affects them. Great leaders develop the skill of empathy by actively listening to and understanding the perspectives and feelings of others to build stronger relationships and make better decisions.

As we discussed, part of a CISO's role is to assess the various parts of the organization by identifying gaps and solutions to remediate them. You will be quite comfortable with this process if you come from an IT or Security Auditor background, as an auditor's mindset is to find gaps, highlight it and provide feedback. Nobody likes to be audited or to be told their baby is ugly. I have often seen people hide the details of a process or say that a control is in place when, in fact, it may not be, only to escape criticism. The whole process puts a lot of tension on teams. In fact, the word "audit" itself has a negative connotation and brings about auditor trauma. Audit is formally known to be an independent and objective evaluation. A better phrase for an auditor to use when working with stakeholders is "independent assessment" or "independent evaluation." The approach you take to evaluate the organization continuously will determine the level of cooperation you get from team members. Your aim is to work together and not let others feel like they are being audited. In situations like this, it is crucial to understand the effect empathy may have on others and to adjust your approach so that they feel you are here to support them as an extension of their team. The following are some areas you can focus on to work on this skill.

It's Not About Me

When performing security evaluations, internal teams and stakeholders need to learn about you, your process, understand why it's useful, and the outcomes it will achieve. It demonstrates that you have a good grasp of your role and are being customer-centric by making it about them. Your strategy should be to build common ground and to go into a mindset of "it's not about me." Recently, regulatory scrutiny has been a great reason for internal auditors and stakeholders to work well together to achieve a common goal, besides ensuring the organization is secure and operating with an acceptable level of risk. Working together accomplishes common goals.

No matter whom you work with, define expectations early so that they can visualize the same end goal. Remember, you will be requesting to see the skeletons in their closet. During the process, people may still wonder: "What's in it for me." Don't let them ponder over it too long, drive it home to by making it about them as well.

Words Matter

The choice of words is essential as people may misinterpret their meaning. Since people are already apprehensive about being checked, avoid using terms like audit or investigation. Replace those with collaboration, best practices, or establishing baselines.

With the right words and attitude, the engineers will realize that you're working with them as a team and are available to assist in security and compliance. If they show that they don't want you probing around, help them understand how it assists the organization. Additionally, credit them in reports for having controls intact. Finally, put in a good word about their involvement with their management.

Positive Tone

A positive tone with your teammates emphasizes your good intentions, along with the right words. Align your feedback with the security mission and highlight the accomplishments in your reports. Set the tone to be successful upfront. For example, the executive summary of your risk assessment should highlight the achievements of each team and transition into the areas of improvement. This makes it clear that you're not hunting for problems; your goal is to help improve security posture. Next, present your inquiries and your findings professionally. Compare the report to previous years so that it shows progress. Finally, ensure remediation steps are agreed upon and documented.

Walk In Their Shoes

During your security evaluations, you will interact with many different people from various departments. An effective way to show empathy is to listen and understand other people's challenges in their job roles. For example, working with a CFO, Human Resources (HR), or team leads in the past allowed me to understand their concerns and processes. Likewise, coming from a technical background helps you understand network engineers or system administrators better by speaking their language. It is always a good time to listen to people's concerns, no matter how familiar you are with them. It gives you a glimpse of their world before asking security-related questions. With this approach, you have the opportunity to tie their concerns with your security initiatives.

LEADERSHIP

As with all other skills, leadership comes with knowledge, training, and experience. While some people are born to lead, others must develop this skill. There are many great books written on leadership. You can also attend training and seminars to learn and practice leadership skills.

All individuals have unique qualities and personalities that build up their leadership styles. A good first step is looking at some leadership styles to see what fits you best. Below are some examples of leadership styles you may have witnessed and are looking to develop. In some cases, you will notice your own strengths and weaknesses in these styles. A CISO with a dynamic leadership style can reach places they could not have imagined.

- **Collaborative Leader:** Leaders cannot achieve anything great without their pack. Any leader needs to walk the walk to be able to talk the talk. John Maxwell states: "A leader is one who knows the way, goes the way, and shows the way." If the leader wants to influence their teams, they must show they are collaborative. Some examples of collaboration that I have seen from my previous Directors include, but are not limited to:
    o Creating a vision for the team that aligns with their purpose and guides the team through it.
    o Building future leaders on the team and including them in critical conversations and decisions.
    o Being transparent and opening the flow of information.

- **Passionate Leader:** I recall patiently waiting, ready to hear a presentation among my colleagues by one of the leaders in the company about our quarterly results. When the leader walked in and started speaking about the program and results, they captured everyone's attention. They were passionate and genuine, which was clearly noticeable in their vibrant body language, enthusiasm in their voice, and clarity of their message. Folks came out of the presentation proud to have such a leader. When a leader speaks from passion and experience, their position is not questioned as they display competence and love for the job. A passionate leader can also help reach the vision quickly and swiftly. In the book "The 21 Indispensable Qualities of a Leader," John Maxwell states: "A great leader's courage to fulfill his vision comes from passion, not position."

- **Servant Leader:** According to Simon Sinek's book "Leaders Eat Last," "The rank of office is not what makes someone a leader. Leadership is the choice to serve others with or without any formal rank." When you find someone speaking to you that you admire, it makes you feel good. These leaders also tend to empower those they lead because they are personable and willing to help. These leaders know that they can serve if they place the needs of others above their own. This skill is not something everyone can do until they train themselves to reach the wisdom of helping others succeed. Servant leaders can also be influential. According to John Maxwell, "A leader who produces other leaders multiplies their influences." People who benefit from servant leaders spread their name and their ideas. Maxwell further concludes: "If you want to be the best leader you can possibly be, no matter how much or how little natural leadership talent you possess, you need to become a serving leader."

You can do a couple of things today if you want to become a leader. Reading popular books about leadership is the easiest step. Reading will get you up to speed on the basic constructs of leadership. Taking a crash course is another great way to practice these skills and get feedback from an instructor. You can also take small steps toward demonstrating leadership in your company by starting an initiative. Finally, something everyone can do is contribute more to conversations and group meetings. Having an opinion shows you care and want to move things forward.

Whatever position you are in, if you actively initiate ideas with your management to kickstart relevant cybersecurity initiatives, you can prove your leadership qualities to yourself and others.

You will also allow yourself to be vulnerable and open to feedback. While being critiqued can be painful, leaders must also learn to assess and respond to feedback professionally and unemotionally. There is no better place to practice your leadership skills than where you currently are. Ask your peers and your managers for constructive feedback.

Finally, think of yourself as a tv station or podcast; will people tune into you? Do they look forward to hearing from you? Build your leadership brand so that you add value to others, and your ideas are contagious for people to share.

ENVIRONMENT

Positive

"Small minds discuss people. Average minds discuss events. Great minds discuss ideas." – Unknown. You generally want to stick to idea development and not dwell on things you cannot solve or don't contribute to your development. Talking about people, events, or theoretical scenarios will be like quicksand. It will only fog your vision and take you further away from your goal.

Being around other leaders is the best way to develop your leadership skills. These people bring you positive energy and will push you to do better. They will discuss ideas with you and allow you to think differently. Their perspectives may give you ideas for improvement.

Start by attending more leadership-focused events. These could be your company events or public events with guest keynote speakers. Have side conversations with speakers or leaders in your company, as they will be more approachable. Network with like-minded people. Connect on social media platforms that they are on and try to interact with comments and questions. Most importantly, choose to socialize more with people with ideas. When attending one of the many three-day conferences, I make it a habit to go out for lunch with someone I can learn from. As a result, I'm continually increasing my pool of opportunities; you never know which one may be fruitful. It may not be easy entering such circles, but little steps every now and then open more doors. The goal is to spend more time in front of influential people to uplift you and less time in front of people who bring you down or ignore you.

Toxicity

Not all environments with leaders are conducive. I've been in small leadership events where the purpose was to promote ideas and build a community where we all supported each other. It ended up being a platform for people who only wanted to boast about their success on stage. I questioned the organizers about how it would benefit me as an aspiring leader and entrepreneur. I was looking to talk to the presenters, look for mentorship, discuss takeaways, get introduced to prospects, talk about my ideas, and look for referrals. Some of these opportunities were also not available as the presenters didn't stay back after their lecture. How is this better than watching a YouTube video of a famous inspirational leader? It's not. These are called mixers. Some do it well but others are a waste of time if you want to develop yourself as a leader. Our advice is to try out multiple groups once, and if you don't feel comfortable, move on to the next until you find a group that helps you towards your goals.

Unfortunately, many toxic leadership environments exist, whether in events or group meetings. People don't talk about them, but they are quite common. For every ten groups I've been a part of, one has proven to be valuable. Sometimes it's worth the struggle to find the right environment. Always ask yourself, "What am I getting from being here? Am I more valued in a different environment?" Push yourself away from toxic environments and pull yourself towards positive ones.

Emotional Intelligence

Emotions play a significant role in how we deal with people. Being aware of our emotional state of mind can help us make decisions. Having control of our emotional responses is a tough skill to acquire, but as a leader, it can help us in difficult situations.

We have historically measured our thinking abilities with IQ (Intelligence Quotient). IQ tests are used to evaluate logical reasoning, memory, and comprehension. However, your intelligence is not just measured by IQ. Your ability to deal with pressure, hostility, or pushback has to do with your EQ. EQ (Emotional Quotient) is your ability to control your feelings. Both IQ and EQ are teachable skills.

Leaders with high EQ know what they're good at and where they fall short. As a result, they are not afraid to ask for help and collaborate with others.

Daniel Goleman, an emotional intelligence expert, developed a framework of emotional intelligence that is divided into four quadrants.

The quadrants are:

1. **Self-Awareness:** Can you read and recognize your emotions?
2. **Social Awareness:** Can you sense, recognize and understand other people's emotions?
3. **Self-Management:** How do you manage and keep your emotions under control?
4. **Relationship Management:** How do you influence and lead others?

Self-Awareness and Self-Management refer to our personal competence. Social Awareness and Relationship Management refer to our relation to others.

There are many ways to develop emotional intelligence. The following are some general tips everyone can benefit from:

- **Mindfulness:** Be self-aware of your emotional state. If someone's criticism makes you angry, realize what it's doing to you and act accordingly. If it's an email, reply after an hour when you cool down. If it's a conversation, pause and choose your words wisely. You can incorporate words like "I understand your situation; here's where I'm coming from." Any time you feel that your comments may escalate the situation, remain quiet until you find a better approach.

- **Accept feedback:** One of the biggest roadblocks to self-improvement is a person's pride or ego. It can take a hit on your reputation and trust from other leaders. Learn to listen to feedback without getting defensive. Instead, ask for clarification so you can take action on improving yourself and thank the person for their feedback. If you're not getting any feedback, it could be because people fear your reaction. In this case, you should create a comfortable environment to solicit it, like during a one-on-one conversation over coffee or lunch.

- **Develop empathy:** The best way to know your employees is to sit with them during a private one-on-one conversation and ask them questions about their future, how they feel, and where they need help. By knowing others' problems and struggles, you develop a deeper emotional connection with them. This gives rise to mentorship as well.

- **Self-Management:** People will notice how you react to news, criticism, or comments. Be conscious of how you present yourself in public, as it will influence how people deal with you. Your peers will look for calmness in you in times of a breach. Take pauses before meetings, display positive body language, have pleasant expressions, and choose the best words to convey your message. For example, one of the best comments I've ever received after giving a cybersecurity presentation was related to how calmly I described a cybersecurity threat and how to deal with it. The comment read, "Your voice is so calming; I would love to hear bad news from you."

- **Provide Purpose:** People will support you if they see your vision. Tell them why you do what you do. Providing regular updates to your team shows them you care. It motivates and gives them a purpose by looking at the bigger picture. It will end up building better relationships and trust.

Mastering all the different facets of emotions is a challenging task. However, with dedicated practice on individual aspects over several months, notable progress can be made.

There are exceptions to this, as not every leader possesses a firm grip on their emotional intelligence. For instance, we've witnessed leaders of prominent tech firms making impulsive decisions based on their whims and emotions. Nonetheless, having a high EQ earns you greater respect.

As a CISO, your capability to manage yourself and others plays a crucial role in your success. Your proficiency in this aspect is how the organization evaluates your competence. During high-stress periods, key leaders and teams pay close attention to your conduct, and your intelligence is gauged based on your reactions.

Writing

There is a correlation between writing and critical thinking. In our journey to write this book, we discovered that writing requires you to be sequential, organized, and understandable when stating ideas. Part of being a security leader, you will be writing and sharing your ideas internally to the organization and externally. It is a way to describe your thinking and communicate your ideas to the broader audience. It is a skill that provides finesse to your messaging.

Just Do It

While professional training courses are available to develop writing skills, the best way to learn is to do it. One way to practice is to start writing blogs in your passionate field of security. The earlier you start, the more credible you will be based on longevity. Writing is very similar to teaching. Teaching is sharing what you know, including your opinion and thinking style. A great example of a blog is by Phil Venables, CISO at Google. He started writing his blog in 2019 and speaks about everything from career advice to maintaining relationships with regulatory entities and security programs. Writing allows you to express your creativity and what you are passionate about. It is your ability to share your state of mind about the topic. Your blog posts and topics can be influenced by your daily activities or a response to a trending topic or recent breach. Writing will help you develop your brand and demonstrate your leadership qualities and thinking abilities. Another great benefit to writing is that you can refer to it in presentations, emails, or client discussions. This way, you gain some notoriety in the subject and don't have to repeat yourself, especially if it's a lengthier topic.

Your blogs should be independent of the company you represent. You can take a more formal approach and start writing blogs or whitepapers for your company as well. This can always lead to writing lengthier and more organized works like a training tutorial or even a book.

Critique

Once you start writing, you can get it critiqued by colleagues and friends. One of the best ways to receive feedback on your content is through comments. While you may not receive comments initially, consistency is the key to gaining traction. Opinions on your posts can also change over time, and you can always revisit a prior blog post to expand on your thoughts. Moreover, use the critique to improve your content.

Public Speaking

Public speaking is by far the biggest fear among humans. It beats arachnophobia – the fear of spiders! As a CISO, public speaking will benefit you considerably as it shows passion and commitment to your subject matter. You may be required to do it internally to provide updates and awareness.

Like writing, getting into public speaking starts by doing. The best advice to begin public speaking is by joining your local Toastmasters International club – a safe group to practice this art and share constructive feedback. It will allow you to get out of your comfort zone while remaining in a safe environment. Start small and grow your audience. The celebrity voice coach, Roger Love, once said, "All speaking is public speaking whether it's to one person or a thousand." Initially, I attended most of the local security meetups as it allowed me to listen and learn from others and get comfortable with people. I then spoke at my local community centers. They're always looking for speakers and usually have a large diversity of presenters and a non-judgmental environment. Moreover, members at the community centers are not very tech-savvy, so I could get away with minor mistakes. Take baby steps and find an outlet to practice this skill.

Acceptance Rate

As I became more confident in my public speaking abilities, I started applying for speaking slots at security conferences. They advertise it as a Call for Papers, Proposals, or Presenters (CFP). Most people don't apply because they fear rejection. For my first attempt at public speaking, I applied for a local TEDx talk and got rejected. TEDx is a regional version of the popular TED (Technology, Entertainment, Design) conferences. Maybe it wasn't such a great idea to start at such a high bar, but it only motivated me. Then I began to apply to many regional security conferences across the US. I had good material and wanted to present to get better at this skill. I applied to an average of ten talks in a year and got accepted to five. For the past 4-5 years, this ratio has been consistent. 50% is a pretty good acceptance rate and should bring some encouragement to people who hesitate to apply. I've also been on the other side, being part of a small group of CFP selection judges and picking topics and associated speakers who would present at a security conference. I can tell you from being a selector that your chances are very good; if there are 20 speaking slots, 40 people usually apply. That validates my 50% acceptance rate. However, when you enter the bigger arena, hundreds of people are applying for a handful of speaking slots, so start at the smaller conferences to build your brand, which will help you prepare for the bigger ones. You get better with every new speaking opportunity. With cybersecurity being one of the most popular topics in business, there are plenty of opportunities to talk throughout the year, from small to large venues.

Story Time

Steve Jobs stated: "The most powerful person is the storyteller." Strong public speakers always incorporate a story. If you talk about your experiences and lessons, you will engage with the audience better, and the story will come naturally as you have lived it. Public speaking is a skill; with all skills, it takes practice. We often think of public speaking as a formal and serious form of delivery. However, comedians are also public speakers and storytellers, and while their jobs seem hard, they make it fun. Similarly, there is nothing wrong with being a little humorous or informal in a professional environment. In fact, it makes everyone more comfortable and allows you to display your personality.

To make an impact with storytelling, the main idea of your story should not be lost in the details, and the lesson should be clear. The storyteller should focus on the audience, especially in terms of how they receive and perceive the information. You, as a storyteller, should also be conscious of the mood of your audience. You can judge this with their expressions, attention span, and body language. If you notice you are losing their attention, adjust your delivery method. For example, you could introduce long pauses, crack a joke, vary your pitch and volume, or ask a question. Based on the response from the audience, you can ensure your message is delivered properly. Effective storytelling is about emotionally connecting with the audience and involving them in the shared experience or lesson. There's a Chinese proverb, "Tell me, I'll forget. Show me, I'll remember. Involve me, I'll understand." The audience may not remember the details of your presentation or even the name of the topic, but they will remember a story that resonated with them. You will find examples of remarkable storytelling in public speaking in TED Talks.

Public Speaking is a prevalent fear, and storytelling is one way of conquering that fear. Building other powerful habits related to public speaking can also help boost your confidence level. One such habit is reading a book out loud for ten minutes a day and recording yourself. Listen to the recording, and over time you will learn how to get comfortable with your voice but, most importantly, how to control your voice in tone, pitch, and pace. Prepare and practice, and don't make perfection your goal. Your aim is to grab the audience's attention in the beginning and end with them inspired and remembering the lesson. Soon public speaking will become second nature.

Like leadership and writing, public speaking can be incorporated into your current role. You can start practicing it today. Is there a subject in security you have always wanted to learn? Prepare a video and share it! When you are ready, do it live with an audience. Is there an experience from which you believe others in your role would benefit? This could be presented in front of your colleagues at an informal lunch-and-learn session. Over time you will get valuable feedback allowing you to build your confidence and public speaking skills. Before you know it, you will feel comfortable being on stage with less preparation. You will notice that people will call you to speak because you have put yourself out there. Take advantage of those opportunities and begin building your brand now. Public speaking allows you to be creative and communicate your ideas by literally giving you the stage. Remember that your story has a purpose, you have something to share, and your audience will benefit.

Talent Acquisition

In Chapter 3 - Role, we talked about how stakeholders value a CISO in aiding them to fill the resource gap. Talent acquisition is a challenging process but a skill that will make you more valued. Hiring the right resources stems from defining the job description accurately. Many jobs are filled by reaching out to your network. Recruiters can also help narrow down the candidates. Then it comes to the interview process. Some things to look for in candidates are their passion and growth mindset. Passion can be determined in several ways, including volunteering at a local non-profit to improve their security posture, working on multiple high-impact projects to benefit communities, writing educational articles online, or even reporting vulnerabilities through bug bounty campaigns.

The hiring process is a two-way street. It is a competitive landscape, and candidates will look beyond just the compensation. Be interested in your candidate and ask them what they are looking for. In an interview, I was once asked, "What will keep you with us for at least a couple of years?" My answer was, "To have the autonomy to make impactful decisions and not be micromanaged." Candidates are attracted to training opportunities, career paths, work-from-home flexibility, inclusiveness in decision-making, and empowerment. Make sure you are having candid discussions about these upfront.

Don't be afraid to take chances on candidates with unique background skills outside of cybersecurity. Their perspectives may be valuable to the team. Cultural fit is another aspect to consider when connecting with candidates after they are hired. Finally, ensure you allow them to strive in the work environment and determine how to support them, so they give you the best work. Their success will be your success.

Hiring suitable candidates to build your team is a challenging skill. However, by incorporating these ideas in the hiring process, you can get better results and retain great talent.

Takeaway

Your value will be determined by the versatility of your skill sets. Continue learning from degrees, certifications, seminars, on-the-job training, and experience, but remember that soft skills are equally essential to make the transition to a CISO. A combination of the various soft skills discussed in this chapter, differentiate Security Experts from Security Leaders.

11. TECHNICAL SKILLS

Jack of all trades, master of "some"

Effective communication and collaboration require strong soft skills, but technical skills are fundamental to the field. The better you understand technology, the better you are positioned to solve problems. Dedicating time to understanding the value of technical skills is essential, as many CISOs have management experience but very little hands-on technical know-how.

A CISO doesn't need to know every detail, just enough to be dangerous. These skills make you independent and shorten the decision cycle as you understand the various layers of cybersecurity. As you recall from the introduction, we discussed the importance of asking why we want to become a CISO. After understanding the roles and responsibilities, it provides you the answer to the "Why?" The previous chapter and this chapter, Technical Skills, will answer the "How?" Let's look at the following areas from a technical lens.

INDEPENDENCE

CISOs should understand their technical environment and the types of technological solutions that would help fill those gaps. CISOs with high dependency on their architects or third-party vendors struggle with finding a solution that helps to address the gaps. For example, suppose a technical CISO is concerned about vulnerability management in the organization and meets with a third-party vendor. The expectation is that the CISO has done the homework before the conversation to answer simple questions by the vendor that describe the company's architecture, such as, "What hypervisor is the organization using?" If a CISO requires multiple follow-up conversations from their technical resources, it delays the process and shows that the CISO was unprepared to have the conversation. A technical CISO, in this scenario, saves time by avoiding a couple of follow-up calls.

As a technical systems engineer, I was invited to meetings that wasted my time. I was required to attend them, but my participation was optional and unnecessary. It was common to meet with a variety of teams. These teams can include internal teams, contractors, and vendors to discuss security controls. By paying attention, you can infer the roles that the attendees in the meeting play. Unfortunately, not all roles need to be present, resulting in confusion and meeting fatigue. If you are a technical CISO, you can avoid having technical staff on certain calls as you can handle the technical questions. People respect and appreciate your level of understanding by getting straight to the point on topics like software engineering, server infrastructure, networking design, or system administration. As a technical CISO, being on a call with technical staff, I've often heard them say, "Finally, someone who understands!"

DEFENSE-IN-DEPTH

As an advisor, a client once requested a ransomware solution. They were looking for a single product quote. I told them that a one-stop solution did not exist. They insisted on an endpoint security product, like an Endpoint Detection and Response (EDR) or a Managed Detection and Response (MDR) solution. Some vendors had convinced them that their products were the only solution. This is where understanding technical processes become useful. I told them they needed a layered security approach to combat ransomware as there's no silver bullet. The client thought I was just trying to sell them multiple products. Here's how I explained to them how to stop ransomware. I only hinted at a few technical terms but defined the flow of the attack along with potential solutions at multiple layers.

1. **Email Security:** Ransomware usually starts with a phishing email link or a malicious email attachment. Email security controls can help detect and stop it.
2. **User Awareness:** If the user clicks on the attachment, user awareness training can help identify malicious emails and report them.
3. **User Privileges:** If the attachment is downloaded, the user should not have administrative rights to execute the malware.
4. **EDR:** If the attachment is executed, Endpoint Detection and Response software should be able to detect and destroy the malware.
5. **DNS Security:** If the malware remains undetected, it should not be able to get instructions from its command-and-control center by blocking DNS requests to known malicious sites.
6. **Micro-segmentation:** If the malware manages to execute and spread, the ransomware should not be able to spread to different computers. Limit the spread by containing it in logical network segments.

I provided a solution using the defense-in-depth approach, as no single solution is foolproof.

If you can explain a threat in terms of technical controls with solutions that fill those gaps in a logical flow, you will demonstrate your knowledge holistically and leave a good impression.

Kill Chain

A similar concept is the cybersecurity kill chain, originally developed by Lockheed Martin. The cybersecurity kill chain outlines the stages of an attack. It outlines a framework for defenders to incorporate security controls at each point to detect, prevent, or intercept the attack.

1. **Reconnaissance:** The criminals gather email addresses, IPs, and social media accounts to create a target. They look for vulnerable systems to attack.
2. **Weaponization:** They load an exploit into a deliverable payload like a pdf attachment. When opened, they can have remote backdoor access into your network.
3. **Delivery:** They find ways to send their payload to the user through emails, websites, or USB drives.
4. **Exploitation:** This phase executes the hacker's code on the victim's systems and exploits some vulnerability.
5. **Installation:** This phase installs the malware on the target system. This can allow persistent access to the hacker.
6. **Command & Control (C2):** The hacker's server communicates remotely with the victim's machine and executes further instructions.
7. **Actions:** In this step, they perform their objectives by either installing ransomware, gaining access to other systems, or exfiltrating data.

Modern-day attacks may combine these into four or five phases over a period of time. The point here is to understand the core foundations of an attack so we can plan our defenses accordingly. Knowing the details of each phase is optional and based on your interest.

If you incorporate this mindset into your cyber strategy, your approach will be considered very thorough. You will also be able to plug your gaps better by determining which solutions and vendors fulfill the various layers of security.

TECHNOLOGY

How do we get to that level of becoming technical? Although a deep understanding of each technology or cybersecurity domain is optional, a broad approach is necessary. This is why we emphasize being a jack of all trades and a master of some.

Core Technologies

Understanding core technology gets you closer to being technical and understanding how they all work together. These include but are not limited to the following:

- Programming
- Networking
- Storage
- Backup/Restore
- System Administration
- Wireless
- Voice-over-IP
- Data Center
- Service Provider
- Databases
- Virtualization
- Web Development

Anyone with backgrounds in these core technologies has a head start because they overlap within cybersecurity. In a corporate environment, you would expect to have most of these core technologies in place. In addition, each one will need security controls to protect them. The better you understand these core concepts, the easier it will be for you to tackle them.

To get up to speed on core concepts, you can take free online courses from introductory to advanced. A good place to start is with the technology you are most familiar with. For example, if you've previously worked with databases, look at the database in use at your organization and learn how attackers compromise it. Then look at the network infrastructure and familiarize yourself with ways to protect it from the most common attacks. Over time, you will know a little about everything in your environment. The research and learning process is perpetual and should become part of your routine.

Product Knowledge

After understanding core concepts, you learn how to apply them. This involves awareness of multiple vendors and products used to implement the technologies. Product knowledge is usually not taught in technical certifications unless they're vendor-based. Vendor certifications have their blind spots as they only focus on their products, marketing themselves, and disregarding the competition. When researching products for the sake of building knowledge, pay attention to the following factors for it to add value in your consultations:

- Competition
- Price
- Support options
- Product age and roadmap
- Chatter on blogs and reviews
- Third party test results

There's always more than one way to close a gap. We must refrain from starting a sentence with "The only solution is…" A good first step to finding a product is to read online articles, blogs, and reviews. These provide a great first-hand user perspective, something you won't find in product brochures. A great way to check product features is to research competitors. Some vendors have competitive battle cards that compare their top three competitors. These are a great way to get up to speed with the features and arm yourself with good questions. Sometimes the best product may be the costliest. In that case, the price may steer us towards another product. There are also enterprise-level open-source solutions that cost nothing but may not have any support for troubleshooting or opening tickets. Furthermore, many new products boast features and roadmaps that may not be fully baked, sometimes marketing puts it on their website to look complete. Moreover, some products may not be around after a few years. We have witnessed products that get acquired by companies and either get discontinued or altered.

As you can see, a lot goes into gaining product knowledge. Start with the products you currently use and expand your knowledge. Always keep an eye out for alternatives. Keep good relations with multiple vendors. Your loyalty is to the security of the organization and not a trademarked name.

Immersive Learning

Your work will help you gain some technical knowledge through on-the-job training, as there are certain things you can only learn through experience. These include training on a product, working with a team on an implementation project, and understanding the pitfalls based on trial and error. If it's not required by work, you would probably not be learning or training on the technology on your own time unless it is meant to reach your personal goals.

Immersing yourself in technology is a quick way to learn. Following are some learning opportunities that can help you get technical knowledge without being an expert.

- **Demos:** Attending online or in-person demos provides a summary of the experiences of others. These can be product demos or demonstrations of hacking techniques.
- **Network:** Networking with technical folks in group projects can garner a lot of knowledge as you take the back seat in technical problem-solving. Ask questions about the timeframe, caveats, or best practices. That level of surface knowledge is sufficient.
- **Participate in hackathons:** CTFs (Capture The Flag) tournaments are a great way to be immersed in an environment with people from different skill levels, all with the same goals. These are judgment-free environments, and everyone there is helpful. You do not even need to compete to get value out of it. You can be part of groups and cheer others. You can also volunteer to be a judge. Through team interactions, I have always made a few friends from every CTF event I've attended, whether online or in-person. I often follow up with them later to clarify concepts or ask for assistance with a problem. Some of these events are not very technical and involve skills like open-source intelligence and finding answers using just a web browser.
- **Workshops:** Some vendors provide hands-on workshops that utilize their product lines. It is interactive, and you typically follow along with the instructor. This is yet another great way to learn technology using virtualized environments. The systems are pre-configured, and you can play with them freely without worrying about breaking them.

CERTIFICATIONS

While experience is essential in combating cyber threats, it can have gaps without a solid background and understanding of core technology. Certifications are one way to provide a seal of approval that you have a good enough understanding of the subject matter. Certifications can be for yourself but are typically attained for others, like to fulfill job requirements, partnership agreements, or compliance. It's also noteworthy that certifications do not prove competency in performing any role. However, the knowledge gained from the certificate, critical thinking, and experience will help you succeed in your role as a CISO.

There are differing views about certifications; traditionally, they have played a significant role and have been a standard practice for all cybersecurity professionals. However, vendors and certifying bodies have abused their positions and flooded the market with all types of courses and exams primarily to make money. So let's look at the good, the bad, and the ugly part of certifications.

The Good

Certifications have an important role to play in our industry. While I am not a big fan of the certificate "money shilling" industry, it provides some roots to understanding and validating basic technology concepts. While some individuals learn better with a course outline and a test to gauge their understanding, the rest view it as adding more stress to an already busy schedule. Vendor-agnostic certifications are most valuable as they touch on theory, technical terms, tools, and tactics. Introductory-level certificates in cybersecurity or a core technology concept like networking or programming help you learn the concepts in a formal, structured format. Certification providers test your knowledge and validate your learning through a certificate.

Vendor-specific certifications can also be beneficial if the organization utilizes those products. It is also good to have a variety of introductory vendor certifications under your belt to show the breadth of product knowledge. As a CISO, you will be involved in many vendor meetings and possibly partnerships. Having certain certifications brings additional value to the organization as they will get discounts or special pricing if some employees hold valid vendor certifications.

Certifications provide validation that you have a good understanding of the subject matter. Furthermore, certifications help in your career progression within an organization. There are also advanced-level certifications that require either some prerequisites or a certain number of years of experience in the field. This knowledge investment demonstrates a long-term commitment to your professional career, as achieving them takes time and energy. As a CISO, it will give you additional credibility.

The Bad

The certification industry has developed a tiered system of progression in its ecosystem. Pick any certifying body, and you will see an extensive list of options divided into paths. Each one of those paths will have a basic, intermediate, and advanced option. It is easy to get consumed within one ecosystem and develop a strong bias towards one certification body. For example, holding ten industry certifications in one subject shows expertise and specialization but may hinder your understanding of the bigger picture. To grow into a CISO, you should diversify your formal training and certifications to become a well-rounded professional. Invest in a mix of the following: technical skills, business skills, communication skills, theoretical and practical knowledge, sales, and vendor-specific certifications.

Some big-name organizations take advantage of their brand and charge between $4,000 - $8,000 for a one-week training course. You can attain the same subject matter on YouTube or other free online resources but without the brand reputation to back it. Furthermore, certification exam fees may cost an additional $300 - $1,500. You typically should not be paying for certifications out of pocket. Since companies have training budgets, utilize them by obtaining the appropriate credentials over the initial years. The high costs of materials, certification exams, and Continuing Professional Education (CPE) are tailored for organizations to foot the bill, not individuals. The easiest way to tap into a training budget is to ask. I should have asked about training budgets in my first few jobs. Halfway through my career, I discussed it with my manager, and they said they would pay for any certifications and courses as long as they made sense to the company. Since then, I've taken at least one course sponsored by the company annually.

The Ugly

Pursuing certifications for the sake of collecting accolades is not beneficial. A reason or work experience should back up each certificate. Remember the concept of asking "why" before we start anything. If you don't see a certificate adding value to your career, don't pursue it. Unfortunately, plenty of "certification junkies" have many acronyms after their name but minimal experience to back them up.

I'm also not a fan of renewing every certification and running after CPEs to actively maintain a certification status annually. Most, if not all, are a money grab for the certifying body. If you've proven once that you have the skillsets and acumen to pass an exam, then repeating that every few years for a fee doesn't hold much value. The only exception is if the organization benefits from current certifications for certain agreements and discounts. I have only renewed a few of the 20 to 30 certificates I've passed over the years. This is because their value deteriorates over time as more people achieve it, or they get discontinued. Paying $300 to $500 every two to three years to renew each certificate is impractical. The few I retained were because some organizations valued them in terms of backend rebates, discounts, or compliance. That aspect alone can create a lot of job security and personal value for employers. Focus on keeping those for the long term.

Certifications alone provide only a baseline understanding. Anyone who's been through the courseware and exams will tell you that a lot of them are outdated and don't reflect real-world scenarios. With readily available test dumps, this industry has become even uglier. Test dumps are screenshots of the questions that someone has taken or memorized after an exam and provided for sale for others to study. This is an obvious violation of the testing policies, but these have been a constant in the industry for as long as I can remember. The pool of questions in an exam doesn't change much and can easily be passed in multiple attempts once you get the hang of it. There is incentive for vendors and large certification bodies to get more people certified to build their following and get more business.

This trend is slowly showing signs of change with many free courses and affordable certifications out there whose business model is to educate more students. At the end of the day, a certification is just one more feather in your cap. A well-rounded individual will complement their credentials with hands-on implementation, up-to-date news, knowledge of the latest techniques, and experience gained from successes and failures in the field.

Takeaway

Being a translator of cyber threats to business impact, A CISO needs to have a solid understanding of the technical side of cybersecurity. This allows the CISO to articulate threats better to technical and non-technical folks. It also shortens the remediation cycle making you more efficient and better respected. You do not need to be an expert but should know enough to be independent and aware of your options. Understanding the layers of security, immersing yourself in learning opportunities, and having some certifications under your belt, all help develop your technical skills.

12. ATTITUDE

You want to test positive for it

You can learn new skills in a short period of time. All forms of education have a defined path, whether a degree or certification. Many larger companies will pay for higher education, like a master's degree, as they train you. Almost all good companies will pay for certifications that benefit them and advance your career. That is why companies don't hire based on education alone. They are looking for something they cannot train you in. That is the attitude you bring.

Developing a positive attitude is attainable with the proper effort. To understand the value of a great attitude, let's first look at something we are all familiar with, a toxic attitude. Then let's discuss ways to develop a great attitude that will benefit every aspect of our career.

TOXIC ATTITUDE

In a corporate setting, the most straightforward task is fulfilling the duties outlined in one's job description. However, this minimalistic approach may not be met with enthusiasm from colleagues. Maintaining a neutral demeanor typically indicates disinterest and a desire to remain inconspicuous. These individuals tend to lack collaboration, inquisitiveness, and an inclination to exceed their primary responsibilities. Undoubtedly, we can all identify individuals, including ourselves, who have demonstrated such behavior.

A detrimental or toxic workplace atmosphere materializes as a result of individuals adversely affecting those around them, resulting in mental or emotional repercussions. Examples include individuals who belittle others, engage in office gossip, spread false information to advance their own career, lack sensitivity towards others' needs, or engage in sexual harassment. Certain individuals project negative energy that can impact the team's overall performance, inspire others to exhibit similar behavior, and make management challenging. One's attitude can impact how they are treated by others and can be contagious. In some cases, leaders' attitudes or their failure to foster a positive work environment can lead to a toxic workplace, resulting in negative impacts on employees' mental health. The ability to manage one's attitude to foster a more positive workplace is a leadership quality that distinguishes and influences others.

CULTIVATING ATTITUDE

Positivity is also contagious. Employees can bring a great attitude to the workplace with their ability to stay positive, respectful, optimistic, and enthusiastic. When we see someone aiming high and talking about doing more, we always encourage them and try to remove any roadblocks from their path. It makes us feel better for supporting a positive attitude. Moreover, encouraging others to be optimistic also grows on us and makes us want to do the same. The net effect is that it inculcates feelings of optimism in everyone around. You feel enthusiastic at work and want more of this feeling. There are always a few people in the workplace that have this great ability to spread this enthusiasm. Those are usually leaders or potential leaders.

It takes a conscious effort to bring a good attitude. The best way to cultivate it is to surround yourself with leaders that have a positive attitude. They will provide an environment where you can brainstorm ideas free of judgment. This will help you grow, be noticed by others, and build your leadership brand. "People may forget what you said, but they never forget how you made them feel." – Buehner.

Below are some examples of displaying a great attitude that you can learn from and incorporate into your life.

Problem-Solving

Once, I was asked at an interview how I would solve a problem at work to which I didn't know the solution. Without hesitation, my answer was, "I'll Google it." A lot of people told me never to say that and that it's not a professional answer. But it is the reality; that's what everyone does. At the same time, I also put it into context by saying that my goal is to get the correct answer in the fastest and most efficient way possible. So, I would first Google it; if I weren't content with it, I would ask a peer in a similar job function, and then consult my reporting manager in that order. While googling is the first step, the purpose of discovering the solution is to research and apply appropriate critical thinking skills to get to the conclusion within context. My answer was well received, and it displayed my attitude toward problem-solving.

We are trying to solve problems every day. Try being conscious next time you're explaining a problem and resolution. Outline it and see if you can work up a good mental flow. Review some of your problem-solving this week and ask yourself if your attitude or response could have been different. Many projects also have a lesson-learned session after they close. You might get feedback or be providing input on attitude. Your attitude towards different experiences can change the outcome.

Go-Getters

There are thinkers, and there are doers. In the field of cybersecurity, there will be many small tasks throughout the week. They will never be the same. This will always keep you on your toes. This is also the best part of the job as it prevents boredom. The only thing that continues to help you solve everyday challenges is your attitude toward them. You cannot ponder over issues for too long and cannot rely on anyone's assistance, go after them head-on.

The go-getter is driven and motivated. When approached, especially in cybersecurity, they are ready to dive in and answer, "I'll figure it out." If they don't know the answer to a question, they are prepared to figure it out with action steps. Whatever the action, the go-getter is also aware of timelines and priorities. It is very easy to get distracted by other challenges or new concepts in a role where multitasking is necessary, so write them down and prioritize them, but stay focused on what's essential for the day.

No Regrets

I get excited when I see a challenge that falls into my domain. My first reaction is, "how am I going to resolve this?" Your mindset towards the challenge should not be a matter of "if" but "when." I know I will do it, but I just don't know when or how yet. I envision success and work myself backward. With enough time and focus, this works almost every time. If it doesn't work out, your positive attitude saves you from the regret of not trying different methods.

Whenever you encounter something you want to achieve, think about what will happen if you don't try. Is it worth the struggle? How would you feel if you failed? These questions should help spark some of the fuel inside you to give it everything you've got. At the end of the day, failure is only part of the experience, and you come back wiser.

Nurture It

If you're reading this and telling yourself that you don't have that drive but want it, there are some ways to develop it over time.

Self-reflect and identify your interests. What are you passionate about? I define passion as something you would do even if no one ever paid you to do it. It is easy to struggle for something you love doing, hoping to find the answer eventually. For example, you can have passion for a coding project, a hardware setup, building a team for a specific task, presenting at a big event, or any new idea you want to try.

Next, take a problem in your task list that you are not too excited about but still need to do as part of your job. Think of the bigger picture and how it affects something else you care about. For example, it may make your manager happy, help you gain the respect of another colleague, be an experience you can talk about later, or be a skill you can add to your resume. The idea is to focus on the byproduct or effects it will have to keep you motivated to finish the job.

As a solutions architect, I assist my sales team in responding to RFPs (Request for Proposals) from clients who want my company's services. RFPs are dry, dull, and full of ambiguous language. However, as part of my responsibilities, I am required to respond to them. I am motivated when my colleagues notice the work that I've put into reviewing and responding to the RFP. This improves the relationship between my sales team and the client. Even though most RFPs don't produce results, my management sees my efforts and appreciates the hours that I put in for them.

Visibility

An important aspect of cultivating attitude is enhancing your visibility. Any effort you put in to nurture a positive attitude should not go unnoticed. You should make the right people know what you did. This may not sound humbling, but it is also not considered boasting. Your management needs to see your energy and how you operate in the work environment. This is one of the attributes that they judge you on without really telling you. One of the reasons why some people get let go is due to the lack of visibility or a bad attitude in the workplace Attitude is not something measurable, but it is noticeable. So, if you're doing something great, let your management know. Don't feel bad about displaying it by subtly talking about your accomplishments in conversation or forwarding an email to ask for advice. Without visibility, it did not exist in their eyes.

One of the best ways to be visible is to introduce a creative concept to your team to help them grow. This will show your attitude towards the team and your collaborative nature. For example, while working in security audit, I introduced a security newsletter to share security themes and current news with auditors of different backgrounds. I involved my immediate team to contribute, and it was received well. We continued to produce this consistently with the goal of being creative, collaborative, and engaging. As a result, team members enjoyed working on it together. We also became more aware of what was happening in the cybersecurity industry, which helped us in our work. The newsletter also became a conversation starter, allowing us to build relationships with other security teams. This was a win-win on many fronts. Everyone, including higher management, noticed it.

Takeaway

A good attitude will differentiate you from all other employees. People will remember you by your attitude at work. When was the last time someone asked you about an ex-colleague, and your immediate answer described their attitude? Use it as a superpower, get noticed, get liked, and get promoted.

13. HUMAN NETWORK

Your network is your net worth

In this industry, a significant factor and hidden secret in career success is not only what you know but also who you know.

Individuals face their unique set of obstacles when building their career paths. Some rely on their expertise and abilities, while others rely on their professional network. We often observe the immediate benefits of utilizing our network to bypass certain steps. However, establishing a network takes years of effort. It can start as early as high school or be inherited through family connections. Regardless, creating meaningful connections is a deliberate choice that allows us to leverage them when necessary. Jim Rohn's statement, "You are the average of the five people you spend the most time with," emphasizes this idea.

As a CISO, tapping into one's network is crucial for hiring individuals, seeking guidance, seeking project assistance, and grooming the next generation. In the following sections, we will examine how the different elements of our network impact our careers and how to capitalize on them.

CATALYSTS

Plenty of things speed up the process of developing professional relationships. All that is required is to spend time pursuing these with persistence and perseverance. Consider these as catalysts for building your network.

Peer Groups

You can be part of professional groups to meet with like-minded people in roughly the same profession and social status. The people in these groups share ideas through presentations and meetups. They discuss issues common to their industry and share with their peers how they tackle them. For example, I've seen peer groups consisting of local government IT administrators discussing security controls and sharing ideas and contacts. There are study groups based on certification such as for the CISSP credential. Regular meetups are usually at informal venues like community workplaces, bars, or restaurants. Someone's work may also host or sponsor their conference room for the meetup.

The big advantage of such groups is that everyone wants to help their peers as they all share a common struggle. I once signed up for a software security meetup where they had a three-hour, in-person CTF (capture the flag) competition. We all sat around a few tables with our laptops, chatted, had some pizza, and tried to solve challenges to win prizes. Halfway through the event, I briefly got to know the person beside me. Out of nowhere, he mentioned that he had a job opening for a security engineer role at his workplace and that I would be the perfect candidate. He said if I were interested, he would put in a recommendation, and the job was confirmed. Things happened so quickly because I was part of the "tribe." This is how many positions are filled; through employees and their peer groups. All that is required is a certain level of trust and getting comfortable with the person. A typical 30-minute interview has no time or environment to create that trust or rapport.

Social Networks

Social media is great for connecting different people, their ideas, and multiple resources but can also waste time. For career growth, you should only stick to certain platforms and activities to take advantage of their benefits.

As of the publishing of this book, LinkedIn is probably the most useful in making connections. At the same time, don't add anyone and everyone you notice; be selective. Choose quality over quantity. My two rules of adding or accepting a connection are: (1) The contact may be useful to me in the future (2) I may be able to help this connection. Many may disagree with me, but more is not always good; you do not want to muddy your social network with random additions. Not everyone has your best interest, and scammer profiles are also out there. You also don't want to be associated with everyone. If your social media feed is too messy, you lose the benefits of this platform.

I will usually add people to my network whom I have met in person at a conference or meetup. Half of your LinkedIn contacts should consist of such people. The remainder should be from discovering new connections based on interactions on posts or expanding your network based on your industry or skills. Recruiters will post relevant jobs on LinkedIn and will reach out. You may also have people connect with you based on your comments or posts. These can be anything from simple gratitude, asking questions, invitations to speak, or applying for a position that has yet to be advertised to the public.

Professionals can leverage a few other social media networks and communication platforms to share knowledge, track feeds, and get their peers' updates. The general principle is simple: follow security professionals from whom you want to learn and get updates. Also, post updates on relevant public events that will benefit your network. Refrain from engaging in non-productive small-talk or conversations, like religion, politics, or current affairs. When used right, social media platforms can become a place to showcase your projects or interactions and show legitimacy and passion in your field. Occasionally, you will find meaningful connections that will transition into phone conversations and in-person meetups. This is a good gauge to see if you are getting any benefits from social media. For example, many of my mentees have contacted me through my social media profile and based on my post updates. This usually leads to a quick audio or video call.

Other communication platforms used professionally allow you to create social media groups. These platforms include WhatsApp, Signal, Telegram, Discord, Matrix, and similar. I'm part of a few focus groups on some of these platforms, where we discuss events, meetups, job opportunities, or assist newcomers. It's easier and quicker to message a person directly in these groups for a brief one-on-one conversation. Larger platforms like Discord usually have event or training-based groups where peers can interact and benefit from the quick discussions. In these types of groups, there's always someone available to answer questions.

Social media is a double-edged sword. So, take advantage of it as it benefits your career, but refrain from all non-productive things that become a time drain. If you are part of too many groups and play a passive role, prune them down to only the ones that provide you with quality and vice versa. I guarantee it will give you back many precious hours in a day.

Mentorship

Developing a professional network takes time, and the results may not be the same for everyone. This is where finding a good mentor supplements your efforts for professional growth. Unfortunately, most people wait too long to find a mentor. There are plenty of reasons for this, including ego, thinking you have the time for trial and error, or not realizing the value a mentor can provide.

While it is challenging to find the right mentor, once found, it can be very beneficial. A mentor can show you shortcuts. In my career, I've mentored numerous kids entering the field. Most struggle to get their first job or to switch fields into cybersecurity. One consistent piece of advice I've given them is to develop their network, hang out at meetups and events and make friends. Unfortunately, not many have taken that advice seriously. Then years later, when they make the right contacts and get the right jobs, they realize the value of the network.

Wasta

I'm sure you're familiar with the saying, "I know a guy." People in powerful positions in a company have a tremendous influence in deciding who gets hired or gets a contract.

When I was applying for my first job in the Middle East, I did not have many credentials besides a bachelor's degree. I applied to over two hundred jobs online and kept track of the responses on an excel sheet. A few months in, I had gotten an automated response from about twenty of them saying they had received the email. The remaining did not respond, which was frustrating. Then my dad reached out to a few friends in large companies on my behalf. Suddenly I had five interviews lined up the following week and job offers from two of them. I accepted the best offer and started immediately.

Three months into the job, I was invited to an interview with another company. The IT Manager had my resume on the table when I noticed the name of the VP scribbled on the top corner. After a brief interview, he asked me how I knew the VP. I told him that he was my dad's friend. He told me, "The job is yours. You meet the qualifications, and this was merely a formality. Your recommendation came from up top; we cannot reject it." Six months later, I switched to another job. After that, I continued to gain experience from multiple jobs through my professional contacts, using them as Wasta.

It's not always what you know; it's who you know. In the Arab world, this is known as Wasta. In Arabic, it is loosely translated to influence, power, or authority of your connections. They say that when you apply for a job in the Middle East, you must not forget to take your vitamin-W, a.k.a Wasta. Nothing happens without Wasta. It's an open secret and often called out during introductions. It's considered a shortcut to developing trust (Refer to the concept of "chain of trust" in Chapter 7 - Power). You develop it by having good ties with that person, family connections, favors, or just being present at the right time and being helpful. In the Americas, the concept of Wasta exists as tightly knit connections and referrals.

While this may seem unfair, it happens everywhere. In some places, it is more overt and almost a requirement, like in most places in the Middle East, while in others, it is more subtle. In some job interviews in the Middle East, I've been flat-out asked about whose recommendations I had come with. The answer to that determined if I got the job or not. Some may refer to it as nepotism or favoritism. I agree; it is an unfair practice. I have seen people on the job who did not even meet the minimum requirements, and everyone wondered how they got there. This is an abuse of power, and on a broader scale, this practice creates division, racism, sexism, nepotism, and other potential biases. I am against this. When in a position to hire, consider merit first, which includes qualifications, skills, and cultural fit. The tie-breakers are things that establish trust and minimize risk, like recommendations.

Unfortunately, Wasta is a reality. While we may not like it, we can come to understand a small element of it. Let me explain: If you are in a hiring position, it is difficult to blindly trust the candidate without knowing them. Even shortlisting candidates based on their resumes provides you with too many options, and there's no way to judge past performance, history, habits, or cultural fit. If a peer recommends a candidate fit for the role, you will take it seriously as your peer has an existing established trust with the candidate and can generally vouch for that person. They may only praise their attitude, which may be enough (Refer to Chapter 12 - Attitude). This is usually the first question you ask them, "do you trust them?" Their trust in the candidate compels you to trust them as well. This is trust by proxy; even though you don't know much about the candidate, you consider them for the role due to the established trust in your contact. If the candidate fits the predetermined shortlist of requirements, then there is no need to look any further. It is the safest option for you. And that is usually how the process flows for most positions of responsibility or where there are just too many candidates against very few job openings.

Lately, this process of Wasta isn't holding much weight as there is more transparency and accountability. Moreover, there is a shortage of qualified candidates and many more jobs to fill in cybersecurity. This is good as it shifts the balance towards skill sets instead of connections.

However, the fact remains that networking, building relationships, and obtaining recommendations will always exist and become increasingly important as one advances in their career. The level of importance will depend on factors such as job scarcity, the significance of the position, company culture, and geographical location. Consequently, it is crucial to consider and identify the appropriate individuals to contact when necessary. It is worth remembering that you may also serve as a valuable contact, or Wasta, for someone else.

Recommendations

In my first role as a Security Practice Lead, the CEO at the interview said that I exceeded every qualification they had on paper. Moreover, when they inquired from their peer networks about me, many people knew me and had very nice things to say about my character. That convinced them to stop their search and focus all their efforts on hiring me. Recommendations hold value. In this case, they acted as a catalyst to speed up their internal decision-making process. I had no contacts, only my reputation that resonated through unsolicited recommendations.

On the flip side, if you are an unethical person at work, always talking bad about people, backbiting, taking bribes, and full of negative energy, it will bite you. People will not recommend you due to your toxicity. You will not see the enthusiasm in their tone when they talk about you. This could be enough for the hiring person to lose faith and trust after learning about you.

I have been in a situation where a hiring manager candidly asked me if I would hire a certain person I knew. Without telling them specifics, I recommended not hiring them because of their work ethic. My opinion was enough for the hiring manager to pursue another candidate, even though they fulfilled the requirements. People's opinions matter. You may lose opportunities when you don't build a network.

Getting genuine positive feedback from people in your network is relatively easy. Simply be a nice person. We've said before that people don't remember the details of your work; they remember how they felt when working with you. When I think about some people I've interacted with in the past professionally, I will often completely forget what we worked on or talked about, but I will remember that we had a great time.

Unfortunately, people seem to remember others for the worst things, often associated with emotions. So, make people feel good around you. They will have no problem recommending you to others on their own accord. You can do this by avoiding controversial talk. This includes anything people are very passionate and opinionated about, like sports teams, political views, or religious beliefs. This is not to say you shouldn't talk about these things with colleagues. If you do discuss these topics, do not debate. Do it in a neutral way that does not appear offensive or polarized but instead seems educational or inquisitive.

References are different from Wasta. Wasta is often seen as a way to navigate systems that are based on bureaucracy or rules, and it can involve using one's social status and family connections to get what one wants. On the other hand, references can speak to your character, abilities, or qualifications. In some contexts, such as when applying for a job, references may provide additional information and perspective on your skills and experiences and can help support your application.

Reality Check

As you work on your human network and incorporate more techniques to create catalysts for success, you will have to come to terms with harsh realities somewhere along the journey. So, let's spend some time reminding ourselves of these to remain grounded and better prepared when facing them.

Loyalty

Every few years, the big tech giants undergo massive layoffs. Then shortly after, they start hiring again. This trend affects the industry at large and creates unnecessary gaps in the job market. There is no such thing as absolute job security. There's no concept of tenure in this field. While most companies have a policy of providing two weeks of notice before they let you go, when the difficult time comes, they will revoke your access within minutes of providing you with a notice. This is a standard security policy. It almost always comes without warning. Some companies will provide a severance package to avoid any bitterness. This varies and can come in the form of anywhere from one to three months' worth of salary, sometimes more based on time spent working in the organization. Whatever the case may be, this concept of employee loyalty does not make sense. Ideally, employees work because of a combination of money and their existing skill sets. We may fool our brains by saying we are loyal to the company because we like the people and love our work. Will your loyalty remain if the company stopped paying you but still required you to work?

Loyalty goes both ways. A company needs to show commitment to its employees as well. In one of my interviews with the hiring manager, I was asked a final question: "We see you've worked at a lot of places and haven't stayed around for more than a few years. What will prevent you from doing the same thing here?" My answer was: "Every role change demonstrated my professional growth achieving a better position or salary. If a company values me enough, they will show it by doing what's in their power to retain me. If someone else values me more, I will naturally go there. Can you guarantee that you will not fire me as long as I perform my duties?" Needless to say, I got the job a few days later.

Companies will play the loyalty card all the time in their favor. So, what can you do to avoid this? Unfortunately, not much. Companies won't think twice before letting you go due to downsizing or budget cuts. You should also not be emotionally attached to any job. Your loyalties should be to take care of yourself first. But never burn your bridges. Continue to stay on good terms with everyone at your past, current and future workplaces.

Family

Many managers and companies may lure you by stating that "everyone is treated like family here, and you will be part of our family once you join." In reality, would you fire a family member? Would you resist negotiating a better salary or pay them better than the market rate?

The concept of "family" at work could not be further from the truth. This is business; your days are numbered when you are no longer valuable to the organization, misaligned with shareholders, or are no longer profitable to the company. The family talk is simply a psychological method to prevent you from leaving when instead, they should be employing better tactics to keep you.

In one of my early jobs, I built great relationships with my peers and manager, and the company benefited immensely from my presales work. I asked for a raise knowing I was being underpaid, but I was politely denied. After exactly a year of working for them, I found another job that would pay me 30% more with a better position. When I told my manager I would take that offer and provided him with one month's notice, he became furious. He told me we were like family, and "this feels like you are cheating on us simply because you found someone better." He told me it felt like a divorce, figuratively. I calmed him down as I wanted to leave on good terms, but they felt the pain as they would not find a replacement for me. I also held a few very important certifications that benefited the company financially. They could have simply offered to match the pay, and I may have changed my mind, but they never made any effort to retain me. My value was clearly elsewhere for the time being. They played the family card with me, and I did feel bad momentarily but got over it the next day. A month later, I discovered that my ex-manager had also left the company right after I had for a better role. So much for "family."

Professional Jealousies

People don't warn you about this when you first enter the workforce, but through experiences, you realize that not everyone has their best interest at heart for you. When you join any new company, all eyes are on you. There will always be someone with feelings of spite or jealousy toward you. This could be because you are more qualified, younger, bring a positive attitude, or the fact that they have been eyeing that position for a while.

Envy is characterized by wanting what someone else has due to competitive instincts. In contrast, jealousy creates a sense of threat, causing one to believe that others are trying to take away what one has. The consequences of professional jealousy can be damaging, as individuals with such feelings may seek to diminish your accomplishments and tarnish your reputation by speaking ill of you to others. Regrettably, even managers may become envious of their subordinates, obstructing team performance and impeding overall business objectives.

Professional jealousies are inevitable. The following are some things you do to minimize it in others.

- Try not to boast about your qualifications, experience, or skills to everyone. Those can already be seen on your LinkedIn profile if you have one. The only time it was required to discuss them was at the interview. Try to stay humble; otherwise, people become defensive and competitive. You want collaboration, not competition.

- If they get to know you personally before they know you professionally, it will help curb professional jealousy. Usually, it's the other way around; you get introduced formally, and people get to learn your personality after weeks or months. This is why it's important to start building good relationships with everyone you interact with in the company from day one. Of course, you don't know what someone thinks about you and why, but you can try to change their perspective early on by being cordial and friendly, regardless of their attitude towards you.

- Don't discuss your next steps or your great ideas with everyone. Keep it to only those who are involved and need to know. Office gossip can unintentionally become toxic. Sometimes it is difficult to keep initiatives secret. For example, you will notice that most executives only announce updates and changes in quarterly meetings.

While you cannot control what's in someone's heart, you can manage and control your emotions. You should only compete with yourself. Most importantly, you should aim to be better today than what you were yesterday. Also, don't compare your situation with anyone else's. There's a reason we're called individuals. We all go through unique experiences that affect our thinking. Keep your emotional intelligence skills strong.

Imposter Syndrome

While building your professional network, you will meet people of all sorts. You will meet peers with better skills, experience, knowledge, and connections. Therefore, it is a natural feeling to question your self-worth and whether you belong amongst them.

Imposter syndrome is a psychological phenomenon in which an individual doubts their accomplishments and feels like a "fraud" despite evidence to the contrary. People can experience it at any level. We discuss it in depth in chapter 15 - Imposter Syndrome.

Stay focused on developing your network. You are not there for competition. In fact, you are there to embrace the range of skills and experience in your network and learn from them. You can learn something from everyone. If you look deep enough into the individuals in your network, you will find people better than you and in situations worse than you. You will have something they don't have and vice versa. You will then realize that everyone is unique and appreciate diversity in everything.

How does this reality check affect your path to becoming a CISO? You will face these struggles at many points in your career. Betrayal, jealousies, and questioning your self-worth are things everyone goes through but don't highlight. Every time you experience these harsh realities, it toughens and prepares you for your progression.

WHAT YOU SHOULD **NOT** DO

While much of this chapter focused on things that build a better professional network, avoiding certain practices that hinder these efforts are also noteworthy. You do not want to undermine your efforts as you grow your network. Be wary of the following:

Don't network without purpose: People always have their guard up. When an unknown person approaches you, you will question their objectives in your head and feel threatened until they give you a reason to be at ease. This is called the fight-or-flight response. So, have a justified reason for adding someone on social media or meeting them. Furthermore, come prepared by researching who they are and why you are professionally interested in connecting with them. When you reach out to them, they will most likely ask themselves. "What do they want?" So, open a dialogue by praising them for their work, showing curiosity about a subject that relates to them, or asking for specific advice. Additionally, don't be focused on the short term or be too transactional. Networking should be viewed as a long-term investment in your career. Focusing only on short-term gains can lead to missed opportunities for building meaningful relationships. If you only reach out to someone when you need something, it can come across as insincere and opportunistic. Finally, don't be overly self-promotional. If you only talk about yourself and your accomplishments, people may perceive you as self-centered and not interested in forming genuine relationships.

Don't flatter excessively: Compliments produce dopamine in the body, but the effect is temporary. When the drug wears off, management will know if the compliments are genuine or if they are to gain an advantage. While compliments are necessary to build good rapport, don't overdo them, as they can have a negative effect, such as the perception of insincerity. If you give too many compliments, your manager may begin to think that you are not being genuine or sincere. This can lead to a lack of trust between you and your manager and damage your professional reputation. Management will see right through individuals who try to butter them up. They may think you are only complimenting them because you want something. Overall, while giving your manager positive feedback and appreciation is important, do so in a balanced and appropriate manner. Maintain professional boundaries to avoid creating unrealistic expectations or a negative workplace environment.

Don't be overly aggressive: Relationships are a two-way street. They should be mutually beneficial. In cases where that is not viable, it is usually a mentor/mentee or student/teacher style relationship. Even in those scenarios, one can consider it mutually beneficial, as a mentor or teacher wants the satisfaction of imparting knowledge or helping others. This can backfire if you are overwhelming them with questions. For example, after my virtual talks, I get messages on LinkedIn. These messages begin with compliments, but then I get bombarded with questions. If a leader has opened the opportunity to chat with you, don't turn it into an interview. This could lead to either a delayed response or being "ghosted" on LinkedIn or other professional platforms. Remember, you will not be the only one interacting with the other person. Respect everyone's time, be patient, and do not burden them with questions. Being pushy or aggressive when networking can be off-putting and may turn people away from wanting to work with you.

Takeaway

Your success relies not only on your skills and experience but also on the quality of your human network. To build this network, it is crucial to establish meaningful connections, maintain a humble attitude, and seek out authentic recommendations. It is important to avoid toxic individuals and situations that could damage your reputation.

14. PHANTOM CISO

All Cattle No Hat

There's a famous saying in Texas, "All hat, no cattle." Sometimes you have all the roles and responsibilities of a textbook CISO without the title. You're all cattle and no hat.

> **The Phantom CISO** manages cybersecurity risk and programs without the official title of a CISO.

Congratulations, you made it this far! While reading this book, if you can relate to the roles and responsibilities outlined in the previous chapters, you are a Phantom CISO. This realization is the first step in moving towards the role of a CISO.

As we have mentioned before, influence is one of the critical aspects of being a successful CISO. Knowing how much impact you have in your current role is essential in determining the confidence people will have in you as a CISO. As a Phantom CISO, you may ask yourself the following: 1) How am I communicating issues to management? 2) Do I have a seat at the management table? 3) Do I need more technical staff? 4) How do I balance my role and priorities between a manager and an individual contributor? 5) How do I transition to a leader? These are great questions, demonstrating that you are on the correct path.

Are there current CISOs needing clarification about their responsibilities? Have they skipped some of the training and experience you received? Absolutely. They may not have been a Phantom CISO like yourself.

How do you transform from a Phantom CISO to a recognized CISO? In preparation, we've discussed various topics in this book, including responsibilities, leadership, skills, and types of CISOs. First, we will discuss why qualified individuals don't realize they are proper CISOs and remain trapped as a Phantom CISO. Then, we'll talk about how they can shift and emerge as a CISO or an equivalent security leader. It's time to take off the mask!

SUPPRESSION

Let's start by addressing why qualified individuals remain unnoticed and hesitate to take over the reins. There are quite a few factors that prevent a potential CISO from emerging. Some elements, like budgets, security culture, or threatened leadership, may not be in your control. We can work on other things like skills development and confidence. Let's go over some factors that keep good security leaders from emerging.

Weak Professional Development

We have discussed developing diverse skills to become a good CISO. However, the lack of skills development is the most crucial factor preventing good people from coming to the top. For example, these individuals may excel in a few technical skills but must catch up on other types of skills, such as soft skills. Moreover, our profession and daily workload may prevent us from tending to needed professional development. There is the phrase, "you don't know what you don't know." This refers to the idea that there are many things we are not aware of and hence, don't think about them. This includes knowledge from within our profession and areas where we could grow or improve. This lack of awareness contributes to the problem.

When I decided to pursue the CISO career path, I evaluated the gaps in my skills and started to work on them. Working in many pre-sales and consultancy roles, I became proficient in technical controls and product knowledge. I got primed for the position but noticed I needed to gain business skills. So, I took on some leadership training which taught me about risk. Furthermore, sitting in board meetings and listening to the pain points of CFOs and CEOs allowed me to talk about security in the language they would understand. Professional development allowed me to realize my potential and what I could be. Once I spent enough time developing business skills, I was ready to move on to the next step in my career.

Underselling

A common reason for staying in your role may be that you still need to articulate your value to your leadership, as they may not realize what impact you make based on your activities. This includes performing self-assessments and managing one or multiple security programs such as vulnerability, threat, and patch management. You are likely also involved with remediation activities, overseeing projects, and delegating tasks. As a Phantom CISO, your ability to actively demonstrate your impact to the organization and showcase it to senior management is crucial. Do not rely on them to realize your value. If all your work goes unnoticed by senior management, you are being undervalued because you are not upselling your capabilities.

Low Security Maturity

Low Security Maturity means that the organization has not recognized security as a major business factor and has not developed its security program. The business owners may have ample budget, but they don't see value in allocating it to security initiatives until they suffer a breach.

Good security talent goes unnoticed due to low security maturity in organizations. You can work with management to emphasize the importance of security in the organization and explain why it's also important to develop yourself in this area. In situations where you do not have the company's support for development, continue to develop yourself, improve your abilities and find better opportunities. You are not only hurting your career growth by staying, but you are devaluing yourself by being around people who do not value your skills. Worse yet, when a security breach happens, all fingers will point at you to save face.

Understaffed

You may have the support of your management to enhance and improve security controls in your organization, but they may not be able to justify hiring more personnel to focus on enhancing security controls. Many for-profit companies must pay more attention to security and invest more in human resources. They may be slow to realize that security protects their investment and that they need the appropriate technical resources. For this reason, they should value your role and appreciate your willingness to protect the organization, and you should take the opportunity that management provides. The freedom to call your shots is significant, even without the staff or budgets. You can start with little changes. It will enable you to elevate your status and become a security leader from within. Likely, you will never be an official CISO in an organization that cannot invest in security personnel. So, you will eventually have to move on to a better role at a different company when the opportunity presents itself.

Threatened Leadership

It is common for someone in the leadership team to feel threatened by an upcoming leader from within their organization. It is the most unfortunate position for a prospective CISO. Everyone is dispensable in any organization with a fair degree of redundancy. With this uncertainty, everyone watches their back and tries to protect their position. I've been in situations where the leadership did not encourage their reports to progress. This included disapproving training and not allowing them to shadow others. They fear that they could be training their next replacement. This attitude exists in small and large organizations alike.

Threatened leadership is yet another situation that keeps competent, and future CISOs suppressed. The only way up is out.

No Entry

Finally, in some organizations, a CISO is not welcome due to the territorial behavior of overlapping positions of a CIO or CTO. It could also be that the organization is not ready for one, as they don't fully understand the value of a dedicated security role. Other organizations may not need a CISO. At best, they need occasional assistance from third-party resources, which could come from a fractional or virtual CISO (vCISO) or a managed Security Services Provider (MSSP).

In organizations where a dedicated security leader is not welcome, there is no path to becoming a CISO. Instead, you should identify this early, pack your cape and move on to an organization that values you. Once you realize your potential, it is time to come out of the shadows.

Next, we present some awareness and techniques you can adopt to help with this transition.

TRANSITION

Transitioning into a first-time CISO role requires some preparation. While you may have the skills and experience to do the job, you must be mentally ready to take on the responsibilities. In addition, you need to change your mindset and utilize your resources to make that transition.

Mental Preparation

You will see countless jokes about CISOs having sleepless nights and getting frustrated about employees not following basic security practices. Furthermore, a CISO is also constantly worrying about the next breach. In talking to many CISOs and being in that role, I can tell you all that is entirely true.

Before applying for a CISO position, the first step is to realize what you are signing up for. It is more than just a matter of understanding the technical or business aspects of the role. The job's substantial mental burden prevents many individuals from taking responsibility. Therefore, you must be mentally strong and patient to make it past day one in the role.

If you are intimidated, don't be. Every CISO goes through the initial stress and overcomes it. Mental preparation comes with time, experience, failure, and dealing with problems. Experience is a critical component of being in any leadership role. I often hear newcomers in cybersecurity put forth goals of being a CISO in two years which is entirely unreasonable. You may be able to cram multiple technical and business training in two years, but that will not prepare you for dealing with human behavior, stress, meeting deadlines, and the pressure to perform. The average CISO is employed between 18-24 months at an organization at one time before transitioning to another organization, primarily due to burnout.

Pace yourself as you plan your future initiatives. Sticking to the plan will help you cross the hurdles. Of course, there will be times when the nature of your work will be ambiguous, and you will need to use your experience to navigate through it. Nonetheless, your patience and self-motivation will keep you going.

Be Bold and Opinionated

Leaders have opinions, and they are not afraid to stand by them. This quality of your opinion alone will differentiate you from the rest and allow you to be heard. Being opinionated is the first step towards thinking like a CISO. Without an opinion, you are like sheep, blindly following the herd.

Many people will be conscious of what others think if they speak up. There is nothing wrong with having a justified unpopular opinion. There will always be multiple views on security strategy. My perspective was always – "What would a hacker do?" This viewpoint did not sit well with some of the "tenured" Business CISOs with little hands-on technical skills because they focused on policy and process. To comfort them, I emphasize that we are on the same team with the same goal of minimizing risk and can have different points of view. This brings us to the next important topic, where we discuss the changing perspectives of our times.

Alter Your Perspective

The goal of security is to secure yourself and your organization from internal and external threats. In most cases, those threats are from ill-intentioned hackers. While an organized and systematic approach is excellent, you must constantly alter your perspective and understand what the adversary is thinking. Hackers are not going through a security framework checklist or the OWASP Top 10 to launch their attack. To beat a hacker, you must think like a hacker. This perspective does not mean changing your strategy entirely, but it does call for altering it with the evolving threats.

Those security leaders who ignore exploring different perspectives fall short of their defenses. A CISO must check their ego at the door and broaden their perspective. Tabletop incident response exercises, third-party pentests, unrestrictive spear-phishing campaigns, and external controls reviews help provide an outside perspective on your security defenses. When a CISO says, "I have everything covered in-house; we do our testing, our reviews, and our phishing campaigns; we don't need outside assistance," they show their insecurity for constructive criticism and fear of accountability. This attitude will undoubtedly allow for biases in the approach and expose gaps in the security strategy, eventually enabling the adversaries to win.

A mature and successful CISO embraces varying points of view on security controls without prejudice. For example, if you come from a business background and are a BISO (Business CISO), don't be afraid to take advice from technical expertise. On the other hand, if you are a CISO with a technical background (like an Ethical Hacker), engage deeper with the business leaders to understand their process and mold your strategies accordingly.

There's a famous Urdu saying: "The branch that doesn't bend breaks." It's essential to be adaptable in your strategies. You will never know everything, and you don't need to. Authentic leadership comes when you listen and learn. It is a continuous cycle of improvement. Adapting to your adversary's thoughts, what motivates them, and their tactics will help you win the battle.

Friends

The previous chapter focused on the importance of the human network. You never know where people end up in their careers and whom they decide to help. Your professional network began to grow the day you realized the advantages of having a network. You will often see people prosper in environments with an established network of friends and colleagues.

With remote work more prevalent in our society, geography still plays an essential factor in creating a network of acquaintances. Knowing the right people typically happens by chance, so you should seize the opportunity to connect with people that cross your path. You may miss a lot of opportunities by staying in your comfort zone.

Also, remember that not everyone will have your best interest in mind. You will need to know who your allies are to nurture those relationships long-term. There are different levels of friendships. Some friendships at work are conditional and may end with your work contract, while others will last longer. Regarding career advancement, having solid relationships with colleagues can be beneficial. For example, if you have a good rapport with your coworkers, they may be more likely to recommend you for new opportunities or put in a good word with management or hiring committees. Additionally, having a network of supportive colleagues can make navigating the challenges and politics of the workplace easier and provide valuable support and guidance as you progress in your career. You will also need a good network of friends in related fields to assist you in security initiatives as you try to establish yourself as a CISO.

While friendships at work are not a requirement for success, they can undoubtedly be valuable assets in terms of referrals while contributing to a positive and fulfilling work experience.

TAKEAWAY

Your environment will play a significant role in deciding your future. If you are already performing most of the responsibilities of a CISO, then it's just a matter of upgrading from a Phantom CISO. Be aware of what's holding you back. If it's your environment, then transition to one where you can make the most influential impact. Also, be prepared to understand what's expected of you and learn to adapt to the changing values, cultures, and times. Make the right friends and avail the right opportunities. This is how you will step out of the shadows.

15. IMPOSTER SYNDROME

CISOs worry they're going to be "found out"

Individuals experience feelings of imposter syndrome in all professions. CISOs are no exception.

> **Imposter syndrome** is a psychological phenomenon in which an individual doubts their accomplishments and feels like a "fraud" despite evidence to the contrary.

It is often characterized by self-doubt and a fear of being exposed as a fraud. You feel you will be "found out" and don't deserve the title, accolade, role, or position. This feeling is natural when you start a new and deserving role. People who don't know you may doubt you. Moreover, your perception of what people think about you worries you. This perception is likely the most significant cause of imposter syndrome.

CISOs may be particularly vulnerable to imposter syndrome due to the high level of responsibility and expertise required in their role. For example, they are responsible for ensuring the security and integrity of an organization's information systems and data, which can be a significant pressure. In addition, cybersecurity is constantly evolving, and CISOs may feel pressure to continually learn and stay up-to-date on the latest threats and technologies. These factors can contribute to feelings of self-doubt and inadequacy.

CISOs need to recognize and address imposter syndrome if they are experiencing it. This may involve seeking support from colleagues, professional help, or ways to build confidence and recognize their achievements and strengths.

REAL OR MADE UP

While we may talk about imposter syndrome as an issue in career development, it is important to note that not everyone experiences it to the same degree, and some individuals may not experience it at all. In addition, some are very good at keeping it at bay, while others are affected by it.

Imposter syndrome is often more common among high-achieving individuals who may feel pressure to meet high expectations and tend to focus on their weaknesses and shortcomings.

While the term "imposter syndrome" may not be found in all psychiatric or psychological diagnostic manuals, it is generally recognized as a valid and legitimate concept within psychology. It is not considered a mental disorder in and of itself, but it can cause significant distress and impact an individual's daily life and well-being if not properly addressed.

For the individuals that don't experience imposter syndrome to a noticeable degree, consider yourself lucky because, for those who do, it hinders their progress significantly. Nonetheless, it is still essential to understand this state of mind to assist in providing an encouraging growth environment for everyone.

WHAT CAUSES IT

To understand how to control it, we must first understand what causes it. Several factors may contribute to the development of imposter syndrome. These may include:

1. **Expectations:** Pressure to meet high expectations, whether self-imposed or external, can contribute to imposter syndrome.

2. **Weaknesses:** Individuals who tend to focus on their weaknesses and discount their strengths may be more prone to imposter syndrome.

3. **Perfectionist:** Individuals with a perfectionist tendency may be more likely to experience imposter syndrome. They may hold themselves to unrealistic standards and feel like a failure when they make mistakes.

4. **External Validation:** Individuals who do not receive external validation or recognition for their achievements may be more prone to imposter syndrome.

5. **Setbacks:** A history of failures or setbacks may also contribute to imposter syndrome, as individuals may feel like they are not capable of achieving success.

6. **Self-Doubt:** Self-doubt kills more dreams than failure ever will. Once you begin believing in yourself, you ignore all obstacles in your mind and focus only on your goal.

7. **Pluralistic Ignorance:** The phenomenon in which an individual may perceive inaccurate beliefs about the group due to the lack of communication. For example, one may perceive that others in a group have a certain level of expertise or knowledge they do not possess. It is the fear of looking or sounding dumb in front of our peers when most people around you may share the same feeling. This false notion can make an individual feel like an "imposter" or out of place. It makes us overthink everything, take smaller and more calculated risks, be less creative, and hold back on ideas. Therefore, it is important for individuals to be aware of the potential for pluralistic ignorance and to strive for open and honest communication within their group or organization.

8. **What Others Think:** Most people are afraid to ask questions because they are afraid to reveal their ignorance. They may also feel intimidated by the brain power in the room. While it is natural to care about what others think to some extent, it is important to recognize that their opinions do not reflect your worth or value as a person. Competent people will not judge you as they have likely gone through the same transition and are willing to give others a chance. By focusing on your goals, values, and achievements, rather than worrying about what others think, you can build self-confidence and self-esteem and be more resilient to negative feedback or criticism. As you continue to ask questions to learn, you will be on the trajectory of becoming a person that will be more competent.

9. **Confirmation Bias:** Confirmation bias, which refers to the tendency to seek and interpret information that confirms one's existing beliefs and biases, can contribute to imposter syndrome. They focus on remembering instances where they made mistakes or did not meet expectations while discounting cases in which they were successful or exceeded expectations. This bias can lead to a distorted view of one's abilities and accomplishments, reinforcing feelings of inadequacy and self-doubt. Such individuals need to be aware of this bias and evaluate their achievements and abilities more objectively. They can seek feedback from others, keep track of accomplishments and successes, and be mindful of how they interpret and remember events.

10. **Stereotypes:** A stereotypical CISO profile is a Caucasian male in his 40s or 50s, with a degree in business and a few high-level technical and managerial IT Security certifications. Not only does this stereotype cause confirmation bias during the hiring process, but it also feeds into the problem of imposter syndrome. Individuals internalizing this stereotype may be less likely to seek opportunities or take on professional challenges because they believe they are incapable. Let's challenge and break such stereotypes.

11. **Overqualification:** Imposter syndrome often stems from individuals feeling underqualified for a job, but the opposite scenario of being overqualified can also lead to similar feelings of not fitting in. Consequently, individuals may not even consider applying for a job, assuming they are too overqualified. Additionally, some managers may not promote highly qualified individuals due to feeling threatened by their skillset, causing employees to conceal their advanced degrees or numerous certifications.

It is important to note that individuals in any profession can experience imposter syndrome, and there is no one specific cause. Instead, it is often a combination of factors contributing to its development.

WAYS TO COMBAT IMPOSTER SYNDROME

Now that we have recognized the various factors contributing to imposter syndrome, we can tackle it head-on. Some strategies that may help manage it include:

1. **It's Normal:** It is essential to recognize that imposter syndrome is a common experience and that many individuals, including successful professionals, have struggled with it at some point in their careers. You will notice a lot of talks on it at tech conferences. The more we talk about it, the better we can manage it.

2. **Seek Support:** Talking to a trusted friend, mentor, or professional can help manage imposter syndrome. Having someone who can provide perspective, encouragement, and support can be helpful. In addition, their experiences can give us the confidence to help overcome imposter syndrome.

3. **Celebrate Accomplishments:** Setting and achieving small, achievable goals can help build confidence and combat feelings of inadequacy. However, it is also necessary to take the time to celebrate and recognize your accomplishments, no matter how small they may seem. These small victories build up over time and create a history of achievements that help change your confirmation bias to an overall positive experience.

4. **Practice Self-compassion:** Be kind to yourself and recognize that it is normal to make mistakes or have moments of self-doubt. Instead of being overly critical of yourself, try to practice self-compassion and recognize that everyone makes mistakes and has moments of uncertainty. For example, I recently ran a vulnerability scan on two thousand IP addresses, and I had guaranteed the helpdesk team beforehand that devices on the network would not be affected by the scan. To my surprise, twenty printers reacted to the scan and wasted paper, ink, and labels costing the company a few hundred dollars. This took a bigger hit on my ego as it questioned my competency.

5. **Professional Help:** If imposter syndrome is impacting your daily life and causing significant distress, it may be helpful to seek the support of a mental health professional. A therapist or counselor can provide guidance and support in managing imposter syndrome and building self-confidence.

6. **Self-Worth:** Be comfortable with yourself. Self-esteem is when you value yourself. Self-confidence is when you believe in your abilities. These two things usually go hand in hand with people who can conquer imposter syndrome. You can develop self-confidence by focusing on your skills and examples of accomplishments from the past.

    Having a positive attitude in life is the basis of self-esteem. Let go of the little things in life and focus on the bigger picture. Keep a calm composure even when faced with failure because people will notice your attitude and pass judgment based on that. Once you value yourself more than what others think of you, people's opinions will also change. Remember, you cannot change how people think; you can only change how you think about yourself.

    Comparing yourself to others will harm you as you will always find someone more competent than you in any skill. Only compare yourself to your past to judge your growth. Try newer and better things to grow your self-worth. As a result, your self-confidence will increase.

7. **Reframe Your Vocabulary:** Changing your vocabulary may not directly affect imposter syndrome, but it can be a helpful tool in managing and coping with it. Words have power and using positive and confident language when discussing your abilities and accomplishments can help shift your mindset and build self-confidence. Positive self-talk has a tremendous effect on the mind. For example, instead of saying, "I'll never be good enough," try saying, "I'm making progress. I'm proud of myself for that." Even changing one letter can alter the tone, like "I've got to secure the organization" versus "I get to secure the organization."

    Your choice of words affects how your mind behaves. Your mind is susceptible to emotions, and you can influence it by altering your tone and words. To remove any self-doubt, remove or reframe the following:
    - Remove:
        o Obviously (it's condescending)
        o Never (reduces trust and energy)
    - Reframe:
        o Exchange "But" (it's contradicting) with "and"
        o Use "Possibilities" instead of "Impossible"
        o "Try" implies a possibility of failure. Instead, use decisive words like "Do" or "don't"

- Change "I'm not good at" to "I'm learning"
- Replace "I'm frustrated" with "I feel challenged but determined"

8. **Intellectual Humbleness:** Imposter syndrome is believing you're a fake. A straightforward strategy to overcome this is to not actually be phony. Stay humble, and don't presume more than you know. Learn to say, "I don't know," or "Can you help me." These are powerful statements, as your ego will tell you not to use them. You will be surprised how many people will reach out to help. Overconfidence will only make you look arrogant and hurt you in the long run. Humility will always create a better long-term reputation.

9. **Exposure Therapy:** Imposter syndrome is often characterized by feelings of self-doubt and inadequacy. It can be helpful to confront and challenge these feelings by taking on tasks or challenges that may initially seem intimidating or beyond your abilities. This is known as exposure therapy.

"If somebody offers you an amazing opportunity but you are not sure you can do it, say yes – then learn how to do it later!" – Richard Branson.

By exposing yourself to things you are afraid of, you can gradually build confidence and become more comfortable taking on new challenges and stepping outside your comfort zone. This can be particularly helpful in building resilience and reducing the impact of imposter syndrome.

It is essential to approach exposure therapy in a gradual and controlled manner and to work with a coach or therapist if you are interested in using this approach. It is also important to recognize that exposure therapy may not be appropriate or suitable for everyone.

We always test products in a controlled environment or a sandbox. Put yourself in a sandbox and be vulnerable. This sandbox environment will have safety nets or limitations so that you cannot fall far and can bounce back immediately. That is one of the best ways to remove your fear of being in uncomfortable situations. For example, if you're afraid to perform your first risk assessment for a client, perform a few for your friend's company or a non-profit. Your comfort level will be there as you are doing them a favor, you do not have time constraints, and the environment is not hostile. You only need to focus on your performance now; none of the other elements distract you.

Before I started full-time in cybersecurity, I did plenty of assessments, ethical hacking engagements, vulnerability scans, and security configuration reviews, all for free. I thought I would make many mistakes, but I quickly realized there was nothing to fear. I initially feared looking incompetent, but I realized the people I was performing the work for knew little about it and appreciated my help. They were also not in a position to judge my competence. This environment created a safe playground for me to practice and build my confidence and experience.

10. **Adaptation**: Building on the previous point of exposure therapy, you need to challenge yourself every now and then. Look for challenges to motivate yourself. For example, you might find yourself in uncomfortable situations, like solving a problem for a difficult client. As you struggle through it, learn from it, ask for help, and adapt strategies to deal with the unknown. There are multiple approaches to solving problems. Mental preparation helps you handle uncomfortable situations better.

11. **Positive Environment:** You can choose to be in certain situations that are conducive to your mental health. For example, regular reinforcement of your abilities is good for building self-confidence. So be around people who bolster you and provide encouragement and do the same for them.

    There are many ways to pick positive environments. For example, speaking at a tech conference on a topic you are already very skilled at builds confidence. You know in the back of your mind that everyone in the room is here to listen and learn from you. Seeing people nod and clap at your presentation is probably the biggest self-esteem booster. It makes you value yourself more and provides you with reinforcement that others respect you as well. They don't have to say a word; their presence is proof. Another approach is to teach, lecture, mentor, or volunteer. All these environments put you in a situation where your role as a subject matter expert (SME) has already been established.

    On the flip side, do not create an echo chamber that feeds your ego. We want a balance to foster humility.

12. **Criticism**: When constructive feedback is given in a supportive and respectful manner, it can help individuals recognize and acknowledge their achievements and areas for improvement and set realistic personal and professional development goals.

    However, negative or overly critical feedback can have the opposite effect and contributes to feelings of inadequacy and self-doubt. Therefore, it is important for individuals to be open to feedback and to view it as an opportunity for learning and growth rather than as a personal attack or criticism.

    It is also important to filter out unwanted criticism and not care what everyone has to say. Everyone around you may think they're entitled to advise you on your career journey. Don't take criticism from anyone you don't take advice from. The reality is that most people offer advice based on their own experiences and background. Jealousy may also fog their judgment. You will never be good enough for the wrong person. The reality is that only a small percentage of people will genuinely want to see you succeed. By seeking out and incorporating feedback into your personal and professional development plan from trusted colleagues or mentors, you can build self-awareness and confidence and reduce the impact of imposter syndrome.

Untapped Influence

Your imposter syndrome may tell you that you don't want to be in a leadership role and that it's not for you. However, you may not be aware of your influence on the people around you or the organization. If you don't want to be a leader for yourself, be a leader to help others.

It is important for individuals to be aware of their strengths and abilities and to seek out opportunities to utilize and share them. You can do this by pursuing leadership roles or taking on additional responsibilities, seeking feedback from colleagues, and building a solid support network. By doing so, individuals can tap into their untapped influence and significantly impact not only their personal and professional lives but the lives of others. For example, you could demonstrate your abilities to achieve milestones faster through your collaboration and team-building skills by replacing someone who worked alone and got a lot of resistance. As a result, you would positively affect many people's careers and mental health.

Overconfidence

Overconfidence is an overestimation of one's ability to perform a task successfully. It often originates from a fear of failure or seeking the pleasure of acceptance of others. For some, it acts as a defensive mechanism to combat imposter syndrome.

Being overconfident can have its own set of challenges and drawbacks. Overconfidence can lead to several adverse outcomes, such as taking unnecessary risks, making poor decisions, and failing to recognize and learn from mistakes. It can also create problems in interpersonal relationships, as others may view an individual as arrogant or lacking in humility. Overconfidence is like a drug that should be taken with precaution, as an overdose will eventually cause cognitive bias that will have the opposite effect; You will lose self-confidence due to failure.

What's worse is the Dunning-Kruger effect, a type of overconfidence that occurs when people with low ability in a certain area overestimate their ability. It is named after a 1999 study by psychologists David Dunning and Justin Kruger. They found that people who performed poorly on a test of humor, grammar, and logic were more likely to overestimate their test scores and believe that they did better than they actually did. This is because they lacked the skills and knowledge necessary to evaluate their ability accurately, so they could not recognize their incompetence. This incompetence can lead to overconfidence, as they may overestimate their ability and take on tasks or make decisions beyond their capabilities.

It is generally more beneficial to strive for a healthy level of self-confidence, which involves recognizing and acknowledging one's own abilities and accomplishments while also being open to feedback and learning from mistakes. This can help individuals to be more resilient, take on new challenges, and achieve their goals while also being mindful of the potential drawbacks of overconfidence.

It is important to distinguish overachievers, who are individuals that consistently exceed expectations or goals. They tend to be highly motivated and driven to succeed. In terms of the Dunning-Kruger effect, overachievers fall on the opposite end of the spectrum. They may have a high level of ability in a certain area and be able to accurately evaluate their own competence, leading to a more realistic assessment of their abilities. Their history of success keeps them confident in their abilities and fuels them to go further.

Takeaway

People become wiser and more confident as they get older. This is because life's experiences teach them to value themselves better and filter out the noise. But we don't have to wait; instead, we can take proactive measures toward building a positive self-perception and reducing the impact of imposter syndrome.

16. INSECURITY

The dark side of security

This book primarily focuses on helping you build the skills needed to advance your career in cybersecurity. However, it is crucial to address some of the aspects in this field that harm security. This chapter will discuss the dark side of cybersecurity, including ways to prevent or handle such situations.

From a security controls standpoint, cybersecurity professionals have this infamous saying about end users: "People are the weakest link." From the standpoint of gatekeeping the cybersecurity field, some cybersecurity professionals can become the weakest link because of their insecurity in security.

Compared to other fields, cybersecurity is still maturing, and the pioneers of the various cybersecurity tools, frameworks, and techniques are still around and developing them. As a result, there is no established path for career progression. This creates organic growth and rapid progression as technology advances. There is naturally a lot of competition because of its demand and growing nature. Heavy competition creates new problems like professional jealousy, lack of recognition, vendor friction, lack of transitioning paths, and peers or superiors threatened by overqualified individuals.

Let's look a bit closer into some of the issues preventing professional advancement and how best to address them.

GATEKEEPING

The cybersecurity field has seen tremendous growth and development over the years, thanks to the hard work and dedication of countless individuals. These individuals have devoted their time researching, teaching, mentoring, and promoting the field. They have also been willing to stand up for their beliefs, even if it means facing jail time, and have worked to pass new laws, raise awareness, and provide free resources and training to others in the field. We are grateful for their efforts and the impact they have had on the field of cybersecurity.

> **Gatekeepers:** People with influence within a company who define the entry into the field.

Gatekeepers who witnessed and became involved in the advent of the cybersecurity field earned their positions through hard work and trial and error. Generations later, people in the field can now hold credentials and qualifications that the gatekeepers were previously not able to display. These qualifications didn't exist when the field was in its infancy. Now specialized certifications and degrees have appeared in the last few decades focusing on cybersecurity. In the days past, there were Computer Science or Computer Engineering degrees and a handful of certifications. There are now thirty to-forty areas of cybersecurity specializations and hundreds of certifications. There were also not a lot of ways to showcase your feats or accomplishments in security. Today you have professional networks, conference talks, blogs, video tutorials, simulations, webinars, open-source tools, CTFs, and bug bounties.

The reality is: while you may have laid the foundation as a gatekeeper and spent twenty years developing your skills and earning your badges, it takes a fraction of that time to train yourself with the guidance, tools, and roadmaps that exist today. At the same time, technology is constantly changing and evolving, and the cycle of gatekeeping will be continuous. Nonetheless, we should pay our respects to the original gatekeepers who made it easier to transition into the cybersecurity field today.

Negative Gatekeepers

You would think that "birds of a feather flock together." However, in the cybersecurity field, some individuals have insecurities, primarily those that have spent decades developing themselves and their companies to the comfortable place they are in today. They now see others benefiting from the fruits of their labor by learning faster and showing potential to climb up the ladder by skipping a few unnecessary steps. These "gatekeepers" don't like that others don't have to go through the same hurdles they had to when the field was still immature. So, they try to raise the bar higher to keep them in their positions longer and the "threats" at bay. These individuals are known as negative gatekeepers. The terms "gatekeeping" or "gatekeepers" has received a negative connotation due to such individuals.

Positive Gatekeepers

Individuals or groups can act as gatekeepers in a positive or beneficial way. Gatekeepers can help to maintain standards and quality within a field by controlling access to certain resources, opportunities, or information. They can ensure that only the most qualified or suitable candidates are given access, which can help maintain the field's integrity and protect the interests of the professionals already established.

It's also worth noting that being a gatekeeper is not always a conscious decision. People may not be aware of the impact they have on others and that some gatekeepers may act as such without any negative intent. Instead, they may just be following their own set of rules and protocols.

The key is finding a balance where gatekeepers can help maintain standards and quality while assisting new professionals in entering the field and advancing their careers. They should be willing to share knowledge, provide guidance and mentorship, and be open to new ideas and perspectives.

Ways Around Negative Gatekeepers

While you cannot convince a person not to be a thorn in your career development path, you can still continue to develop yourself.

If you happen to work with such individuals or encounter them in interviews, the following tips may help:

- Avoid confrontation in technology. Egos will be hard to get past. Instead, listen and pose any objections inquisitively. For example, instead of saying, "I found a more modern way to do it," try brainstorming the idea with them first and getting them to agree for you to try it out. Their approval will make it seem like they had something to do with it.
- Stay humble. You don't need to correct everyone or be right all the time. It is not a sign of weakness; it is a sign of wisdom. There is always a lot to learn. You may know much more than your superiors in the company but never display it. If they mention your unique qualifications, brush it off to avoid jealousy.
- Continue to grow your skills even if you don't get support from your boss. Study and research topics in your spare time, attend events, meet new people, create contacts in person and online, and increase your overall knowledge base. The company is not responsible for helping you grow; only you are.
- Avoid interacting with negative gatekeepers. "Out of sight, out of mind." If they don't know what you're up to (developing yourself), they cannot get in the way. Instead, be around people who support your growth goals.

- Find a few individuals who can mentor you without the label of a mentor. These individuals want to see you grow to your fullest potential without asking for anything in return. They are hard to find but once you do, stay close to them.

If none of these techniques work, consult with a professional coach or move on to more positive and encouraging environments.

If you feel you have been "gate-kept," remember that you cannot assume someone's intentions. You must give them the benefit of the doubt. You may be mislabeling someone as a negative gatekeeper. You may have some deficiencies in your knowledge or skills that you may be avoiding, and they may be trying to protect you or even help you. You may also have an attitude problem that reinforces your bias. Unfortunately, there is no shortage of individuals in cybersecurity who are impatient, feel privileged, and ignore advice about experience and skill development. Keep an open mind and do some self-reflection. Only look at facts and keep emotions out of your judgment. The worst path to self-development is to blame or label others.

Burnout

In the tech industry, it is important to address the issue of burnout, which is becoming increasingly common but is often considered taboo to discuss. Some people may feel that talking about burnout is viewed as complaining in our fast-paced and competitive society.

Within cybersecurity, burnout refers to the physical and emotional exhaustion from working long hours, experiencing high stress levels, and constantly being on call to address security issues. This can lead to a decrease in productivity, an increase in mistakes, and a higher risk of turnover in the cybersecurity workforce. To prevent burnout, cybersecurity professionals must take care of their physical and mental health, set boundaries, and practice stress management techniques. Burnout can affect anyone, regardless of their ability to multitask or handle a packed schedule. Recognizing and managing your limits is key to avoiding burnout and maintaining a healthy work-life balance.

Burnout Is Serious

Burnout is a serious problem that can negatively affect individuals and organizations. Burnout causes stress, broken relationships, and severe mental exhaustion. It should not be taken lightly. It also reduces performance, focus, morale, and creativity while negatively affecting your overall job and work relations. Remember that you work to earn a living, have a better lifestyle, be happier, and get recognition for your achievements in your career, but burnout takes all that away from you. Once it happens, it takes a lot of time to recover from it.

Although some people may be more resilient to burnout, it is still vital for everyone to be aware of the risks of burnout and take steps to prevent it. If left unchecked, burnout can creep in. Even if an individual is not currently experiencing burnout, they may be at risk of developing it in the future if they are not taking care of themselves. Additionally, burnout can have negative consequences not only for the individual experiencing it but also for their colleagues, who may have to pick up the slack, and for the organization, which may see a decrease in productivity and an increase in mistakes and turnover. Therefore, everyone needs to be aware of burnout and take steps to prevent it from maintaining their well-being and that of their colleagues and organization. Some of the damage burnout causes include the following:

1. **Physical exhaustion:** Burnout can lead to physical symptoms such as fatigue, insomnia, and decreased immune function, making it more challenging to complete daily tasks and maintain good health.
2. **Emotional exhaustion:** Burnout can cause sadness, frustration, and hopelessness, affecting personal relationships and overall quality of life.
3. **Decreased productivity:** Burnout can lead to a decrease in productivity and an increase in mistakes at work, which can negatively affect the individual and the organization.
4. **Increased turnover:** Burnout can increase the risk of turnover in the workforce, as individuals may leave their jobs due to high levels of stress and exhaustion.
5. **Mental health:** Burnout can contribute to the development of mental health problems such as depression and anxiety.
6. **Physical health:** Chronic stress and burnout can also negatively affect physical health, increasing the risk of developing heart disease and type 2 diabetes.

The long-term effects of burnout are a serious problem; over 59% of employees in large tech companies report burnout, according to an Indeed[1] survey. The COVID-19 pandemic only made it worse as more employees worked from home, worked harder, longer hours, and took fewer breaks. Any tech leader in the making needs to be aware of this problem, take preventative measures for themselves and create conducive work environments for others to prevent it from happening.

Causes

To manage burnout, we first need to understand what causes it. Contrary to popular belief, work overload is only one cause of it. Many other factors contribute to this problem, some of which include:

---

[1] Kelly, Jack. "Indeed Study Shows That Worker Burnout Is at Frighteningly High Levels: Here Is What You Need to Do Now." Forbes, Forbes Magazine, 9 Nov. 2022, https://www.forbes.com/sites/jackkelly/2021/04/05/indeed-study-shows-that-worker-burnout-is-at-frighteningly-high-levels-here-is-what-you-need-to-do-now/.

1. **Performance punishment:** Being great at your work has drawbacks; you get assigned more work. This has a spiraling effect where more work piles up on you and less work gets assigned to low-performing employees. Overworked employees will eventually exit the company, leaving the company with low performers.

2. **Excessive workload:** A high volume of work, tight deadlines, and a lack of clear responsibilities can all contribute to burnout. Working fifty to sixty hours a week, which is close to the US average, is a recipe for burnout. The constant pressure to do more due to competition prevents this number from coming down but the reality is quite different. For example, Iceland successfully piloted a four day, thirty five hours work week for several years without any pay cuts. They noticed a decline in stress and burnout with a better quality of life.

3. **Lack of support:** Feeling unsupported by colleagues, supervisors, or upper management can increase the risk of burnout.

4. **Poor work-life balance:** When there's an imbalance between work and personal life, it can cause one to feel overwhelmed and exhausted. The time you put outside work provides your mind some breathing room along with purpose.

5. **Lack of job satisfaction:** A lack of enjoyment or meaning in one's work can contribute to burnout. Unclear direction or career progression creates less meaning to what you do, and working towards arbitrary metrics and numbers does not provide long-term work satisfaction.

6. **Unclear job expectations:** Not understanding the expectations or goals of one's job can lead to feelings of uncertainty and frustration.

7. **Poor leadership:** Poor leadership that treats employees unfairly or does not handle workplace conflicts properly can contribute to burnout.

8. **Toxic workplace:** Companies that only rewards sales or exceptional results but not efforts or the process leave others feeling less productive. You cannot measure everyone with the same yardstick.

9. **Chronic stress:** Ongoing stress can lead to burnout, especially if it is not managed effectively.

10. **Technology Overuse:** Technology allows us to stay connected everywhere. How many times have you checked your emails on the phone while sitting on the toilet seat? Are you on your smartphone when you take your kids to the park? Be honest with yourself. I'm guilty of it. Most people believe working remotely or from home enables them to be more

productive because they have less distraction from office chatter, coffee breaks, and the office commute. The lines between work and rest eventually become blurred due to instant access to information, no matter where we are. Technology is a double edge sword that contributes to burnout.

Warning Signs

Burnout can creep up on you, but there are ways to catch it early. Now that you have a better idea of the causes and the severe drawbacks of burnout, you should pay attention to some of the following warning signs:

- You become more irritable as you do more work and are unable to cope with time. You develop a negative attitude and lose enjoyment in work.
- You start missing deadlines, and the quality of your work declines as well.
- You stop caring about sleep, exercise, food, family outings, movies, or anything that draws you away from work for extended periods.
- You notice health issues like shortness of breath, palpitations, back pains, sleep issues, tendonitis, stomach aches, or lethargy. You may also see signs of substance abuse and a reliance on alcohol or smoking to cope with the stress.

If you or a colleague are experiencing these warning signs of burnout, it is crucial to address the issue before it becomes more serious.

Ways To Avoid It

Prevention is better than cure. If you are lucky enough not to have experienced burnout, pay special attention to the signs to proactively keep it at bay. Burnout has become a common problem in our field, and it needs to be addressed early on before it gets out of hand.

Don't ever assume that you won't experience burnout or that you will be able to deal with it when it happens. I assumed I would not experience burnout because I was extremely efficient, meticulous, mentally strong, motivated, passionate, and overconfident in my abilities. This attitude delayed burnout, but it didn't prevent it. Unfortunately, there are more discussions related to dealing with burnout rather than the focus on preventing it. After learning from my mistakes, here are recommendations to avoid the onset of burnout and manage it proactively.

1. **Recognize the signs:** If you experience any warning signs similar to the examples mentioned above, don't ignore them, as they will only worsen exponentially. Stop and take action to fix them immediately. Don't think you can come close to fire and not get burned.

2. **Put work into perspective:** You cannot do it all. You must sacrifice some tasks to accomplish others. Don't overload your task list. Instead, create a priority list for the day or week and focus on the top one or two things in that list that affect your job based on demand. Don't cram that list with too many tasks. The word priority is singular; focus on what's most important and work your way down the list. The satisfaction of already completing the higher-priority tasks will produce dopamine, a neurotransmitter responsible for generating feelings of happiness, and will motivate you to stay consistent.

3. **Role Clarity:** Some employers have very vague job descriptions. Once they start work, employees are expected to perform various tasks outside their scope. Your role and responsibilities should always be discussed upfront as it may become harder to negotiate them once you are hired. When asked to do work that is not directly part of your responsibilities, you must discuss it with your management for clarity. They may reciprocate with better bonuses, additional time off, or be more receptive to your future requests. If you do not clarify, you will be taken advantage of and be given similar tasks again. Moreover, work will pile up, ending in frustration and discontent.

4. **Take frequent short breaks:** If you're like me and sit at the computer and work until you are finished with a particular task, you will notice that time flies fast. You can quickly burn through half of the day before you get off the chair. While you may think this is productive, it is not. Instead, inserting short ten-minute breaks every thirty to sixty minutes reenergizes your mind to perform more efficiently. Breaks do not mean watching random YouTube videos, browsing social media posts, checking personal emails, or playing games. Breaks must be off-screen, off the phone, and unrelated to work or technology. I like talking to people around me, going for a short walk, talking with my kids if I'm home, or focusing my eyes on natural sunlight. Some people like to cook or do the dishes as a productive form of stress relief.

5. **Exercise:** A minimum of twenty minutes of cardiovascular exercise daily is all it takes to improve blood flow. Exercise produces happy hormones like endorphins and serotonin. It acts as a distraction and stress relief and provides more nutrition to the brain for the next time you start your grind.

6. **Sleep:** I used to say, "Life is too short to waste it on sleep. I'll have plenty of time to sleep in my grave." Lack of sleep can build stress in several ways. You may feel more anxious, irritable, and moody when you don't get enough sleep. Additionally, lack of sleep can affect your ability to think clearly, make decisions, and solve problems. Finally, lack of sleep can also contribute to physical symptoms of stress, such as increased blood pressure, headaches, and muscle tension, which can further increase feelings of stress and discomfort. Sleep is probably the best thing you can do for your brain when you're overworked. The more you work in a day, your mental capacity declines, and your brain becomes less efficient. A good seven to eight hours of sleep every day keeps your mind

and body fresh. If you cannot achieve that consistently, you should make it up on the weekends. It is also important not to sit late at night in front of a bright screen, whether a laptop or phone, as it suppresses melatonin production in the body. This hormone helps regulate the sleep-wake cycle, which is produced in response to darkness.

7. **Family time:** When you spend more time with your loved ones, you realize there's more to life than work. Don't ignore the importance of friends and family, as when the day comes that you don't have work, get laid off, fall sick, or become retired, you will always have friends and family to support you. Many US workers don't entirely utilize their vacation time off from work. Moreover, studies have shown that employees take fewer days off when companies offer unlimited paid time off (PTO). I've been caught up in this as well. In my previous job, I remember taking only a handful of days off per year as I worked remotely during my vacation. My boss used to tell me that as long as you are not off the grid and are able to check emails every day, I consider you working. This habit encouraged me to respond to every email during my time off. Now I feel the company should cut off email access during mandatory PTO. That's the only way to take a mental break from work. At the same time, there should always be backup and redundancy so that the company isn't reliant on one individual.

8. **Ask for help:** One of the issues with high-performing individuals is that they don't trust anyone else and don't ask for help. When I started asking my peers for support and delegating some of my mundane tasks or projects to others, a lot of the load was off my mind, and I could focus on the outcomes rather than the process. Smart people find shorter ways of doing things; the shortest path is usually by asking for advice. You will be surprised how many people are willing to help if you only ask.

9. **Communicate:** Talk to your management the moment you feel overworked. Together you will find ways to distribute workload, hire more people, or get compensated, like with extra time off. If you do not take the time to communicate your concerns, you cannot blame others for not knowing. For example, once I started getting a lot of projects from my team, I quickly reached out to my bosses and discussed how we should cope with scalability. Initially, they got worried that I may leave, but we figured it out by involving and training others to offload some of my work, along with giving me a pay raise for my broader responsibilities. Others also got a chance to get trained and mentored. It was a win-win for all.

10. **Unplugging:** It is impossible to have a normal conversation nowadays without someone getting interrupted by smartphone notifications. Social media and communication apps compete for our attention. The news always highlights the negatives as it gains them more clicks. Also, constantly looking at other people's achievements on social media may create feelings of competition or hopelessness. Simply getting away from it all is the best cure. Don't get distracted and disconnect yourself from the noise. We all need regular doses of

digital detox as part of our daily routine to decrease stress and increase mindfulness. Depending on your needs, either set a time to get your dose of technology or go for extended periods of time without it to cleanse your mind and regain focus.

11. **Self-control:** Challenge yourself not to work when you're with family, during the weekend, driving, or on trips. The world will not end if you don't work for a few days. Try it if you don't believe me. Ironically, one good thing that happened to me when I got sick with COVID-19 was that I was forced to get off technology for a week as I did not have the physical or mental energy to work or to even look at a screen. Remember that I had not taken more than a handful of days of PTO in the last three years. So, at first, I got worried and thought, "who is going to do my work?" After a week of no work, I realized that no one was affected by my absence, projects were still running as scheduled, clients were all taken care of, colleagues were supportive, and family and friends were around for support. It was a blessing in disguise. From then on, I've been taking it easy by striking a balance between work and life.

Burnout is a reality, but if we learn to recognize the signs and take proactive actions, we can prevent it from affecting our lives and help others.

ENTRY LEVEL

Another topic that hinders progress in cybersecurity is the confusion around entry level cybersecurity jobs. We discuss the lack of availability of qualified cybersecurity individuals, yet we put unreasonable expectations at entry-level jobs. If the bar to entry is so high, it will have a snowball effect on the job market, and we will create the perception of a talent shortage.

You can find plenty of so-called "entry-level" jobs posted by recruiters. Some terrible examples of entry-level job descriptions in cybersecurity might include:

- "0-2 years of experience required in X technology." This should be zero years of experience; that's the definition of entry-level.
- "Preferred certifications: CEH, CISSP." Neither of these are entry-level certifications. Instead, these certifications require two and five years of relevant security experience, respectively, to certify.
- Not clearly outlining the responsibilities of the role or the tasks the candidate will be expected to perform. This results in an unclear direction, and they end up doing a bit of everything.
- Using overly technical language that someone new to the field may not understand. This will deter them from applying.

In one particular job posting, I saw a requirement for "five years of Kubernetes experience," when the technology was only available for three years at the time of the posting.

Cybersecurity is a field that encompasses many different roles, some of which may be considered entry-level and others that require more experience. For example, entry-level cybersecurity roles might include security analyst, threat intelligence analyst, security operations center (SOC) analyst, or a junior position on the compliance team. These roles typically involve monitoring and analyzing security information and events, identifying potential threats, and taking appropriate action to mitigate them. On the other hand, there are also entirely non-technical fields to get started in, such as product sales, project coordinators, policy development and documentation, compliance risk, running education and awareness programs, public relations, and cyber insurance. Internships are a great way to get your feet wet.

However, other roles in cybersecurity, such as security architect, penetration tester, or incident responder, typically require more experience and specialized knowledge.

Rewriting

Entry-level job descriptions need to be rewritten. Some acceptable terms in an entry-level job description include:

- Will provide training. Must be willing to attain certifications.
- Familiarity with the following technology is a plus: VMWare, Linux, and Networking.
- Social skills: work in a team, meet with clients, email and phone follow-ups, participate in vendor demos and events.
- Demonstrate a keen interest and passion for technology.

Every employer wants a "rock star" but is unwilling to pay for one. Employers don't need to lower their expectations; they need to be realistic. Anyone can be taught a product, tool, or process in weeks. Instead, they need to hire for talent, passion, and willingness to learn. That is what will give them quality and sustainability.

With these minor mental readjustments, we can attract more talent and benefit from entry-level candidates rather than scaring them away.

MENTORSHIP

Coaching the next generation is grounds for great mental satisfaction. It is noble and shows your passion and love for the field and the next generation. The condition is that you do not expect anything in return other than gratitude. If the purpose is to feed your ego, it harms yourself and the industry at large.

Goal

The purpose of mentoring is not to teach someone technology or theory or to assign them work. One of the preferred ways to mentor someone is to teach them something they cannot easily learn from books or YouTube videos. These are things like:

- Negotiation skills
- Developing the right skills
- Not wasting time on things that have little career value
- Developing self-worth
- Shortcuts to success
- Long-term planning
- Discussing the pros and cons of their career paths
- Showing them the ugly side of things
- Walking them through the day-to-day activities
- Dealing with difficult situations or objection handling
- Conflict resolution with peers, bosses, or clients
- Helping them look at the bigger picture
- Not letting them cloud their judgment by products, vendors, technology, or buzz words
- Helping them get rid of unconscious bias

While this list is not exhaustive and depends on the individual and their focus, it should give a good idea of the concept of mentorship. You don't want them to go through the same struggles as you did, so you guide them.

Benefits

It is beneficial for people within society to obtain mentorship. Mentors can create a positive outlook and foster healthy relationships. They can boost your self-esteem and self-confidence. Mentorship helps you create goals and ambitions and inspires you to want to be a better version of yourself.

Conversely, the mentor receives respect because the mentee appreciates the knowledge and time the mentor provides. The mentor continues to learn from teaching and gains the satisfaction from helping others.

Disadvantages

Having a mentor in your career path can have some drawbacks, including:

1. **Dependence:** You may become too reliant on your mentor for guidance and support rather than developing your decision-making and problem-solving skills.
2. **Limited perspective:** Your mentor may only have experience and knowledge in a specific field or industry, which can limit the scope of advice and opportunities available to you.
3. **Conflicting interests:** Your mentor's goals and interests may not align with yours, which can lead to disagreements or tension in the mentorship.
4. **High Expectations:** Your mentor may have high expectations of you, which can add pressure and stress to your professional development.
5. **Time-consuming:** Finding a mentor and maintaining the relationship can be time-consuming and may take away from other important responsibilities or activities.

It's important to find a mentor you trust and can learn from, but also to be aware of these potential drawbacks and take steps to mitigate them.

Abuse

Unfortunately, some individuals abuse the concept of mentorship. It's a big word that some people like to attach to their profile to show seniority. They look at it as an opportunity to advance themselves in the field. These types of personalities harm the security profession.

Sadly, some individuals use mentorship to boost their ego, build their personal brand, get publicity and likes on social media, and even use it to push their agendas. This agenda could be to promote their product, business, sponsorship, or to make money. While there is nothing wrong with charging a fee, the act does not become selfless anymore. I'm not against paid engagements; after all, a lot of time is consumed mentoring. However, it is justified if the monetary aspect doesn't affect the goals discussed earlier. There are cybersecurity mentorship programs that charge a hefty fee. Most of these are courses with mass online lectures, video-on-demand self-paced studies, group discussions, or homework with evaluations. While they may work for some people, they fail to focus on the one-on-one aspect of individual development and feedback.

Besides these career-hindering effects of bad mentors, there have been other serious complaints, like reports of online sexual harassment towards the mentees. Some have taken advantage of their influence by exploiting the mentees' willingness to succeed. It is disgusting, to say the least, and undermines the selfless efforts of many other great mentors, most of whom never come into the limelight. These bad apples harm the reputation of security professionals everywhere who want to see others succeed.

Recognition

A long-standing issue has been that cybersecurity is often considered a subfield of information technology (IT) because it involves the protection of digital information and systems. In many organizations, there is usually no dedicated security professional on staff, and security tasks are spread across the IT team. As a result, security is given low priority due to the lack of time and understanding.

It's important to note that while IT is focused on managing technology, cybersecurity is focused on protecting technology and data.

The lack of recognizing it as its own distinct field stems from the notion that cybersecurity is considered a technical field, even though there are plenty of non-technical areas of security like policies, education, partnerships, and projects.

Putting cybersecurity under IT can hurt security in a few ways:

- **Limited Focus**: If cybersecurity is managed within the IT department, the focus may be more on maintaining the functionality and availability of technology systems rather than on protecting against cyber threats. This can lead to a lack of emphasis on security measures, such as vulnerability assessments and penetration testing, leaving an organization more vulnerable to cyberattacks.
- **Limited Expertise:** IT staff may not have the specialized training or expertise in cybersecurity that is required to effectively protect against cyber threats. This can lead to inadequate security measures or a lack of understanding of the latest cyber threats.
- **Limited Accountability:** If cybersecurity is managed within the IT department, it can be difficult to hold individuals accountable for the security of the organization's digital assets. This can be necessary for compliance and regulatory reasons. The lack of accountability can make it challenging to identify and address security issues in a timely manner.
- **Limited Budget:** IT departments are often focused on maintaining and upgrading existing systems and technology, which can limit the budget allocated to cybersecurity. This makes it challenging to acquire the necessary resources and tools to protect against cyber threats.

By treating cybersecurity as a distinct field, organizations can more effectively allocate resources to protect against cyberattacks and data breaches, which can be extremely costly in terms of financial losses and damage to reputation.

Security affects everything and everyone. There is both a business impact side and a technical side to security. That is why it needs to be recognized as its own independent domain and not fall under IT.

Professional Competition

Competition is usually healthy, but only if it uplifts everyone. In the professional field, it is all too common to either envy or despise someone in your field. The growth potential and career paths in cybersecurity are so diverse that it magnifies that feeling.

Professional competition in the workplace can be harmful because it can create a cut-throat environment where individuals focus more on outdoing their colleagues rather than working together towards a common goal. This can lead to a lack of trust and collaboration, professional jealousy, and only staying around people that reinforce your confirmation bias. Such behavior increases stress and tension among employees. Additionally, it can lead to unethical behavior, such as withholding information, taking credit for the work of others, blocking promotions, and eventually hindering overall career advancement for you and others. It can also lead to the exclusion of employees and a toxic work culture. These factors can ultimately harm productivity and lead to high turnover rates.

Let's look at some of these issues stemming from highly competitive environments to resolve or avoid them better.

Professional Jealousies

In his famous book, 48 Laws Of Power, Robert Greene stated, "Never appear too perfect." While we encourage growth through showcasing your accomplishments and uplifting others on social media platforms like LinkedIn, there's a drawback to this exposure; Envy.

People usually only post their successes on social media, rarely failures or embarrassments, which gives the impression to others that your life is perfect, and they wish they had what you have. However, in reality, everyone experiences their fair share of losses and rejections.

The reality is that criticism from some people is a reaction for them being envious of you. Additionally, they may see the negative in everything. They demonstrate this behavior with passive-aggressive comments. For example, an individual tuned into my webinar on social engineering and commented that my definitions of "influence" and "manipulation" were wrong. The best way to counter opinions is with facts. I provided references to the definitions, and I excused myself from further discussion even though the rebuttal continued.

Professional jealousy can be subtle and often unconscious, so it might not always be easy to spot. For example, a friend of mine introduced me as a brilliant entrepreneur to his colleague. Instead of asking me about my services, his colleague began asking me questions like "what is your hourly rate?" When I explained to him, I don't do business in that manner. He insisted that I had an hourly rate and then asked rudely, "What are you worth?" even while I tried to explain to him that I charged a fixed-fee project basis. For the purpose of the conversation, I gave him a fair hourly rate. His immediate reply was, "our engineers charge five times that." He then asked me, "You've been doing this for many years; how come you're not running a big company by now?" I handled it with a smile and found the opportunity to walk away. Sometime later in the year, the same person challenged my hacking methods in one of my public presentations. This time I knew what to expect. I told him, "I stand by my techniques based on knowledge and experience. Feel free to email me why you think I'm wrong and demo your theory as I did." Based on my experience dealing with passive-aggressive behavior, I walked away from the person.

Interactions like this are inevitable. If no one disagrees with you, you are probably not interesting. While you cannot avoid it, you can deflect it. You can learn to ignore it entirely or laugh it off. Some people will use self-deprecating humor to diffuse the situation: "Don't believe some nerd like me who you just met; do your research." Whatever you do, don't get defensive. There's an old saying: "Never argue with stupid people; they will drag you down to their level and then beat you with experience."

Feelings of regret, laziness, or incompetence inside these people bother them, and they want to transfer some of their frustration onto you. They want to momentarily see you feel uneasy and agitated to spoil your day. Don't fall into that trap.

There are also a lot of successful people that keep everything to themselves to avoid such toxic engagements. People also refuse to share their steps to success, fearing that others may copy them, do a better job, and eventually surpass them. They may learn from them and do it in half the time with half the struggle, so they are unwilling to share useful information with others. This threatened feeling differentiates envy from jealousy. These people eventually become "negative gatekeepers" and hinder career growth by limiting knowledge sharing.

Ethnic Bias

This section is not what it sounds like. It's not about the workplace's discriminatory practices against people with different characteristics than you. There has been plenty of research on this and countless books and articles written on the topic. Our concern is the opposite of that; Discrimination that happens between people of the same race, ethnicity, language, or minority group due to competition within. You may refer to it as intra-ethnic discrimination.

For example, within certain ethnic groups, there may be a culture of high expectations and pressure to succeed, leading to employees feeling competitive with one another regarding job performance, promotions, and recognition. In addition, there may be a limited number of individuals who represent the group in certain positions or fields. This can lead to competition among members of the group to be the one who represents them. This competitive behavior within minority groups could result from initiatives like Diversity and Inclusion or a quota for minorities. Other factors that contribute to this include the following:

- **Limited opportunities:** When there are limited opportunities for advancement or success within a minority group, individuals may feel the need to compete against one another to secure those opportunities.
- **Stereotypes and discrimination:** Minority groups may face stereotypes and discrimination in the workplace, leading to a perception that there is only room for a limited number of individuals from the group to succeed. This can lead to competition among group members for the limited available opportunities.
- **Pressure to succeed:** There may be cultural or societal pressures within the minority group to succeed, leading to individuals feeling competitive toward one another in terms of job performance, promotions, and recognition.
- **Internalized discrimination:** Individuals from minority groups may internalize societal discrimination, leading to self-doubt and a lack of confidence. This could lead to competition among group members as they try to prove their worth, which can adversely affect team dynamic and productivity.

It's worth noting that these behaviors are not specific to minority groups and could be present in any group of people. However, the reasons why these behaviors appear could be different and linked to the social and cultural context in which the minority group is situated.

If you are not part of a minority group commonly identified by ethnic background, religion, or gender, you will likely never experience such bias. The root cause of this comes from a history of struggle and being marginalized.

I have noticed two general trends for intra-ethnic biases. First, for some people, the competition to succeed is with everyone, especially their "own kind." You would think that individuals part of a tight ethnic group would help each other unconditionally. While that is the typical case, some will cut you out simply because they want to shine amongst the smaller group they are part of and not share the limelight with anyone else. They have better chances of getting noticed if they don't have to compete with a larger group, and anyone who comes close to their success poses a threat. This is an unfortunate reality.

The second trend is that these individuals want to be like the majority group and be desperately part of their "tribe." So, they consciously try not to show any bias by breaking off professional ties with their own ethnic community. They fear people will accuse them of favoritism if they promote or publicly praise someone from their own group. So, to avoid any bias in the workplace, ironically, they actively ignore and discriminate against their own. For example, such people will not praise you in public nor recommend you to others. They will also not hang out with you in social work gatherings. On the other hand, they will go out of their way to please the tribes they wish to be a part of.

Unfortunately, you cannot change this "wannabe" behavior. Our purpose is not to fix it but to provide awareness of this. Many people get confused when they experience this due to the expectations they hold from people they share commonalities with. Therefore, don't have such expectations as it will save you from disappointment. Instead, focus more on being around people who uplift you regardless of any differences. No matter what side you look at this from, whether it's promoting your identity or discriminating against it, both harm professional growth in security. The only bias you should have is towards the merit and abilities of a person.

Credit

Another byproduct of professional jealousy is not giving credit to others and being overly protective about your work, publications, talks, or slides. Some people are selfish and want to take credit for everything, even if it's a public resource or an idea already discussed. Some feel if they share their secrets, others will surpass them. Many others assume that giving someone credit will undermine their own work and their ability to be considered a pioneer or leader. Again, this is due to insecurities.

For example, I've noticed people write articles about hacking techniques they "discovered." A simple online search shows tons of similar posts from decades ago. Today it is hard to find a novel idea. This does not mean we cannot repeat or build upon what others did. Instead, providing attribution to the inspirational author is good for credibility as it shows you are not afraid to promote others.

I'm never afraid to share my "trade secrets" with anyone for fear of copycats or provide credit where it's due. That's because I have enough confidence in my abilities to execute or explain the idea better than others who may copy it. The internet always leaves a trail.

Echo Chamber

Professional competition can also contribute to an echo chamber, which is a situation where a group of people or an organization is isolated from dissenting opinions or outside perspectives. This can lead to confirmation bias, which is the tendency to seek out and interpret new information in a way that confirms one's existing beliefs or hypotheses. So, you start listening to people who agree with you, reading articles that confirm your bias, and searching for statistics that align with your understanding. This can be a problem in professional settings because it can prevent individuals and organizations from considering alternative viewpoints and making well-informed decisions.

Competition compels people to stay within positive reinforcement groups. They don't like to hear constructive feedback and consider it criticism. As a result, they are depriving themselves of opportunities for improvement. Self-correction is essential to growth. A lot of things blind you due to your perspective. One must not fear opposing views. Instead, broadening your mindset by changing your audience and eliciting constructive feedback contributes to maturity and will humble you. I once gave a talk to a non-technical audience on "Social Engineering awareness."

While everyone learned a lot, the attendees gave me lots of feedback. They told me the title of my talk was misleading as it shouldn't have the word "Engineering" in it, that it had nothing to do with hacking, and that the term "ethical hacking" was an oxymoron. I took mental notes to develop better titles and address basic concepts upfront that may not seem so basic to my audience. Before this experience, I had limited my interactions to within my professional circle. However, by broadening my communication and engaging with diverse audiences and perspectives, I gained a wealth of knowledge and skills in effectively communicating.

If going into foreign territory makes you uncomfortable, you can remain in your echo chamber and still benefit from feedback in a safe and conducive environment. For example, immediately after my speaking engagements, I make it a habit to engage in small talk with people in the audience and ask them for feedback. Naturally, everyone says, "it was great." Nevertheless, I follow up and ask how it could have been better. Most people are still shy to provide feedback, so I start providing self-criticism asking for confirmation. I will pass comments like, "I talk too fast," "I was too technical," "I should engage the audience more," or "my jokes were too dry, no one laughed." If I'm lucky, I get true feedback. The same techniques can be applied to your colleagues after a meeting or your boss during a review.

The following are some ways to address the problem of echo chambers and confirmation bias that can be integrated into your business dealings:

1. **Encourage diversity:** Having a diverse group of people with different perspectives and experiences can help prevent echo chambers from forming and can also help to counter confirmation bias.
2. **Seek out dissenting opinions:** Make a conscious effort to seek and consider perspectives that differ from yours. This can be done by reading or following articles and experts from different technological backgrounds or actively listening to and engaging with people with different viewpoints.
3. **Challenge your assumptions:** Regularly question your own assumptions and beliefs and consider alternative explanations for events and phenomena. Play devil's advocate in group discussions before you agree on a solution. This will ensure you have considered opposing viewpoints.
4. **Encourage constructive disagreement:** Create an environment where people feel comfortable disagreeing and providing their opinions without the fear of sounding disrespectful.
5. **Use decision-making frameworks:** Use structured decision-making frameworks that encourage considering multiple perspectives and options and help identify and mitigate confirmation bias.

It takes time and continuous effort, but a consistent approach can help reduce the impact of echo chambers and confirmation bias.

Career Advancement

Professional competition may harm your career advancement. I've seen colleagues who hide what they do and work alone to get credit. In a management team, if team members are competing against each other for a promotion, they may not be willing to support each other's professional development. They may even sabotage each other's efforts to advance in their careers. I once had a manager who denied my requests for career development training and kept me out of specific meetings with management as they wanted to take credit for my work. It was because I was more qualified than them and was showing rapid signs of progress. I got hints of this with comments like, "You don't need this training; you have tons of experience and a [insert certification]," or "sit this one out, give others a chance as well; We're a team."

Professional competition in the workplace can hinder career advancements by creating a cutthroat environment where individuals are more focused on competing with their colleagues rather than collaborating and working together. This can lead to a lack of trust and communication, as well as a lack of support for each other. Additionally, when competition is intense, it can lead to a focus on individual accomplishments rather than team accomplishments, which can make it difficult for individuals to advance in their careers. Overall, it can create a situation where people are more focused on themselves and their advancement rather than the organization's success as a whole.

People who block someone's abilities to advance due to insecurities will eventually be replaced. Still, some stick around forever due to deep ties with the stakeholders. Either way, you should not tolerate it. Take the signs seriously. Develop yourself with or without anyone's support and maintain a positive attitude to come out on top. Do what you can to navigate the situation and establish good communication channels with your management. If all else fails, get out of this toxic environment at your first opportunity. The goal of this entire book is career advancement. If you cannot remove the thorns from your path, find a different route.

Race To The Bottom

When organizations compete, they may reduce their cybersecurity standards to cut costs and gain a competitive edge in the market. This is termed as a "race to the bottom." As a CISO, this practice affects your budget. On the other hand, a CISO may also be engaged in this practice when they try to save dollars for the company. For example, a CISO may outsource parts of their cybersecurity to a cheaper third-party provider that offers lower prices by cutting corners on their internal security measures. I've seen management invest in the cheapest MDR or SOC solution and throw it out after their contract ended because the service didn't provide what they hoped for. So, they wasted their time and money and even worse, left gaps in their security posture.

Vendors or managed security providers are constantly competing in price. In a "race to the bottom" scenario, organizations may neglect critical security practices, such as regular software updates, employee training, or incident response planning, leaving them vulnerable to cyber attacks. Supply chain attacks often target such vendors of managed service provers. This can result in data breaches, financial losses, and reputational damage for both the organization and its customers. Moreover, it sends a message to their clients that they have enough room to cut costs, and the next time the client will squeeze them further on price. This practice leads to a focus on short-term gains by vendors rather than long-term success.

When choosing security products or services, you should look at many factors. These include staff expertise, competency level, experience, understanding of their problems, depth and breadth of scope, trust, and relationships. There is a difference in value and outcome between a junior pentester, fresh out of college, and a seasoned pentester with 20 years of experience.

MINORITY REPORT

In the previous section, we discussed the negative ethnic biases arising from extreme competition within a minority group. The more significant issue is the lack of executive minorities represented at top roles.

Diversity and inclusion in the technology industry is an essential issue as it can lead to better innovation and decision-making. Lack of representation of minority groups at the top level of an organization can be a symptom of systemic bias and discrimination, making it difficult for individuals from those groups to advance in their careers. This lack of representation can also lead to a lack of understanding and consideration of perspectives of diverse customers and communities. Therefore, it is essential for organizations to actively work towards increasing diversity and inclusion at all company levels.

Global Problem

The CISO is an executive-level position. How many minorities are represented at that level? The designation of minority groups is very different depending on the geography. For example, how many "white" executives would you notice in countries with half the world's population such as India and China? How many Jewish, Christian, women, or non-Arabs will you find as CISOs in the world's wealthiest economies such as Saudi Arabia, Kuwait, Qatar, UAE, and other Middle Eastern countries? The answer to these questions is: very few.

The lack of executive minorities representing top company roles is a global problem. While some might argue that the ratio of executives should reflect the population of the majority in a given country, the real problem arises when there is systemic discrimination. When certain groups are underrepresented in leadership positions, it can result in pay disparities and unequal career opportunities.

Furthermore, when companies lack diversity in their leadership, they may struggle to attract and retain diverse talent, which can hinder their ability to compete in a global marketplace. Finally, underrepresenting certain groups in leadership positions can reinforce systemic discrimination, creating a self-perpetuating cycle that is difficult to break. This can lead to a lack of trust and confidence in business and society, reducing social cohesion and contributing to broader social problems.

Discrimination in the workplace can occur at any level, including in executive positions. However, proving discrimination can be challenging, as it is often subtle and indirect. Discrimination can take many forms, such as gender, age, race, ethnicity, religion, or disability-based discrimination. In some cases, discrimination can be evident in the job application process. For example, minority candidates may receive fewer interview opportunities, or job requirements may be tailored to exclude certain groups, resulting in fewer qualified candidates from underrepresented groups. Additionally, bias in hiring decisions can lead to the exclusion of qualified candidates due to their race, gender, or other personal characteristics. Discrimination can also occur in the internal promotion process. Employees from underrepresented groups may be overlooked for promotions, even if they have the necessary qualifications and experience. This can be due to unconscious bias or systemic barriers that limit opportunities for advancement.

There are obvious benefits to a diversified workforce. The various cultures, backgrounds, and experiences that come with race, gender, age, language, or beliefs all contribute to an open mindset. Companies can benefit from this in their marketing, ideas, and thought processes. However, the company culture sometimes needs to change to accommodate this mindset.

Cultural Fit

I do understand the value of being a cultural fit. Once, I was interviewing for a senior network engineer, the hiring manager told me I would be the most qualified and experienced engineer on the team. After taking the company tour and further discussion, the hiring manager and I agreed that this was not a fit for me. The company culture did not suit me. Everyone was laid back. There was an open floor plan with barstools, high tables, bean bags, pets, bicycles, games, and a lot of after-hours drinking. Most people were from the same city, grew up in similar neighborhoods, went to the same schools, and were of the same age group. Being the only married person with kids who did not get their jokes, did not drink, nor want to sit at the office late to hang out, I was not a great fit for the culture as I felt out of place. So, I passed the opportunity to someone else that would enjoy that environment.

Someone may call this discrimination, but there were other minorities represented. The decision was mutual in this case. What if it was the environment that was causing this natural divide? Employees who share similar values and work styles can help to create a more cohesive and productive team. However, it is important to recognize that the concept of "cultural fit" can also be problematic, as it can be used to justify discrimination and bias and lead to a lack of diversity in the workplace. In addition, the concept of cultural fit is often subjective and can be influenced by unconscious bias. Furthermore, it is important to remember that culture is not fixed, culture is always evolving, and a diverse group of people with different backgrounds, experiences, and perspectives can bring fresh ideas, new ways of thinking, and can help the organization to adapt to the ever-changing market.

If a culture is not accommodating to different backgrounds, it can make it difficult for individuals from marginalized groups to feel welcome and valued. In addition, such an environment can make it harder for organizations to attract and retain diverse talent.

Creating a culture that is inclusive and accommodating to diversity is vital for organizations. It can be achieved by educating employees, training on unconscious bias, providing opportunities for diverse perspectives to be heard and valued, creating policies, procedures, and practices promoting diversity and inclusion, and holding leaders and employees accountable. It requires ongoing effort, commitment from leadership, and a tailored approach that considers the organization's specific needs and realities.

Balanced Approach

From a CISO's career perspective, what should you do? The advice depends on where you are in the process, an aspiring CISO or an existing one.

As an aspiring CISO, you should try to find your tribe. These are like-minded people who share your views. Recommendations usually arise from your professional circles that may land you your next big gig. The power of recommendation is stronger than qualifications on paper because of trust. Try to get noticed and excel in your career with your merit. While it is impossible to avoid some form of discrimination in the workplace, rely on the strength of your network and avoid places where you see no minority representation. It will be challenging to grow in such environments.

As an existing CISO, when you are in a position to hire a team, go out of your way to be fair. Some companies have adopted blind reviews, a method used to hide the candidates' names, gender, location, picture, or profile, as these may create biases in their decisions. They filter out candidates based on qualifications only. Then the final round is in-person or video conferencing to evaluate soft skills. Also, ensure that you are not being narrow in your search for candidates. Most job roles are filled without even being advertised. Provide the opportunity to a broader audience.

While there are different approaches to embracing diversity, an unbiased approach may be a process where the hiring managers' decisions are reviewed by peers before finalizing any candidates to curb any biases that may have crept in. Then, both parties can share comments and clarifications before agreeing to a final decision.

Vendor Friction

The cybersecurity ecosystem consists of security professionals, vendors, researchers, educators, and tools, to name a few. Unfortunately, not all play well together due to competition and loyalties, which ends up hurting the field of security. Some of that friction comes from security vendors.

There is strict competition between vendors to tap into the lucrative security market. Their internal presentations will highlight the 200 Billion dollar market potential and encourage their sales force to get a small piece of that pie. While this sales strategy is fine, as security professionals, we sometimes forget that vendors are sales organizations driven by profits. Every vendor believes they have the silver bullet to solve all problems. They will use buzzwords in their marketing material to create product loyalty, like "100% effective," "best of breed," "military-grade encryption," "novel," "the first," "the only one," or "pioneering." All these words and phrases are red flags and should be taken with a grain of salt as their meanings have been abused.

Negative Impact

Vendor friction and competition in the cybersecurity industry can negatively impact it in a few ways. One way is that it can lead to a lack of interoperability between different cybersecurity products, making it difficult for organizations to integrate and use them effectively. This creates fragmentation in the industry, with different vendors pushing their own proprietary solutions and standards. Clients can get locked into a product portfolio making it difficult for organizations to adopt new technologies or best practices. This can slow down the overall progress of the industry and make it harder for organizations to keep up with the latest developments and trends.

Additionally, vendor friction and competition can lead to a focus on short-term gains and marketing tactics rather than long-term product development and innovation. This can result in a lack of progress in the industry and a failure to address the constantly evolving threats facing organizations.

Vendors will usually not support their competitors' products and often highlight their flaws. When those same individuals change companies and join competitors, their message changes entirely. All this creates more friction among the many great choices and causes unnecessary polarization of views on product selection. It makes it more challenging for security consultants to propose products based on requirements alone. We must consider regional politics, company ethics, brand recognition, or personal preference based on experience. We must also consider country laws. For example, firewall manufacturers must comply with US export control laws and cannot sell to countries on that list due to the strong encryption capabilities built into them. A recent US import ban on certain Chinese manufacturers also affected the hardware supply chain and product choices.

Other negative impacts of vendor friction and competition in the cybersecurity industry include the following:

- **Misleading or false claims:** Vendors may make exaggerated or false claims about the capabilities of their products to stand out in the market, leading to disappointment or even security breaches when organizations realize the product cannot meet their needs. For example, they may claim to encrypt their user data, but a breach may reveal the opposite.
- **Lack of transparency:** Some vendors may be less transparent about their products' inner workings, making it difficult for organizations to assess their security and potential vulnerabilities. Under the hood, they may be using open source products while private-labeling their tools.
- **Lack of customer support:** As vendors focus on acquiring new customers, they may neglect their existing ones, leading to poor customer service and a lack of support for organizations when they need it most.
- **Over-reliance on automation:** Some vendors may push for automation as a solution for cybersecurity, ignoring that human intervention and oversight are still crucial in identifying and mitigating cyber threats.
- **Cybersecurity talent crunch:** Vendor friction and competition may result in a scenario where companies are in a race to hire and retain top cybersecurity talent, making it difficult for organizations to staff their cybersecurity teams.

All these vices can lead to a less secure environment for organizations and individuals. It's important for a CISO to be informed and aware of these negative impacts when evaluating and purchasing cybersecurity products and services, and to prioritize interoperability, vendor transparency, security, and customer support in their decision-making process.

Brain Washing

With so much time and money spent on marketing and product promotions, security folks are constantly bombarded with shiny new security products and features. Without realizing it, we all get influenced to some degree and end up drinking the vendor's "Kool-Aid," in other words, supporting a single vendor's security solution. Did you ever prefer one security product over another because you simply liked the brand and tried to justify it with generic security jargon? Be honest with yourself. I certainly have. When I worked for a vendor for a short time, I promoted their products and used the same buzzwords mentioned previously in every presentation. Biases creep in. I got brainwashed into thinking that there were only a couple of top vendors in the space and that there were only a couple of ways to implement a security solution correctly.

Until I went solo, met other people, researched other options, demonstrated various products, tried different tools, and read comparisons and reviews, I realized most claims only hold true on paper or their websites. Marketing and promotions have muddied the waters. Today I enjoy putting different products to the test and having a "bake-off" to validate what they claim. I can tell you from experience that half of it is usually "marketing fluff."

Unfortunately, loyalty to products and companies often takes priority over finding solutions to keep adversaries at bay. Companies will spend a lot of money on "swag," events, or dinners to increase brand awareness and to convince clients to invest in them. These techniques have a subliminal effect on our choices. Once we realize this, we can differentiate between the effectiveness of a product or solution in our environment versus meeting their sales numbers.

Going Against the Flow

A few companies have decided to take the opposite route. Some develop enterprise-level, free and open-source tools. Others provide free security training without focusing on selling their product or services. They aim to prepare security professionals fast and effectively by delivering bootcamp style training, mentorship, and hands-on experience to hit the ground running. It benefits everyone and showcases the company in good light. There's nothing to lose with this tactic and only respect and loyalty to gain.

It's important for a CISO to be aware of the potential impact of brand loyalty and biases when evaluating and purchasing cybersecurity products and services. They should strive to be objective and impartial in their decision-making and should regularly reassess their current products and vendors to ensure they are still meeting their needs and providing adequate protection.

LACK OF EXPOSURE

Another aspect that prevents individuals from becoming great security leaders is the lack of exposure to different cybersecurity roles. Exposure to multiple roles expands their understanding and experience of the various aspects of the field. For example, a CISO must have a broad understanding of all aspects of cybersecurity, including risk management, incident response, compliance, and technical security controls. Without exposure to these different areas, it can be difficult for an individual to develop the skills and knowledge necessary to lead a security organization effectively and make informed decisions. Additionally, a lack of exposure can also limit an individual's ability to effectively communicate with and manage the various teams within the organization that are responsible for the different layers of defense.

So how do you get security leadership experience without already being a CISO? There are several ways to bridge the gap and gain exposure to different cybersecurity roles:

1. **Professional development:** Seek opportunities for training and education in various areas of cybersecurity, such as risk management, incident response, and compliance. You can achieve this through online courses, certifications, or attending conferences and workshops.

2. **Job rotations:** Consider taking on different roles within your organization or requesting to rotate through other teams within the security department. This will give you exposure, hands-on experience, and a deeper understanding of the various aspects of cybersecurity.
3. **Networking:** Building relationships with professionals in different areas of cybersecurity can provide valuable insights and knowledge. This can be done through attending industry events, joining professional organizations, and participating in online communities.
4. **Reading and Research:** Keep updated with the latest developments and trends in the field by reading industry publications and following thought leaders.
5. **Mentorship:** Seek out experienced professionals in the field who can provide guidance, advice and serve as role models for the skills and knowledge you want to develop.

Combining these strategies can help bridge the gap and gain the knowledge and experience needed to become a great security leader like a CISO.

An important question to ask ourselves is: What causes this knowledge exposure gap between cybersecurity leaders and the people entering this field? The problem comes from both sides; the people who want to become leaders don't have enough time to take on additional responsibilities, and the individuals in leadership positions (CISOs) don't have the time or motivation to mentor anyone. Moreover, job insecurity also plays a crucial factor in creating this roadblock; some insecure people believe they may be training their replacement.

All the various factors presented in this chapter create many obstacles to success.

THE SOLUTION

After reading through some of the top issues that harm the advancement of individuals in cybersecurity, we, as leaders, can do a few things today to remedy this. Change starts with oneself.

1. **Moral Support:** Congratulate your peers and others on their professional accomplishments. This could be as small as a phone call or email when they get a new job, a comment on LinkedIn, sharing their article or story, or even as simple as clicking the "like" button. Again, it takes nothing from you to do these things; it only makes you look better and more supportive in their eyes while providing moral support to others. This is the first step in suppressing envy and jealousy.

2. **Credit:** Provide credit or attribution to those who helped you on your path to knowledge, position, or success. This small step also doesn't take away your hard work; instead, it builds better bonds within the community. In addition, it shows humility and makes the other person feel better and want to help more. Finally, document your work. Keep records of your accomplishments and contributions to the team and encourage everyone to share their successes.

3. **Knowledge**: Encourage open communication and collaboration among team members, and work to create a sense of community within the organization. Encourage a focus on learning and personal development by providing access to training and conferences rather than competition and individual achievement. Also, reward collective accomplishments. It will address professional competition, jealousy and encourage teamwork.

4. **Mentorship:** Provide training opportunities to help team members develop their skills and advance their careers. Create a mentorship program that matches mentors with mentees based on their skills, interests, and goals.

5. **Biases:** Address any instances of discrimination or prejudice that you become aware of and work to create a fair and equitable work environment. Widen your perspectives by actively recruiting and promoting individuals from underrepresented groups.

6. **Culture:** Address the cultural issue by actively promoting diversity, inclusivity, and cultural understanding within the organization.

7. **Burnout:** Educate yourself and your team on burnout and mental health and promote a healthy work-life balance. Encourage team members to take time off when needed and provide resources and support for stress management and self-care.

8. **Gatekeeping:** Address gatekeeping by promoting a culture of openness and inclusivity and actively seeking diverse perspectives and ideas. Talk about it with peers and encourage feedback.

9. **Stay professional:** Avoid gossiping or talking negatively about your colleagues and stay professional in all interactions. Moreover, if you see someone else gossip, change the subject or avoid the conversation. There's nothing good that comes out of it.

10. **Watch your words**. In this cancel culture society, you can't say anything without offending someone. It doesn't mean you shouldn't say anything at all. Listen to opposing viewpoints and say what you believe in without offending the opposing argument. It's not what you say, it's how you say it. Avoid derogatory terms, provocative statements, harmful speech, and useless debates. The internet always remembers. So, think twice before posting something online or participating in a debate. If it doesn't help you or anyone else, avoid it.

11. **Embrace competition**. Your competition should only be with yourself. Never feel someone is a threat to you. Practice self-awareness and mindfulness. Recognize when you feel jealous or resentful and take steps to manage those feelings. Have faith in your abilities, trust your teammates, and create an environment of collaboration. Instead of getting caught up in comparing yourself to others, focus on your work and goals.

12. **Don't depend on others**. Believe in yourself. Having mentors and shortcuts is great, but nothing beats hard work and strife. You learn from your successes and failures. Fail fast so you have more opportunities to succeed. Seek the company of people better than you to create an environment that uplifts you.

13. **You get what you give**. Don't expect anything from anyone. Always have the attitude of giving. Give gratitude, advice, assistance, and support, even if you never got it. It will eventually come back to you when you least expect it.

14. **Do your research**. Before sharing information, make sure to conduct thorough research. Avoid spreading rumors, falling for sensational buzzwords, clickbait articles, or false promises made by anyone. Instead, verify the information's authenticity before disseminating it. Keep the broader context in mind and understand that products and companies are continually evolving. Articles may be disproven, and people's viewpoints can shift over time. The media's objective is to generate revenue or garner attention, whereas your objective is to provide sound security guidance.

If we all play our part and consciously avoid things that harm the security practice, it will have a compounding effect in advancing this great field.

Takeaway

Insecurities in security are common. However, it's important to keep in mind that these issues are complex and multifaceted, and addressing them will likely require a combination of different approaches and ongoing efforts. A complete strategy includes both developing yourself as well as avoiding anything that hinders progress.

17. SUPPLY & DEMAND

Change the competition

This is a great time to be in cybersecurity. No matter when you read this book, I can guarantee this statement will never get old.

After two decades of being in this field, I still feel it is growing and changing as I wake up every day to new breaches, adversarial techniques, technology, tactics, products, and solutions. There will always be a high demand for individuals with cybersecurity skillsets at all levels. It is the supply that needs to keep up.

The supply of qualified individuals is always a struggle. According to CyberSeek[2], which tracks active open jobs and available talent, the US national average supply and demand ratio is 68%. This means that if every qualified cybersecurity individual filled up the positions required by those companies, there would still be 32% unfilled cybersecurity roles. There's more than enough pie for everyone, even considering that many cybersecurity professionals moonlight and have active side gigs.

This is excellent for those who are passionate, work hard, and want to excel in this field, but not so great for companies or employers seeking to protect their environments from bad actors.

PROBLEM

While malicious hackers primarily create demand, the problem of supply is created by both the system and the employers.

---

[2] "Cybersecurity Supply and Demand Heat Map." CyberSeek, 1 Feb. 2023, https://www.cyberseek.org/heatmap.html.

A few factors create this problem, but one of the most important ones is the education system. The education system is too long and unnecessarily structured, and employers have unreasonable demands and requirements for hiring candidates with degrees, certifications, and experience. While at the same time, most malicious hackers are in their teens and are not bound by these prerequisites. This one-sided constraint hinders progress. When was the last time you read about a notorious hacker's profile with a master's degree, multiple cybersecurity certifications, and over ten years of experience in a relevant field? Unfortunately, the bar of entry for malicious hackers to commit crimes is much lower than for cybersecurity professionals to defend.

Another factor that contributes to the issue is the ever-changing threat landscape. Cybersecurity threats are constantly evolving, making it difficult for organizations to keep up with the latest threats to protect their systems and data. Again, it leads back to education and hands-on experience, as there are not enough qualified individuals to keep up with the skills and understanding to keep threats at bay proactively.

Technology is a double-edged sword. As technology becomes more integrated into business and daily life, the race to introduce products and services often skips security and privacy protections. As a result, more vulnerabilities are introduced and cause frequent hacks. The haste in technological advancement increases the need for cybersecurity, putting more pressure on organizations to find qualified professionals.

Lastly, companies need to budget appropriately for cybersecurity. In all my security risk assessments, I supply the client with a budgetary sheet matching all the recommendations from the assessment. Then, I ask them to use it in their next budgetary meeting so they can set realistic cost expectations.

The supply and demand challenge will constantly change over the years. In the next section, we will focus on taking advantage of our environment and becoming the demand in the field of cybersecurity to help progress in our careers.

Environment

There is no doubt that we learn better in a conducive environment. We pick up things faster when we have more intelligent people in our group. Some people perform better in a competitive setting as it gives them the determination to improve. On the other hand, it sometimes also makes it harder to rise amongst the rest and stand out in such a competitive space. A different approach to this is to level the playing field instead.

Lower The Bar

If you cannot beat your competition, change your competitors. This advice is only for early in your career, not when you are in a mature and senior position. For junior roles, there is naturally more competition as there are more qualified individuals to fill those positions. On the other hand, as you get more senior, the competition filters out. Logically, there are far fewer CISO roles available than security analyst roles.

If you work in a company where you are considered the smartest person in the room, you may have a false sense of being appreciated and respected. On the other hand, you will also have more opportunities for promotion. Senior roles still need to be filled, and when companies have a smaller pool of candidates, you have a higher chance of being picked.

In an ideal scenario, one should choose a geographic location with **high** demand and **low** supply. There's an old saying in the Asian Subcontinent: "In the land of the blind, the one-eyed man is King," meaning that you are considered the top candidate for a position if there are no better choices available. I have often taken advantage of this by pure coincidence. For example, in some of my previous jobs, I happened to be in an environment where there were not a lot of tech savvy individuals with industry standard certifications to pick from, so my competition was drastically reduced, allowing me to stand out.

Take advantage of your environment and grow other skill sets while you have the opportunity so you can continue to remain the smartest person in the room. For example, involve yourself with more public speaking engagements, obtain the appropriate skills, network with executives, interview with local newspapers or media outlets, and create better relationships with vendors. These activities would be much more challenging to accomplish for a junior or mid-level cybersecurity professional in competitive environments.

Disadvantages

There are clear disadvantages to being the only qualified person. The major ones are that you can get too comfortable in your bubble, it can hinder your growth, feed your ego, and you may feel threatened by people smarter than you. This is why it is advisable to go only in low-competitive environments to facilitate quick career growth. When your growth hits a plateau, you are ready to move to a higher competitive environment.

I've seen this strategy applied in either non-profit organization or government departments low on budget. The compensation may be quite low in such organizations, but the opportunities to grow within are much faster due to the lack of competition and the willingness to retain talent.

Think Regional

There are opportunities everywhere because this field continues to rapidly grow. This may be an unpopular opinion, but if I were to start fresh in my professional journey and climb the ladder faster, I would stay away from areas where there is the most competition. For example, in the US market, I would not start my career working in large metropolitan tech-hubs like San Francisco, Los Angeles, New York, Chicago, Houston, or Atlanta. Instead, I would work in relatively less technologically progressive cities or suburbs where I would have a better chance of success, statistically. Once I have the confidence and experience, I would take on more challenging territories.

Think International

The strategy of choosing a high demand and low talent supply regions is not limited to the US. Until recently, Middle Eastern countries were ideal for this. Gulf countries like Saudi Arabia, UAE, Qatar, Bahrain, and Kuwait have accepted expatriates with open arms and have provided attractive benefits and hefty salaries in these tax-free countries since the early 80s. Many expatriates have taken advantage of this job influx to advance their careers. They have gone from entry-level positions to senior executives in a few years rather than decades due to the region's explosion of industry and wealth and the desperate need for foreign expertise. It is no wonder that most of these Middle Eastern countries have a higher expatriate population than locals. My family was part of this wave of expatriates, and I used those opportunities as a springboard to excel in my career faster than I ever could as compared to other parts of the world. So, don't limit yourself to certain geographic regions, explore other countries if you can for better growth opportunities.

Remote Work

Remote work has affected the supply and demand issue for better or for worse. The global pandemic of COVID-19 affected many jobs. Organizations were forced to have their employees work remotely. Moreover, companies whose business model could not support remote work went under. Schools adopted remote learning as well, and we had to re-think how to operate work and education. Many people lost their jobs, but a lot of new jobs were also created or re-purposed. Let's look at the pros and cons of remote work and how we can use it to our advantage.

Good

The IT and cybersecurity fields weren't affected as much by going fully remote. These fields have always had an element of remote work for at least the last two decades. The good part is that more opportunities have opened for an already thriving market, as most jobs now cater to a work-from-home culture. Due to cybersecurity roles being available for remote work, individuals from various geographic regions have the opportunity to pursue cybersecurity careers without relocating. People have traditionally relocated due to their jobs. Now people are leaving high-tax states and countries to move to places where they can either save more or have a better quality of life with family.

While more opportunities opened, remote work also created more competition. As a result, recruiters have gotten more access to job seekers. In addition, employers unable to attract good talent due to their locality, city, or state now have a larger pool of candidates by allowing remote or hybrid work. This is especially beneficial to companies who are in a place with high-income taxes, high housing prices or rents, bad city traffic, or rural areas with low resources.

Bad

Cybersecurity has been affected in the sales, marketing, and networking departments.

In-person meetings always have a much higher effect on the sales process. We've been taught in every public speaking class that over 80% of communication is non-verbal. The ability to see people's expressions as you talk through risks and costs is lost over web conferences, where most people multitask and do not turn their cameras on. From experience, we know that attendees are distracted by multiple browser tabs, email windows, or documents during web conference meetings. Most people are partially to fully distracted every few minutes. I know I am.

On the contrary, it is not easy to multitask in an in-person meeting where all parties are fully engaged. Networking events are very productive as they provide a relaxed environment where you can engage freely with partners, vendors, and new technology without any pressure. I've developed contacts unexpectedly at vendor booths after following up with them on products and having detailed discussions. That would never happen on a cold call with a CISO.

In-person cybersecurity events are excellent for creating new connections. The same applies to speaking opportunities. On the other hand, the engagement and chit-chat after a speaking event can be non-existent when the event is virtual.

Remote work can create a lack of visibility for yourself when attempting to obtain new opportunities. For example, you are less likely to build good rapport with your colleagues by missing out on brainstorming opportunities, which could lead to creative ideas.

When you combine all these factors, the lack of non-verbal communication, focus, one-on-one conversations, and networking all contribute to an inferior experience that ends up in lost opportunities.

Hybrid

Once individuals get a taste of remote work and realize they can get much more done at a home office, it is hard to go back to a corporate office setting with distractions and that requires hours of commuting to and from work. It simply does not make sense. A happy medium is a hybrid work environment. It decreases the poisonous micromanagement nature of some organizations and allows opportunities for trust. Regular company gatherings, events, trips, in-person training, and client or vendor meetings at different venues all make for a great mix of a hybrid work culture. This creates the strongest values and highest efficiency for employers and employees.

Taking Advantage

With the many pros and cons of remote work, how do we take advantage of it in our careers? You can create visibility online by being active in professional chat groups or social media. Look for opportunities, remote or hybrid, that could lead to a CISO position. The occasional travel may be worth it even if you live in a different city or state. The flexibility of remote or hybrid jobs can build your career much faster than traditional on-premises-only roles. If that lifestyle doesn't suit you, eventually settle down in a place and company where you are comfortable.

Also, take advantage of the work-life balance it brings you. Hopefully, working from home, even partially, allows you to spend more time on yourself and with your family. Also, note that working from home can consume you as the boundaries between work life and personal life can be blurred. So, incorporate proper time management skills and frequent breaks, so you don't get burned out.

TAKEAWAY

As you build yourself as a capable and qualified cybersecurity professional, consider exploring new environments to give yourself an edge. While this is not the strategy one should lead with, it is something many have done successfully, and you should consider if you are not seeing the rate of progress you desire.

18. COMPENSATION

Show me the money

The best advice in career development is to follow your passion. Because if you love what you do, you don't work a day in your life, but money matters. We all need to pay the bills. The world's workforce is structured around money, and the days of the barter system and alternate means of compensation are essentially over.

Before we get into career planning, let's go over the compensation topic, as it tends to motivate many people, especially those looking to switch fields into cybersecurity. The fundamental question you should ask is: what gets you paid more? Is it your knowledge, skills, experience, or your responsibilities?

The position of a Chief anything Officer (CxO), is considered the highest executive role in that field. It comes with the highest responsibility. Your pay is directly proportional to the amount of risk you handle. This is true in any industry. For example, some of the highest-paid professions in the medical field are anesthesiologists, surgeons, and psychiatrists. In business, it's the CFOs and chartered accountants. We put a lot of trust in certain roles like pilots, flight safety engineers, lawyers, and judges. With great responsibility comes great compensation.

We focus a lot on brand-name degrees or industry-recognized certifications. The truth is all those are important and help build a foundation on which we stand. Still, it's the specific responsibilities we choose that dictate how much we get paid. We all know some extremely competent individuals in our lives that get paid mediocre salaries. On the other hand, we may also know people with no formal education who are multi-millionaires. There is no straightforward rule for high compensation. Fortunately, we are on the right track as the CISO is one of the highest-paid positions in cybersecurity.

To maximize our growth and earn to our highest potential, we need to understand the compensation structure, what others are making, negotiation tactics, objection handling, and many other factors that influence where we end up on the money scale.

Structure

CISO compensation typically includes a base salary, performance-based bonuses, and benefits such as health insurance, retirement plans, and stock options. The specific structure of the compensation package can vary depending on the company and the individual.

During interview negotiations for a CISO position, the compensation package and contract terms can play a significant role. For example, candidates may want to negotiate for a higher base salary, more generous bonuses, or additional benefits such as more vacation time or flexible working arrangements. They may also want to negotiate for more favorable performance metrics or termination provisions.

The Data

We need data to back us up before we start negotiations. There are several ways to find out your market value as a CISO:

1. **Research industry salary data:** Websites like Glassdoor, Payscale, and Salary provide salary data for various jobs and industries. This data can give you an idea of the typical salary range for a CISO in your region and industry.

2. **Network with other professionals in the field**: Talking to other CISOs in your industry can provide valuable insights into the current job market and the typical compensation packages offered.

3. **Consult with a recruitment agency:** Recruitment agencies have access to a wide range of job opportunities and salary data and can provide guidance on what to expect in terms of compensation and benefits.

4. **Job listings:** Reviewing job listings for CISO positions on websites like LinkedIn, Indeed, or ZipRecruiter can give you an idea of the salary ranges offered by different companies.

5. **Crowdsourced data:** An online search will result in many open discussion platforms, such as Blind and Quora, that allow employees to share their salary information anonymously. This can give you an idea of what people earn for similar roles in different companies.

It's important to note that the data you find may not be specific to your region, industry, or experience level. So, it's best to use multiple sources to get a more accurate picture of the market.

Average

The pay range of a CISO varies depending on the country, experience, industry, or size of the organization. The highest-paying ones typically include the financial, manufacturing, or IT sectors. From a geographical perspective, large metropolitan areas in the US, like San Francisco or New York, will have a higher average than other cities. Online searches show a wide range for the average annual salary of a CISO; between $200,000 to $350,000. Additionally, sign-on bonuses can range from $50,000 to $100,000. Larger companies also provide equity in the $150,000 to $400,000 range.

It's also important to consider that the salary for a CISO is not just a reflection of the base salary but also includes bonuses, profit-sharing, and other forms of compensation that can significantly increase the overall wage.

Outliers

You will also find outliers to these ranges depending on where you look. For example, I have seen CISO salaries advertised on LinkedIn for $150,000. At the same time, an ethical hacker was being paid more.

The highest-paying CISOs will make significantly more than the average CISO salary, of course. The exact wage for these outliers will depend on various factors, such as location, company size, and industry. However, some estimates suggest that the highest-paying CISOs can make upwards of $500,000 or more per year, including bonuses and other forms of compensation. A survey done by Heidrick & Struggles[3] in 2022 collected responses from 327 CISOs. It revealed that the median compensation in the United States was $584,000 across a broad industry spectrum. With bonuses and equity, that number went up to $1 million.

Some CISOs working in large tech companies, startups, finance, healthcare, and consulting may have the potential to earn higher salaries. In addition, CISOs with a proven track record of success and who have held leadership roles in multiple organizations also have the potential to earn higher salaries.

As a CISO's role becomes more critical, these exorbitant salaries are creeping into the averages. The same survey also revealed that the top two concerns of a CISO for deciding to depart their role at a company were burnout and stress. The concern of a breach was the third. It further highlighted the difficulty of keeping a CISO in their role long-term, even with such high compensation.

---

[3] "2022 Global Chief Information Security Officer (CISO) Survey, Heidrick & Struggles, 4 Feb. 2023, https://www.heidrick.com/en/insights/compensation-trends/2022-global-chief-information-security-officer-ciso-survey.

Negotiation

From my experience, the salary and compensation conversation with peers is taboo. Furthermore, there is little public discussion on it. I've always wondered if I was making enough because I did not have an idea of what others in my position were making. Most job postings still do not mention the salary. At best, they may put in a broad range next to "willing to negotiate for exceptional candidates." One of the ways to keep up-to-date with the salary numbers is by continuously interviewing in the market and having recruiters provide insights on compensation for certain roles. During this process, people may realize they are underpaid and decide to change jobs.

It's crucial to understand salary information when it comes to negotiating. Negotiations can involve an awkward dialogue that involves a lot of back-and-forth between the recruiter and candidate. Both sides are highly strategic and may even evade disclosing actual figures. However, discussing salary ranges and other compensation benefits is still essential to arrive at a mutually agreeable number that satisfies both the candidate and the company.

Once you receive your first offer, know that a company will not give you the best and final offer on the first attempt. Most employers have a specific budget allocated for each role and will try to stay within that budget while offering a competitive compensation package. Job candidates need to be aware of this dynamic and be prepared to negotiate for fair compensation. Justifying your market value and demonstrating the value you can bring to the company can help you negotiate a more favorable compensation package.

Remember that salary negotiations are a conversation, not a monologue; there is always room for negotiation. You need to be realistic about what you're asking for and be able to justify why you believe you're worth a certain salary. It's also essential to listen to the employer's perspective and be willing to compromise. For example, suppose there's no leeway on the base salary. There's always room for movement on other elements of the compensation package, like commissions, sign-on bonuses, performance bonuses, perks, equity, stock, time-off, flex policy, remote work, expenses, and training. Our goal is not to leave anything on the table and be fair to ourselves.

CHEAP TACTICS

During the negotiation process, as an incentive, sometimes companies will try to highlight the value you will get in your career for working with them when denying you a better financial deal. Don't give in to this tactic. It's a two-way street; both parties benefit from an employment agreement. The goal is to arrive at a happy medium where both parties are satisfied.

Companies may use several tactics to try to drive down the salary of job candidates, some of which include:

1. **Low-balling the initial offer:** Companies may initially offer a salary lower than the market rate to leave room for negotiation.
2. **Focusing on the candidate's lack of experience:** Companies may try to argue that the candidate is not as experienced as they claim to be and, therefore, should not be paid as much. This may be one reason they write high numbers in the years of experience required in the job description.
3. **Playing the "market rate" card:** Companies may argue that their salary offer is in line with the market rate, even if it's below what the candidate is worth. Their source of information may be based on the lower salaries they found online.
4. **Budget constraints:** Companies may argue that they have budget constraints and can't afford to pay more than their initial offer.
5. **Using the "we have many candidates" card:** Companies may argue that they have many qualified candidates for the position and that the candidate should be grateful for the opportunity, regardless of the salary offered.
6. **Using non-salary benefits as a trade-off:** Companies may offer non-salary benefits such as flexible work arrangements, better health insurance, or more vacation time to reduce the overall salary offered.
7. **You benefit more:** Companies may try to position the offer in a way that seems they are doing you a favor. They may use phrases like:
   - "You will have the privilege of working with top-tier clients."
   - "We value you like no other company; you will be highly respected."
   - "You will learn a lot. You will have access to all our systems, demo gear, and resources."
   - "You get to build your own team from the ground up."
   - "You have the freedom to do it your way."
   - "You get your own office space." However, working from home would be more appealing.

These influence tactics help tip the scale in the employer's favor. However, these are not added benefits to getting the job. Instead, these are common, available to most, and are part of the role, no matter who gets it. They are bargaining chips that don't count towards salary and should not be the basis for negotiating your total compensation.

Another tactic or trade-off employers use to offer a candidate a lower salary is by offering a one-time sign-on bonus instead. For example, suppose you ask for $250,000 on a $200,000 base salary offer. The company may counter that by saying they can accommodate by offering a $50,000 sign-on bonus and a $200,000 base salary, essentially making it the same offer. However, it is not the same, as from year two, your earnings will decrease by 20%.

Others may offer a guaranteed bonus of $100,000 after one year. In subsequent years, company policies on bonuses may change, or there may be lots of terms and conditions around growth, and you may not be eligible again. Be careful of future promises. I've had many managers in the past promise me growth opportunities. In most cases, they left the company before I did. Always have commitments written down on paper or email as evidence. Make sure there are clear timelines and qualifications for which you can measure and hold them accountable. Otherwise, they never materialize.

Overall, focus on the long-term benefits rather than giving in to short-term monetary gains.

READ THE FINE PRINT

Additionally, you should review the contract terms carefully to ensure you are comfortable with the job responsibilities, reporting structure, and other details outlined in the agreement. Finally, you may want to negotiate for changes to these terms if they are not in line with your expectations or preferences. Remember, a contract is an agreement between two parties, always up for negotiation.

At a closing interview, the management once gave me approval that I could continue my side hustle as long as I wasn't stealing their customers. We all agreed it benefited the company as I was bringing them more visibility and sales leads this way. However, when I read the contract, I refused to sign it as it had a vague moonlighting clause stating that I could not work anywhere else in a similar field while I was employed with them. They told me to ignore the verbiage as it was standard contract language, and to sign it as we had an understanding. I jokingly said that I don't need to sign an employment contract either, as we also have an understanding that I start on Monday. As a result, the manager sent me a confirmation to my personal email address stating his approval, on behalf of the company, to allow for this exception. A year later, when management changed, I proactively shared the clause to my new reporting manager, who appreciated it.

It's also important to consider non-compete and non-solicitation clauses, as they may limit the candidate's future career opportunities if they leave the company. Candidates may want to negotiate for more reasonable terms or exceptions to these clauses.

The interview cycle takes time. The final phase is signing the contract, so take your time in reviewing the fine print. Most incentives are offered in good faith. Try negotiating the best deal possible because it will be much harder to re-negotiate after joining.

In general, it's important for candidates to have a clear understanding of their priorities and to communicate them effectively during the negotiation process. It's also important to be willing to consider the company's perspective and constraints before finalizing your decision.

BALANCE

Strike a balance between your passion and monetary compensation when evaluating job opportunities, especially for a senior position like CISO. Money is only a means to an end and should not be the sole focus when making career decisions. You should also consider other factors such as job stability, skill development, work-life balance, and mental health.

Think about how each job opportunity will affect your future career prospects, whether it will provide opportunities for growth and advancement, and whether it aligns with your long-term goals. Also consider how the job will affect your personal life, including travel, family time, and overall well-being.

More importantly, a CISO's role is a high-stress job. Think about how the job will affect your mental health. Stress and burnout are common in the field of cybersecurity at all levels. So, it's important to find a role that will be challenging and rewarding but not overwhelming. Always remember that you are in control of your career especially when it comes to making decisions for the purposes of aligning with your values and goals. Based on my personal experience, communicating my priorities and concerns during the negotiation process and working with the employer to find a mutually beneficial arrangement has worked for me. For example, during the discussions regarding an offer, I negotiated to work remotely for three to four days a week for at least the first six months, as I needed to manage personal commitments.

Objection Handling

Concession

A popular concept in influence tactics is conceding and expecting reciprocity. Concession is a specific tactic used in the bargaining process where one party makes a concession (or compromise) to induce the other party to reciprocate by making a similar concession. Concession involves sacrificing something in order to reach an agreement, while bargaining involves exchanging offers and making compromises in order to find a mutually acceptable solution.

An example of concession in a salary negotiation will be if an employee agrees to work longer hours in exchange for a raise in pay. The employee is making a concession (working longer hours) to induce the employer to reciprocate by offering a raise. Another example will be if an employee agrees to take on additional responsibilities in exchange for a promotion.

This tactic may not always work and can backfire if the other party doesn't reciprocate. For this tactic to succeed, it's important that both parties should get something of value out of the negotiation.

Starting with a higher ask creates more room for negotiation and compromise, which can lead to a more favorable outcome. However, you should also be prepared to make a concession to induce the other party to reciprocate.

Don't be afraid to ask for more than what's offered. If rejected, you can concede and ask for something lower instead. The recruiter will then try to reciprocate your concession by trying to make the original offer more attractive. For example, if your ask for a 20% increase in the base salary was denied, you can ask for additional time off or a flexible work schedule instead. The goal should be to get an overall better deal. This only happens if you try the concession/reciprocity tactic.

It's also important to remember that the other party's needs and interests should be considered when using this strategy. For example, if you ask for something unreasonable or your request is too great to be fulfilled, it may be difficult for the other party to reciprocate, and the negotiation may become less productive.

Rescinding Offers

Unfortunately, companies can retract their offers due to unforeseen circumstances. What's worse is that they can leave you hanging between two jobs if you have already informed your current employer.

There are several steps you can take to protect yourself if a company rescinds an offer:

1. **Get it in writing:** Ask the company to provide written documentation outlining the reasons for the rescinded offer. This can help you understand the situation and be used as evidence if you decide to take legal action. Keep all documents and communications related to the rescinded offer, including emails, letters, and notes from phone or in-person conversations.

2. **Seek legal advice:** If you feel your rights have been violated, you should consult an attorney. An attorney can advise you on your legal options and help you navigate the process of taking legal action if necessary.

3. **Re-Negotiate:** If the company has valid reasons for rescinding the offer, try to negotiate a new offer. This can be a good way to resolve the situation in a mutually beneficial way.

4. **Get in touch with references:** Reach out to the contacts you provided to the company and let them know what happened. They may be able to provide a positive reference for you in the future.

5. **Keep your options open:** Keep looking for other job opportunities in case the rescinded offer is not resolved. Don't close your doors too soon.

Another option is to add a clause in the contract for financial compensation in case the offer is rescinded. This may be essential to you to guarantee a smooth transition. However, it is uncommon in employment contracts and may be difficult to enforce. Therefore, it's also necessary to consult with a lawyer before including such a clause in a contract to understand the legal implications and ensure that the clause is enforceable.

While companies may rescind an offer, it's not common, and there's usually a valid reason for it. It's also essential to communicate with the company and understand the reasons for the rescinded offer. The company may be willing to work with you to find a another solution.

Layoffs

Layoff Resistant

Every so often, companies go through significant layoffs for many reasons, like restructuring, mergers and acquisitions, economic downturns, or automation. This causes a temporary panic in the overall industry. So, what can we do to shield ourselves from this? First, realize that if you have been laid off, you cannot do much as it happens unexpectedly. Not all industries are affected by it to the same extent. For example, some of the following verticals are less prone to layoffs and could be a place to work for long-term stability:

1. **Government and Public Sector:** CISOs working in government and public sector organizations are less likely to be laid off due to taxpayers' stable and consistent funding.

2. **Healthcare and Medical:** The healthcare and medical industry is relatively stable and less prone to layoffs. This is due to the high demand for healthcare services and the constant need to protect patient data and medical records.

3. **Cybersecurity Consulting and Services:** CISOs in cybersecurity consulting and services companies are also less likely to be laid off. This is because the demand for cybersecurity services continues to grow as more and more companies seek to protect themselves from cyber threats.

4. **Cybersecurity Research and Development:** CISOs working in cybersecurity research and development organizations are also less likely to be laid off because these organizations are focused on developing new technologies and solutions to protect against cyber threats.

5. **Financial Institutions:** Financial institutions are also less prone to layoffs for CISOs, as they have a high demand for cybersecurity professionals to protect their client's financial and personal information.

Preparation

It's worth noting that the job market and economy are constantly changing, so it's essential to keep an eye on industry trends and be proactive in seeking new opportunities. Some ways to prepare include:

1. **Build a strong network:** Building relationships with other professionals in your field can help you stay informed about job openings and new opportunities. As previously mentioned, most positions are filled through word of mouth.

2. **Stay up-to-date:** Staying informed about new technologies and best practices in your field can help you stay relevant and attractive to potential employers.

3. **Diversify your skills:** Having a diverse skill set in different areas of cybersecurity, such as risk management, incident response, compliance, or ethical hacking, can make you more valuable to your organization and increase your chances of being retained during a layoff.

4. **Build a positive reputation:** Building a positive reputation within your organization and a personal brand in the industry can make you more valuable to the organization and less likely to be laid off.

5. **Keep an open mind:** Be open to new opportunities, whether in a new role, company, or industry.

6. **Demonstrate value:** Continuously demonstrate your value to the organization by delivering results, contributing to the company's goals and objectives, and being a positive and productive team member.

7. **Updated resume:** Ensure your professional profile is up-to-date on LinkedIn or your website and highlights your skills, experience, and achievements.

It's important to remember that layoffs can happen anytime and to anyone. By taking these steps, you can increase your chances of being retained during a mass layoff and position yourself for future opportunities in the cybersecurity field.

Takeaway

There are a few valuable lessons you can take away from this section. They all involve being fair to yourself, fighting for your worth, and striving to have a strong earning potential. Be proactive in building yourself to be resilient in difficult times. Know your market value and always be up-to-date in your field. Also, don't be afraid to ask about what was not offered, and be prepared to reply to tricky negotiation tactics. People are willing to give; you just need to ask.

19. SELF PROMOTION

Don't forget to like and hit the subscribe button

Once you embrace self-worth, you must find a good way to tell the world. Self-promotion is essential to career progression, as it allows you to showcase your skills, accomplishments, and value to your employer and others in your field. By promoting yourself, you can demonstrate to your superiors that you can take on additional responsibilities and deserve advancement or other opportunities. Self-promotion can also help you build a solid professional reputation and increase your visibility within your industry, leading to new job opportunities and other career advancements. However, it's essential to be mindful of how you go about self-promotion and to avoid coming across as arrogant or self-centered. Instead, focus on your achievements and let your work speak for itself rather than making exaggerated claims about your abilities or accomplishments.

AWARENESS

You may be the smartest person on the team, but if your management is not aware of your actual accomplishments, their perception of your impact at the company will be misconstrued. During my early years, my manager maintained a rating system for his trainees. He ranked me as the number one performer out of twenty interns. In the following quarterly review, he ranked me number ten. I was surprised and I consulted with my manager. He asked me why he thought I should still hold the top spot and if I had contributed any value in the past few months to deserve it. I mentioned some of my contributions including the coordination of study groups with students, supporting them at work, and surpassing the certifications quota per quarter. He said that by being unaware of these things, he couldn't rate me appropriately. I told him I perceived it as boasting, which goes against my humility. He advised me to learn the art of conveying every small professional achievement because it would directly affect my promotion and career growth. Since then, I've always found a subtle way to share my achievements in casual conversations with my managers. It has helped me immensely in my career progression over the years.

You are responsible for informing the right people about your professional skills, achievements, and activities. This may sound like boasting and not being very humble. There's a fine line between self-promotion and showing off. Self-promotion aims to develop your personal brand and provide you with future opportunities. In contrast, the goal of boasting is to feed your ego. If your goal is to open more doors for yourself while staying humble, then this section is for you. It will build self-appreciation while at the same time gaining the genuine respect of others around you.

Next, let's look at some techniques to help develop your brand and mature it over time.

TECHNIQUES

You will need to utilize multiple techniques for self-promotion. Most of these techniques are primarily used for giving back to the community, but you can hit two birds with one stone.

Start A Blog

We have all been in a position where we have spent countless hours scouring the internet to troubleshoot a problem. Finally, through trial and error, we get to a solution. Why not write about it and save the next person the trouble? They will thank you and love you for it. Some of my best finds on the internet were step-by-step articles with screenshots about troubleshooting and solving the same problem I was experiencing.

Starting a blog is a great way to showcase your dedication to the field. It's good to pick a theme for your blog, like hacking, coding, hardware, security controls, or IoT. It's also good to be consistent and current in your writing. You can use popular blogging websites like Medium, LinkedIn articles, or WordPress to enhance your reach further. A blog can also self-serve as you can refer to it for your own use, especially if it's a tutorial.

If you are regular and want complete control of your content, website, and branding, build your blog using a custom domain. You can use popular hosted blogging platforms like WordPress that offer an easy Content Management System (CMS) or GitHub Pages, if you're comfortable coding.

Create Free Video Tutorials

There are always multiple online videos for any single problem or question discussed online. Remember, it is quality that shines over quantity. So don't be discouraged from creating a short tutorial of something already published online. Your approach may appeal better to some people. Giving others the options to explore multiple solutions are always worthwhile.

The bar to entry for publishing videos online is extremely low. You don't need to have expensive equipment or even show your face. The easiest way is to screen-share your computer and discuss a topic with either slides or a browser window. If you go down this path, my advice would be first, to keep it short, as people have less patience, and second to get a good-quality microphone. No matter how good the content is, if the audio is low quality, people will tune out within a few seconds and look for an alternate video with better audio.

Remember that your goal is not to be the next YouTube star; if that happens, don't forget to give this book a shout-out. Instead, your goal is to display a glimpse of your expertise and establish a footprint on the web.

Vendor Events

As a subject matter expert, speaking at company-sponsored events is a great way to build credibility. Even better is speaking at vendor events as a guest. Vendors love to hear stories of how their partners or clients solve particular issues and how specific products and services aid them. People also love to attend panel discussions to listen to first-hand experiences.

With the abundance of webinars, you have many more opportunities to participate. All you need is a good microphone and camera. Take advantage of your vendor relationships and seek opportunities to speak. You can also step out of your comfort zone and consider speaking at independent cybersecurity or IT conferences.

I received my first job in the US when my manager found a professional video interview of me at a large vendor conference. My manager said he watched it before interviewing me and liked my confidence and how I carried myself. The resume became relevant only after I had already caught someone's eye.

Presentations

As discussed earlier in Chapter 10 - Soft Skills, one of the best ways to display your passion in your field is to talk about it publicly. Public speaking is still considered the greatest fear for most people. Today, many events are virtual, giving you the advantage of not noticing the audience's reaction to prevent nervousness. Some are even pre-recorded, which allows you to do many takes before submitting the talk.

For self-promotion, it can be beneficial to build a highlight reel. This could be a short 15-second video compilation of your talks or a picture collage of you speaking at different events. Some events also promote video introductions of a speaker on social media. To the person looking at your profile, it shows them that you have the confidence to present your ideas to a broader audience.

CFPs (Call for Presenters, Papers, or Proposals) is the industry term used to invite people to speak at conferences. Most of the local security conferences encourage first-time speakers, so take advantage of being involved as most people do not apply due to impostor syndrome (discussed previously in Chapter 15 - Imposter Syndrome).

I have not only spoken at numerous local and national events, but I have also been part of the selection board. From experience, the chances of your speaking proposal being accepted are better than you think. One reason is that not enough people submit them. Another factor is that some proposal submissions can be similar, and only one of them gets accepted. So, if you have something interesting and specific, submit your proposal on a topic you are passionate about. The title and content of your topic will attract the selectors' attention, so be creative. For example, the content description can resemble a short movie synopsis, leaving the reader wanting to know more.

CFPs are often published six to twelve months in advance. A good way to keep ahead of the submission deadlines is to run a quick online search for "CFP" and "cybersecurity" to see upcoming announcements for presentations. Look at previous topics to get an idea and apply to a few of them every couple of months. Keep track of your submissions including the content you submit, the biography you provide, and key dates related to the event. You can re-use the topic to apply to many other speaking events if you get turned away.

LinkedIn

An easy way to display an keen interest in your field is to be active on professional social media platforms like LinkedIn. Its purpose is to showcase yourself first and communicate with other professionals. Commenting and sharing relevant posts to benefit others gets you noticed. To stand out, you need to be a content creator rather than a consumer. This involves writing original content like articles and posting images or videos that help solve a problem or encourage others to dive deeper in a subject area.

To maximize your LinkedIn profile presence, take a professional photo to make a good first impression. In your headline, state your role. Every company has a value proposition, and so do you, so be sure to state or display it in the banner. Utilize the about section to display your characteristics, skills, role, and passion. Also, provide a link where they can contact you or ask you something.

Don't be afraid to share your achievements on LinkedIn, no matter how small. People will comment, which spreads it to their network feeds, bringing it in front of people outside your network. That's how the algorithms work. Also, don't be disheartened if no one likes or comments. That is not the goal. Try several avenues to network and avoid spending too much time on it, as it can consume your day. Also, never overdo it, as it will become apparent and backfire. I have muted many contacts who will write and share too many times in a day. Sometimes I question if that is their real job; posting content continuously.

Above all, be sure to keep your posts professional and career-related. Whenever someone shares a political, religious, ethnic, philosophical post or comment unrelated to enhancing my career, my brain automatically tunes out. This results in "unfollowing" or muting them, and their arbitrary online rank drops a few notches lower in my online world.

Ensure you separate your professional online presence from your personal one.

Podcast

Podcasts have become a popular medium for listening to news and people's opinions. It's a longer freeform format as compared to videos and blogs. If you feel adventurous and are confident hosting, start a podcast. Plan out ten episodes and if you can see yourself scaling it to thirty, then start immediately. If you're feeling less adventurous, be a guest! A great way to build a professional brand is to be invited to someone else's podcast as a guest. The best part is that no planning is required; you simply need to show up! Podcasters are always looking for guests. If you have something good to share and someone has a podcast on that subject, don't hesitate to reach out to them, as they may just be looking for someone like you. You won't know until you try.

Book

The most time-consuming and arguably the strongest of all these techniques is writing a book. It may seem hard, but the book you're reading right now is also the first one we've ever written, and it was self-published. The courage to write this book was built over time after utilizing small-form techniques such as writing blogs, creating video presentations, guesting on podcasts, and being involved in interviews. The bar to entry of being an author is low. If you can write twenty blog articles, you can write a book with twenty chapters. You just need to put in time to arrange your thoughts, structure the content, keep it relevant, and proofread it. Using editors and proofreaders is beneficial if you have the time and budget. Some authors hire ghostwriters to organize their thoughts and write the book for them. We discourage this path because it doesn't fully represent your words and opinions. More importantly, it becomes more challenging to defend or comment on later. Nonetheless, if you have an opinion and want to spread your knowledge, you have grounds for writing a book.

The reason we stress writing a book is because the title of "author" puts you in a league of its own. How many people do you know in your professional circle who have written books? We don't judge a book by its cover, but we do give additional value to the person who wrote it. The person will still be considered an author, whether the book is popular or not. Imagine being introduced to a company, talks or events as the author of a book. It elevates your position in the eyes of others and shows you are dedicated to your field by setting aside hundreds of hours to write a book. It is an excellent tool for self-promotion. Use it when you're ready.

Maturity

As you incorporate multiple techniques to engage with the public and highlight your successes and failures, you will need to develop the following characteristics to be taken seriously.

Build Confidence

If you're not sure, don't talk about it. Sometimes it is better to remain silent than to have an opinion about everything. If you don't sound confident, the audience will notice. To build confidence, try the following:

1. **Practice:** The more you practice your writing or speech skills, the more self-assured you'll feel. An excellent technique to engage your audience when speaking is to employ vocal variety, which entails altering your tone, volume, and pauses.
2. **Use Humor:** Humor can lighten the mood and remove judgment. It allows you to relax and express yourself freely, whether in writing, speech, or video.
3. **Positive Self-Talk:** Remind yourself that you are prepared and capable. Tell yourself that people will benefit from what you put out there.
4. **Know Your Material:** Your confidence level will depend on how well you know the material. If you know it well enough, your preparation will be minimal, and you will feel comfortable answering live questions. Also don't present too much information to the listener, it may distract them from your main point.
5. **Visualize Success:** Imagine giving a speech confidently in front of board members or at an event. Also, imagine how good you will feel after it's done. This will reduce your anxiety.
6. **Be Yourself:** By being authentic, you will allow your personality to shine through. Don't try to mimic someone else.
7. **Be Flexible:** Learn to adapt your speech or writing depending on the situation. If you encounter problems with a speech, learn to improvise. If you face criticism in writing, remain calm and handle it with poise. Don't respond to every comment.
8. **Know Your Audience:** Adjust your message according to your audience. The same topic can be presented very differently to a technical or business crowd.
9. **Seek Feedback**: Get feedback from others on your writing and talks. This can help you identify areas for improvement and build your confidence.

Have An Opinion

Opinions can be important for self-promotion, as they can help you stand out and establish your personal brand. By expressing your thoughts and views on a particular subject, you can show your expertise and knowledge on the topic and attract people's attention to that field. People also love stories, so mix them in as examples to support your opinions.

However, ensure that your opinions are well-informed and backed up by evidence, as expressing misguided or uninformed views can damage your reputation. It is also essential to be respectful and considerate of others' views.

Be A Problem Solver

You will see a lot of trolls on the internet who want to spark controversy or incite friction to get some short-term attention. Stay clear from such involvement. Also, avoid publishing "click-bait" articles to get attention. Your goal is to build a positive reputation. If you're not solving a problem or providing clarity to a complex topic, you are not contributing any value to anyone.

Opportunity Cost

You will do most of the things mentioned in this chapter in your spare time. However, there are only so many hours in a day, so you will need to prioritize. Writing, speaking, and working on yourself will be unpaid work. There will be a cost of choosing one option over another. Realize the immediate or long-term value of hours you put in for developing yourself, as it may be taking away time from earning money and attending to clients or your family. You will need to prioritize, give up a few things, and learn to create a balance.

Takeaway

To stand out from the rest, you should develop a personal brand that showcases your qualifications and sets you apart. While it is not a competition, you must be fair to yourself to open the right opportunities. Think of yourself as a salesperson, and your product is yourself. Finding a balance between highlighting your strengths and remaining humble is essential. Building maturity in your personal brand is a long-term process, but you can start taking small steps toward this goal today.

20. CAREER PLANNING

Mission for Recognition

Planning is crucial to career progression. A lack of planning is often the biggest obstacle to career advancement and promotions. It's essential to set goals early on and consistently plan for your next steps.

Your career should be a series of stepping stones, each building upon the previous, towards your ultimate goal of becoming a CISO. It's essential to be realistic in your expectations and take things one step at a time, remaining persistent and adaptable to change. Patience is vital as advancement in any career takes time and effort.

Whether you're in the early phases of becoming a CISO or looking to advance in your current role, the tips and advice provided in the rest of this chapter can help you incorporate effective planning into your overall career strategy. By following these guidelines, you'll be well on your way to achieving your goals and advancing your career as a CISO.

STEPS TO SUCCESS

Dividing your goals into many smaller sub-goals will help structure your progress. You will also be able to measure how far along you are in the path. Smaller goals are also much easier to achieve and, with time, build the foundations for something bigger.

For someone pursuing the leadership role of a CISO, your career plan should include achieving tasks that are expected of a polished CISO. Here are some steps you should aim for in your career planning:

1. **Foundation:** Build a strong foundation in cybersecurity through experience and education. Identify your gaps in knowledge and fill them over time.
2. **Experience:** Gain experience in different aspects of cybersecurity. Try a bit of everything to get hands-on product and technology experience.
3. **Certifications:** Acquire relevant certifications, such as Security+, CEH, CISSP, or CISM.
4. **Leadership:** Seek out leadership roles in security teams and demonstrate success in those roles. Prior leadership experience will help qualify you for this role. It will be very challenging for the employer to hire a CISO who has yet to lead a team.
5. **Network:** Network and build relationships within the industry through attending conferences and events. Remember that the connections you make today can open doors for you tomorrow.
6. **Updated:** Stay up-to-date on cybersecurity technologies, trends, and best practices.
7. **Skills:** Develop skills in risk management, communication, and leadership. Continuously assess and improve skills through professional development and ongoing learning.
8. **Strategy:** Most people will attain tactical skills from technical jobs, but a CISO needs more strategic thinking. Gain experience in business operations and long-term strategic planning.
9. **Mentors:** Seek out mentorship and guidance from experienced CISOs.
10. **Diversify:** Build a diverse skill set, including knowledge of compliance and regulations.
11. **Groups:** Consider becoming involved in cybersecurity organizations and groups.
12. **Brand:** Build a strong reputation and brand within the industry.

This list is only a reference; you do not have to incorporate all of them into your goals. Other tasks may be more relevant to your industry that you may want to include in your list. Nonetheless, the more you have in your plan, the better your chances of success.

EXPECTATIONS

Before discussing specific skills and applying to jobs, we must look at the bigger picture. The journey to becoming a CISO can take time and effort. However, success is often a result of persistence, hard work, and a commitment to continuous improvement.

Many juniors enter the cybersecurity field and get impatient. I've had newcomers ask me, "How do we get to where you are, I've been working hard for two years, and no one will hire me for a senior role." This is not an isolated incident. There were countless times these types of questions caught me off guard. I had to pause a bit and think before providing an answer, as I didn't want to sound arrogant or like a negative gatekeeper. The fact is that it takes time, knowledge, and experience to build a career. Patience and self-reflection help keep us on track. Set your expectations according to your goals and sub-goals.

Stress and mental health issues are also very common in this position. The responsibility to keep the organization safe and to continuously promote a security culture will eventually lead to mental fatigue and burnout. The turnover rates of CISOs are very high as well. Factoring these into your expectations should help you make better decisions. I always advise taking time to think through the role; eventually, you will naturally mold into a security leader.

GROWTH PHASES

As we lay out a plan, we must look at the entire career cycle and chop it into phases. For example, let's say you plan on a twenty-year career. You could start at age twenty or forty; it's irrelevant. Next, you should divide that into roughly four quarters as follows:

1. **Building Phase:** Consider your first five years to be the building phase. In this phase, your aim should be to build your skills based on your long-term plan. This should include getting the proper certifications while your workload is still less. As you are in the learning mindset, with this momentum, attaining certifications becomes achievable as you work full-time. In this phase, you will also network a lot. Attend conferences, make friends in the industry, and learn from others. A typical job in this phase is a junior security professional.

2. **Stability Phase:** In the next five years, you will be at a mid-level in your career. A security analyst or team lead is an example of a role in this phase. You will experience some stability in these job roles. This is also the point in your career where you are comfortable. Most people stay in this phase throughout their retirement, but you must push past this plateau. In this phase, you should start establishing your identity, purpose and look to become a subject matter expert. You should have a good idea of your area of expertise. Use this confidence to start presenting on topics, writing blogs, and networking at events to get noticed.

3. **Management Phase:** By this time, senior-level opportunities will present themselves. This is the time when you should explore roles in management in various areas such as in a SOC, or Incident Response. This will be a tough transition, but your experience, networking capabilities and mature brand will help you land in the proper management role.

4. **Leadership Phase:** Once you have reached this final phase, you should spend time growing within the senior ranks. At this point, you will have learned enough about the various cybersecurity roles and responsibilities, soft skills, products, and vendors. In this phase, you will have the self-confidence and network to become a CISO.

While these are very rough timelines, it provides you with expectations. In reality, the path to a CISO varies from person to person, but it's important to set milestones. A twenty-year span is considered short, especially when you notice people with forty to sixty year careers. Today's generation is impatient but motivated, so the above example is not only achievable but provides an expedited growth timeline. The time you spend in each phase will vary depending on your personality, skills, geography, and contacts.

Exceptions

There will always be specific examples of people who will deviate significantly from this baseline. I've met countless people at events who have been at the same company and job for twenty years. They are comfortable in the "stability phase." Then I've met CEOs that make popular lists like the "Forbes 30 under 30," a list of thirty successful individuals under the age of thirty. From the start of their career, they spent five to ten years reaching an executive-level position, primarily as entrepreneurs.

As you grow in your career, you should create and follow a laid-out plan, so you don't derail. If a career-changing opportunity knocks on your door, accept it, and shorten your growth timeline. Don't let imposter syndrome get the better of you.

Employment versus Business

These growth phases apply to a typical salaried job. The corporate world has unwritten rules about advancing up the ladder. Most people reading this book will be employees at a company, not business owners. If, on the other hand, you are an entrepreneur, this model of growth and career advancement will not apply to you. Instead, your focus will be on the ideas and the product or service you bring to the market. What will matter more is marketing and promotions, business contacts, go-to-market strategy, investment, and many other variables beyond this book's scope. I also encourage everyone to explore the path of starting their own business and paving a new path to success.

Job Application

By this point of the book, you have probably searched for some CISO positions, considering that it's time you realized your potential. Understanding the job description is the key to understanding how your experience matches the role. You may have also noticed that there can be a lack of consistency in job descriptions. Most of them are poorly written, discouraging many people from applying.

Job Description (JD)

While not all CISO roles and responsibilities are exactly alike, you will find many commonalities between the CISO job description, such as:

- Provide strategic advisory services.
- Develop and implement the overall information security strategy for the organization.
- Develop and track a clear, measurable cybersecurity plan
- Develop and maintain strong relationships with stakeholders, including customers, partners, and government agencies.
- Communicate effectively with executive management and the board of directors on security issues and risks.
- Develop content and present at industry events.
- Integrate an information and cyber security risk management framework
- Maintain compliance with industry regulations and standards, such as PCI-DSS and ISO/IEC 27001.
- Develop and manage the information security budget.
- Manage a zero trust cybersecurity framework.
- Stay current with emerging threats and technologies in the cybersecurity field.
- Involve third-party security vendors in assessing their solutions against current or future needs.
- Define and deliver a cybersecurity culture and awareness program.
- Lead and mentor the information security team.

Additional past expectations for CISO JDs may include:

- 10+ years of cybersecurity experience
- 3+ years of leadership experience as a CISO, CIO, or CTO along with references.
- Knowledge of information security frameworks such as NIST 800-53, CIS, or PCI.
- Experience with communicating an effective strategic vision.
- Industry-recognized security certifications like, CISSP, CISA, CISM, or equivalent.

Focus on preparing for these common requirements to set realistic expectations.

Bad JDs

Don't let a CISO job description intimidate you. Often, HR will include a long list of responsibilities for every kind of CISO role imaginable, which can discourage qualified candidates from applying. Sometimes, they even merge the duties of a CIO and CISO. They want you to meet every qualification and experience listed in the job description, but that's not always feasible. They will pull together a combination of requirements from different types of CISOs described in Chapter 9 - Types.

Many CISO job descriptions will focus on the tactical side, which are more in line with a Security Manager's position. You can spot this with requirements like:

- Manage the implementation and maintenance of security systems and processes.
- Monitor and respond to security and privacy incidents.
- Lead the implementation of a secure system development lifecycle.
- Manage security risk assessments and perform regular security audits.
- Manage the day-to-day operations of the technology team and network infrastructure.

As a result, many great candidates will deter from applying to jobs with unrealistic expectations in the job description. Most hiring managers will also disagree with such broad requirements posted in the job description but will let HR use the outdated template, nonetheless. If you feel the company and position is right for you, always apply and let the interview process be the judge. Remember, you have a 0% chance of getting the job if you don't apply.

Real Qualifications

Here's a checklist of questions to help you determine if you fit the bill for a CISO role. You are ready to apply to a CISO role if you can validate sufficient experience for more than 50% of the questions below.

- ☐ Do you work cross-functionally with business units internally or externally performing risk management activities?
- ☐ Do you determine the cause of internal and external breaches and help ensure that appropriate corrective action takes place?
- ☐ Have you assisted in planning, designing, or implementing a security strategy for a company?
- ☐ Have you been involved with analyzing threats in real-time and mitigating the threats?
- ☐ Have you prepared and presented to an audit risk committee, board of directors, or management on breaches, security strategies, or audit and compliance findings for an organization?
- ☐ Have you validated new technology to ensure it complies with security regulations?
- ☐ Do you have experience managing projects and ensuring they are completed timely and within budget?

- ☐ Do you have experience managing people and teams?
- ☐ Do you know how to manage priorities and realign focus on relevant initiatives?
- ☐ Do you maintain relationships with key stakeholders in various business units?
- ☐ Do you attend CISO roundtable discussions or security conferences with the C-Suite at seminars?
- ☐ Do you maintain relationships with key management personnel in cybersecurity at various companies?
- ☐ Do you have strong opinions on implementing various security domains at companies?
- ☐ Have you been involved with a security initiative from the start and implemented a full solution, like a cybersecurity user awareness training, or bug bounty program?
- ☐ Are you a self-starter, and have you measured your influence on security in a company or with management?
- ☐ Are you comfortable receiving critical feedback about yourself and your management skills?
- ☐ Do you have experience interviewing and hiring talent?
- ☐ Have you contributed to publications or conferences related to security?
- ☐ Are you willing to lose your job due to a breach?
- ☐ Have you delivered unpleasant news to a person, team or department?

If you have followed a plan and met some of the requirements mentioned in this chapter, evaluate your situation, and take the leap to apply for a CISO position. Don't let a bad job description keep you from progressing in your career.

TAKEAWAY

A clear plan with achievable goals is crucial to achieving success in your professional career. Start by setting realistic expectations and understanding your strengths and weaknesses. Next, study the growth phases and get ahead by acquiring new skills and knowledge, networking within your industry, and seeking mentorship and guidance. Finally, when looking for new job opportunities, tailor your resume to the specific job requirements, highlight your relevant experience and achievements, and be prepared to articulate your value proposition during the interview process. With a clear plan, hard work, and determination, you can achieve success and growth in your career.

21. YOU MADE IT

Now What?

After transitioning to a CISO, how do you establish yourself and earn everyone's respect?

You may think that this is it, you have found the job you will retire in. Rather, an important question to ask is, how do you maintain, progress, and succeed as a CISO through multiple organizations? Let's pause for a quick reality check. As mentioned earlier, the average CISO lasts in an organization for 18-24 months. There are obviously a lot of reasons that drive CISO's out. Some common reasons are burnout, lack of respect, lack of authority to make changes, lack of internal and external influence, blame, culture, budget, and miscommunication, to name a few.

To help you stay longer and happier in your position, you will need to be aware of all the things that will drive you away. Then take proactive steps to address them. Just like you mitigate security threats for the organization, you will need to reduce job security risks.

For starters, as a CISO, establish a foothold, and be assertive in this role. We aim to go above and beyond our expectations and be the catalyst of change we strived for.

PREREQUISITES

Before discussing what you should do to establish yourself as a CISO, let's discuss some of the considerations for becoming a CISO before you take on the role.

In Sync

Ensure the leadership is aware of your plans to improve the security posture of the organization. Don't feel perplexed if they fail to define it in the job description and have different expectations. You will need to redefine them during the interview and validate that everyone is on the same page. Many misunderstandings happen later as the employer's expectations do not align with the

CISOs. It would help if you inquired why the previous CISO left or why a new position is now open. Some companies are looking for a unicorn CISO to solve all their problems and pin the security responsibility on someone. Your job is to turn that thinking around and help them realize that you are the enabler of business success by minimizing risks that arise due to security incidents.

Budget

Before you sign up for the job, you also need to address the question of budget. Will the organization provide a dedicated budget to assist you in your job? Will they take your advice in redefining it? Who will you work with to make that happen? A dedicated budget is fuel for your projects; Your advice will never come to fruition without it. Shared budgets with other departments will cause friction.

Resources

Ask about the resources at your disposal. I've seen CISOs quit because they had all the great ideas and roadmaps carved out but no one to implement their plan or support from upper management. You should either be given the authority to build a team like a Builder CISO or already have trained resources at your disposal when you join as a Steady-State CISO. Please refer to Chapter 9 - Types.

Who's Calling The Shots?

People assume that CISOs solely call the shots when it comes to securing the organizations, but without, executive buy-in, budget approval, and resource allocation, their hands can be tied. In some organizations, it is the board of directors who provide final approvals; in others, it's the CFO or the Chief Operations Officer (COO). Depending on the situation, you must know who calls the shots and makes the final decisions. Knowing the influencers is equally important as these are individuals who will help you move the needle in your security initiatives. Without having a clear understanding on the chain of command, you may struggle with getting approvals.

RECOGNITION

At this point, we can either be steady in our jobs or make an impact in the industry. We should never settle for mediocracy. We want to take it to the next level. We want to be recognized as someone that brings value to this industry. To accomplish this, we need to be authentic and not some copycat. We can achieve this by having opinions backed by knowledge and experience. Our words and actions need to have a positive effect. We can put a few more things on our list to accomplish.

Points Of View

By this point in your career, you have worked in many environments, talked to many different people, and experienced various scenarios. You should have already developed strong opinions in certain cybersecurity areas, like the ones mentioned below. These points of views drive you to be a better cybersecurity leader.

- Mapping attacks to defensive techniques
- Breach expertise
- Open-source intelligence
- Privacy
- Law and compliance
- Hacking skills
- Social engineering tactics
- Global politics and nation-state hacker
- DevSecOps
- SOC team development
- Business hurdles
- Healthcare industry
- Startups

The list is endless. Identify your area of knowledge and focus on researching it further.

Without an opinion, you may not be influential, and without someone disagreeing, you're probably not saying anything interesting.

Speaking Events

As part of gaining recognition, you should share your point of view beyond your organization. People love to hear the perspective of an expert. Be involved in a mix of speaking engagements, in-person or virtual, and don't limit yourself to smaller geographic regions. Also, take part in panel discussions. If your request to speak is not accepted, try to attend similar events, ask questions and inquire about the opportunities to collaborate. Interact with the current speakers and the organizers. Eventually, you will have a chance to present your ideas and thoughts.

CISO Mixers

There are many events in cybersecurity that cater to specific roles. For example, security professionals attend events like DEF CON, Black Hat, bug bounty competitions, or capture the flags (CTFs). A broader and more regional event will be local conferences (a.k.a. CONs), or local chapters of Security BSides. Like these, many events also cater to technology executives like CIOs, CTOs, or CISOs, along with partners that have solutions to offer. Think of these as a mixer for CISOs and vendors. These CISO-only events are a great place to network with fellow peers, discuss your ideas, listen to others and, most importantly, form new connections. Getting into these "mixers" is not easy as they are usually invite-only. Your chances increase as you apply and speak at various events. It's all a matter of building yourself to get noticed and getting invited through referrals.

Regional Lists

There are a lot of lists that rank the top 10 or top 100 CISOs in a certain category. This could be by region, industry, age, or anything that can help make more lists. These lists are not a means of rating or ranking you at your job. These are also not some elite lists and don't mean much. They are just another tool for advertisement and recognition; we should use them only for that, not an ego boost. To get on these lists, someone either nominates you or you apply. You can also keep an eye out when a handful of judges are seeking applicants. You need to be in certain networks to know about these opportunities and application dates. If you manage to get listed in an article, it can boost your career.

Peer Recognition

As you develop more contacts through mixers, conferences, or meetings, other CISOs will start to know you and recognize you as an industry leader. As a result, your peer CISOs may reach out to you for advice, recommend you, and invite you to events. All this increases your recognition through your peer network.

BE A GOOD LISTENER

"Seek to understand and then be understood." Steven Covey summarizes this perfectly in his book "The 7 Habits of Highly Effective People."

One of the most challenging parts of a go-getter is that they want to hit the ground running. During the first few months as a CISO, you will need to display a lot of patience as you build rapport and understand the culture. Listening to everyone's concerns about the lack of security or the hindrance that it creates is crucial as it will help you define how you tackle security controls later.

A mistake often made by security professionals is their strategy for enforcing security controls. Being constantly abreast of security threats sometimes makes them believe that over-enforcing security controls is part of doing their job. This may hold some weight but it's also important to consider how it may affect existing processes and user adoption. Listening to your peers, and end-users will help you understand the critical work they do, so you assist them by optimizing security controls. Relevant feedback will help develop a better security culture.

They're Watching

As a CISO, you will often be put on the hot seat as you advise the organization on dealing with security gaps. You will then be responsible for helping the organization make those changes. There is little room for error. When everything goes well, you will get all the praise. However, when things don't go as planned, your performance can be scrutinized. Think of all the breaches and public disclosures and what kind of a spot it put the CISOs in. There have been several high-profile cases of CISOs resigning after a data breach or mishandling of a security incident. Here are some examples:

1. Yahoo CISO Bob Lord resigned in 2017 following two massive data breaches that affected all 3 billion user accounts. Within six months in 2015, Yahoo went through three CISOs.
2. Uber CISO Joe Sullivan resigned in 2017 after the company disclosed a data breach affecting 57 million users. Sullivan also faced criminal charges and was found guilty of covering up the breach.
3. Capital One CISO Michael Johnson was demoted from his role in 2019 after a data breach that exposed the personal information of over 100 million customers.
4. Equifax CSO Susan Mauldin and CIO Dave Webb retired in 2017 following the massive data breach affecting 147 million consumers.
5. JPMorgan Chase CISO Greg Rattray and CSO Jim Cummings were reassigned to new positions in the wake of the 2014 data breach affecting 83 million accounts.
6. Target CIO Beth Jacob resigned after the 2013 breach that affected 40 million customers. Target appointed its first CISO after that.
7. Facebook CISO Alex Stamos resigned in 2018 in relation to the 2016 US Presidential election and the Cambridge Analytica scandal, in which a political consulting firm gained unauthorized access to the personal data of millions of Facebook users.
8. Bed Bath & Beyond's technology chief, Rafeh Masood, resigned in 2022 in the wake of their data breach.
9. eBay CTO Mark Carges announced his resignation after the company suffered a data breach in 2014.
10. The US Office of Personnel Management (OPM) CIO Donna Seymour retired following a series of catastrophic breaches in 2014 involving 22 million records of federal personnel and background check.

These resignations highlight the high stakes and significant consequences that can result from a data breach. It highlights the importance of having robust security measures, being transparent in your strategy, and accountable in the face of a breach.

Watch What You Say

Smart people talk less and listen more because people will disagree and dissect every word you say. Ensure you've thought through about what you want to communicate. It is much harder to retract your words as it is stored almost forever on email or the internet. Think about the long-term consequences of what you say. Your sentences may not be controversial today, but a few years from now, someone may take them out of context and point out your hypocrisy when it hurts you the most.

There's a famous saying, "God gave you two ears and one mouth so that you listen twice as much as you speak." Don't respond immediately to negative feedback from users or management, rather take the time to reflect. If you're posting online or speaking, don't respond to trolls because their goal is to get a reaction and bring you down to their level. Almost every comment can be left unanswered and will not change your message or how people think about you.

Conflict Resolution

Pleasing everybody is not possible. Everybody has opinions about what constitutes "good" security.

Let's first realize that we may make people upset or angry based on our decisions. For example, programmers are touchy about their code. They will not like it when you highlight security holes in their code and ask them to follow best practices. It's like calling their baby ugly. Network engineers may question their own competency when we present gaps or misconfigurations from a vulnerability scan. System Administrators will also not like the additional workload of enabling security features in their systems. Moreover, The CIO may have differing views on tech issues than you. Finally, you may put your partners or vendors in a tough spot when you question their methods.

Territory wars are inevitable. I say this lightly, but I have experienced friction by management or peers related to security initiatives, similar to the examples mentioned above. However, I've been able to resolve them reasonably quickly by following some basic guidelines. Conflict resolution can be handled through different modes of communication, including email, phone, and in-person. Some general principles include:

1. When you respond to an email, read what you wrote at least twice before hitting send. In the heat of the moment, your language may be stern. When you take the time to reread it, you will find yourself rewriting it to tone it down. If an improper email is sent, you risk damaging your relations with the recipient and your reputation in the company. It's not worth giving yourself and others the stress. Be polite and mindful in your responses.

2. Meaning can be lost over email or text, so in-person conversations help to clarify and resolve conflict. Body language, gestures, tone, and expressions also help reveal the story. Phone conversations and in-person meetings can help drop the guard and avoid many back-and-forth emails that may embarrass everyone in a display of authority.

3. Always speak politely and professionally. People forget the content but never forget the tone or how it made them feel.

4. Listen fully before explaining your stance. Don't interrupt. A lot can be misunderstood if you don't let people speak their hearts out first. Speaking last at a meeting gives you the advantage of hearing everyone out and thinking of a better response.

5. Negotiate on finding a mutually beneficial solution. Make some concessions and come to common terms. If you're getting pushback on security policy adoption, clear any misunderstandings. Gradually rolling it out in phases may bring about better long-term adoption. Providing rewards and incentives may also help. Overall, celebrate the smaller wins. They all add up to something bigger.

6. Repeat in your own words what you've understood during the conversation to get clarification. It's common for people to think they understand what another person has said, but maybe a minor detail was misunderstood. Also, asking others to summarize the conversation and what the next steps should be will help get everyone on the same page.

7. Trust in people's abilities and provide them space to do their work as they feel. Don't micromanage them. It helps to be in their roles in past jobs to understand their process. If you haven't been in someone's shoes, don't tell them how to tie their laces.

PREDECESSORS

Some conflicts arise because of disrupting the status quo. For example, when security hasn't been implemented correctly, you will need to address the gaps that eventually get discovered. Blaming a predecessor for their negligence is an easy scapegoat. You will likely not know the conditions under which previous decisions were made. There may have been restrictions or lack of support that you have yet to discover.

First and foremost, blame the process and not the person. Then move forward with your initiatives, considering why they couldn't be implemented in the past. Knowing this will help you form a better remediation plan.

Your peers and other employees may be comfortable with the methods and security culture already established by your predecessors. Therefore, you may face resistance when challenging the established norms. Tread carefully, understand the situation, then plan your initiatives accordingly.

Discovery

Bear in mind that you may discover skeletons. Unfortunately, you will have a partial picture from your predecessor, so you will need to perform a lot of discovery to get started. Moreover, the information that was provided to you during onboarding including current documentation may be outdated.

When performing cybersecurity risk assessments, understand the controls that need to be implemented, and dive deeper into checkbox items in a list. For example, as part of a risk assessment, I once asked a network administrator if they had implemented network segmentation. He confirmed that he configured VLANs. However, when probing deeper, the VLAN ACLs were not in place. As a result, the segmentation policies were not enforced. While we attempt to get the full picture, maintaining a discovery process is essential before executing any initiatives.

Dirty Laundry

Security is a sensitive topic. For example, as a consultant, I reviewed the results of a vulnerability scan with the entire IT team. As a result, the network team mocked the server team for their SSL vulnerabilities, while the server team heckled the network team for their insecure telnet ports. System administrators were also put on the spot for their poor patch management practices. As a CISO, we can handle this better by having dedicated team meetings based on the vulnerabilities. The appropriate teams can perform their responsibilities through collaboration to remediate their respective gaps. In addition, compartmentalizing key information based on a need-to-know basis prevents airing dirty laundry and even data leakage.

LONG-TERM EXPECTATIONS

When budgets get approved and projects are initiated, management may only care about getting the project completed on time. A common question I get asked right after the initial assessment phase is, "How long do you think it will take to complete the project?" Take the time to understand multiple factors and present to management a timeline based on proper justification. Remember that other unknown factors, involving people and processes, may be outside your control.

An approach is to under promise and over deliver. For example, if you can ideally achieve a certain goal in one month, like patching all development servers, add some buffer in your timeline. Consider the hurdles introduced by the engineers, culture, bureaucracy, reviews, legal, and pushback from users or management. You are now looking at an actual completion time of three months but promise them four months to build in a buffer. Setting realistic timelines allows you to get many projects completed over the course of the year while minimizing stress.

Brand Authority

As a CISO, it is vital to understand the distinction between your personal brand and your employer's brand. Your professional brand is how you are perceived in the industry and is built on your skills, experience, and reputation. On the other hand, your employer's brand is the reputation and perception of the company.

While your employer's brand can provide a strong platform to launch your professional brand, it is essential to ensure that you are not exploiting the employer's brand for personal gain. The authority that comes with a widely recognized brand should be leveraged to advance your employer's goals and objectives rather than promote your brand.

It is also important to cultivate your professional brand, as it is essential to your career development. After all, it is your personal brand that got you the job. You can grow it by participating in industry events, networking with other professionals, writing articles and blog posts, and speaking at conferences. Doing so will establish you as a thought leader and a subject matter expert in your field.

However, you should always be mindful of the lines between your personal brand and your employer's brand. For example, when using social media or writing articles, it is essential to clearly indicate that your views are your own and not necessarily those of your employer. By being transparent and ethical in your actions, you will enhance both your personal and employer's brands and establish yourself as a trusted and credible leader in the industry.

Additionally, when speaking at a conference, you should clearly indicate whether you are representing your employer or yourself. If you are representing your employer, you can wear company-branded attire and include the company's logo in your presentation materials. Ensure you have communicated with your management that you will be representing the company as well. By doing so, you will demonstrate your loyalty and commitment to your employer while also establishing yourself as a respected leader in the industry.

As a CISO, the authority that comes with your personal and employer's brand can be leveraged in several ways to advance the goals of the company and to build your brand:

1. **Influence industry standards:** By leveraging your employer's brand, you can have a greater impact on industry standards and regulations. You can participate in industry groups, standards organizations, and policy-making bodies to advocate for best practices that benefit your employer and the wider industry.

2. **Secure partnerships:** Your employer's brand can open doors for partnerships and collaborations with other organizations. By leveraging your authority, you can negotiate favorable terms and secure strategic alliances that benefit your employer and advance your professional goals.

3. **Attract top talent:** Your employer's brand can also make your organization more attractive to top talent. You can use your existing contacts and authority to recruit top-notch professionals and build a strong team to support the company's goals.

4. **Enhance reputation:** By upholding the values and reputation of your employer, you can enhance your own personal brand and reputation. On the flip side, you can also uplift your company's reputation. Many companies hire a new CISO, or Post-Breach CISO, to repair their reputation after a breach.

Remember that with authority comes responsibility. You should always use your authority ethically and transparently, lead by example and act in the best interests of your employer and the wider industry.

SOCIALIZE

As you establish yourself, continue to get to know people. This process never stops. Remember, if you are not already a people person, you need to become one now. Networking skills can be used to discover more opportunities, such as developing partnerships or obtaining new customers. Sharpen this skill by socializing more. Don't miss opportunities to meet people in different settings. For example, company events are great opportunities to meet people in an informal setting. Also, spend time talking to the attendees after a presentation.

Your goal should be to bridge the knowledge gap and humanize the business process. We are all social creatures and communicate best with emotions and stories. Personal stories and experiences allow us to look past titles, roles, and corporate barriers.

PC Culture

"Always be authentic and speak your mind. Be transparent," this is the advice everyone gives to build your brand and recognition. However, there needs to be a balance in how much we open up. We can't say whatever we want, or repercussions can follow.

Today, many more opinionated issues have crept into the tech world than a few decades ago. People are offended much easier and take to social media for support. Many people will often blindly support the boycott of an individual or company without doing any investigation. When the claims are false, it can often spread like wildfire, ruining the person's reputation. These are traits of a cancel culture.

> **Cancel Culture:** Cancel culture refers to the practice of calling out or boycotting individuals or entities for their perceived offensive or problematic behavior or beliefs. It can take various forms, such as social media campaigns, petitions, or public statements.

To avoid getting caught up in cancel culture, carefully consider your actions and words, especially in public forums, and be mindful of how they may be perceived by others. You need to be politically correct (PC), in your choice of words to avoid misunderstandings.

You could also be "canceled" because of something you said in the past that may have been the norm, but views on it may have changed in the present. Unfortunately, people will not look at things in context when referring to personal and professional opinions and will be quick to cancel you. It is the unfortunate reality we live in today. If you find yourself in the midst of a cancel culture campaign, it may be helpful to listen to the concerns and criticisms being raised, and to engage in constructive dialogue with those who are calling for accountability.

Ultimately, navigating cancel culture requires a willingness to listen, learn, and engage in respectful dialogue, while also maintaining personal boundaries and upholding your values and beliefs.

Balance

To effectively express yourself, it's important to strike a balance between authenticity and consideration for others. While it's essential to speak your mind, it's equally important to avoid causing undue offense. Sometimes, it may be necessary to be mindful of certain sensitive topics or adhere to "political correctness" to promote a respectful and inclusive atmosphere. However, this should not hinder meaningful discussions or the exchange of ideas. Remember that pleasing everyone is impossible, but respecting everyone is within reach.

Word Evolution

To align with Politically Correct (PC) Culture, specific terms used in IT and cybersecurity documentation have been updated. Some of the common ones are listed below:

Blacklist	to	Deny list
Whitelist	to	Allow list
Master/Slave	to	Server/Client or Primary/Secondary
Master/Branch	to	Main/Branch
Penetration Test/Pentest	to	Adversarial Emulation or Security Testing
Man-In-The-Middle attack	to	Person-In-The-Middle Attack

Here are some terms I have not found alternatives for yet, like "whitepaper," "motherboard," "daughter cards," "male/female connectors," and "grandfathered plans." Even the word "hacker" is disliked by many. So instead, they insist on either differentiating ethical from malicious hackers or using alternatives like "adversaries" or "threat actors."

> **Note:** Some security vendors have changed words like "blacklist" to "deny list" in their configuration settings.

Attractive Views

We all have opinions or biases that stem from our upbringing, environment, and relationships. We may also like someone more if they share our personal views on a topic we feel strongly about, such as a cause, hobby, or sports team. This can lead us to be influenced by them in their professional life, even if their personal views don't relate to their job. As a security leader, you should be mindful of unintentionally influencing others with your personal views on matters unrelated to security. It's important to separate your personal life from your professional role.

Simple Rule

Whenever you find yourself involved in sensitive discussions or feel compelled to post a comment or reply online, it's best to take a moment and consider three essential questions before sharing your input:

1. Do I have sufficient expertise on this topic?
2. Will my contribution be helpful or beneficial to others?
3. Will my input help to resolve the issue at hand?

If the answer to any of these questions is "no," it's best to refrain from sharing your input, as it may do more harm than good and waste your time.

Some argue that cancel culture is a direct consequence of the excesses of PC culture, where the fear of saying something offensive or politically incorrect has led to an overly cautious and unforgiving culture. Others argue that cancel culture is a separate phenomenon, driven by a desire for accountability and social justice, and that it can be an effective tool for holding powerful individuals and organizations accountable for their actions.

While there's no one-size-fits-all approach to navigating PC culture and cancel culture, and the best way to proceed may vary depending on the situation. However, you should educate yourself on different perspectives, listen to others, and apologize if you inadvertently offend anyone.

REMOVE FILTERS

As a CISO, understand that you play a crucial role in an organization's security. Your primary responsibility is to provide an honest and realistic assessment of the organization's security posture to leadership. This includes providing a worst-case scenario, as well as being politically correct and respectful. In addition, it's essential to be transparent and avoid sugar-coating the risks and vulnerabilities. By presenting a clear and realistic picture, leadership can make informed decisions to address and mitigate potential threats.

However, being honest and upfront may challenge the status quo or question past decisions. Nonetheless, you must communicate the truth to protect the organization's security. When a breach occurs, the CISO is the one who is held accountable, and it is crucial for the CISO to be able to say, "We did our best," while providing proper justification.

SME

In becoming a CISO, you learned how to navigate through your struggles. Now, as a subject matter expert (SME) in cybersecurity leadership, you must continue sharing your knowledge and experience in your field. People look to you for guidance and insight, and by sharing your expertise, you can maintain your reputation and continue to be a trusted source of information.

Additionally, you can work with other SMEs to collaborate on projects, co-author papers or presentations, or participate in roundtable discussions. This can help you build a network of peers and expand your knowledge base.

You can further enhance your reputation and impact as a subject matter expert by continuously educating yourself, sharing your knowledge, seeking feedback, and practicing ethics and professionalism. By doing so, you can continue to be a valuable resource for others and maintain your credibility.

SELF-ANALYSIS

As you run gap analysis on the organization's cybersecurity posture, you should also evaluate your skills to determine the best approach to take when it comes to performing your duties effectively. This is known as self-analysis. The goal is to use your strengths to make meaningful changes in the organization, while understanding your weaknesses and working on improving them.

Self-analysis is a crucial step for a new CISO in establishing a baseline for their approach. This can help you hit the ground running and establish a strong reputation from the start. Here are some examples of what you can do during a self-analysis:

1. **Assess your skills and experience:** Identify your areas of expertise and where you can improve. This will help you understand where you can contribute most effectively to the organization and identify areas where you may need external support or additional training.

2. **Evaluate your leadership style:** Determine your leadership style and assess its effectiveness in different situations. This will help you understand how to lead your team and interact with stakeholders. Popular examples of leadership styles include transactional, servant, and transformational.

3. **Assess your communication skills:** Evaluate your ability to communicate complex technical information effectively to non-technical stakeholders. This will help you determine how to articulate your ideas best and ensure that your message is understood.

4. **Identify internal resources:** Seek out internal resources that have expertise in areas where you may have weaknesses. This will help you mask those weaknesses while still getting the job done with internal support.

5. **Seek feedback:** Ask for feedback from colleagues, peers, and past managers to understand your strengths and weaknesses better. This will help you identify areas to improve and further develop your skills.

Self-analysis allows you to focus on your priorities, strengthen relationships, and better align with organizational goals. Overall, self-analysis can help CISOs start on the right foot and positively impact the organization from the beginning.

Buy-In

From a CISO's perspective, getting buy-in from upper management for security initiatives can be challenging, as they may not have the time or interest to fully understand the details. To overcome this, the CISO should focus on gaining the trust of upper management and presenting security as a business enabler rather than a cost center. This can be done by communicating the benefits of security measures and demonstrating how they can positively impact the company's overall goals and objectives. Additionally, the CISO should work to streamline and simplify the process for upper management, making it as easy as possible for them to support security initiatives.

Gaining buy-in from upper management is crucial for a CISO to maintain their position and carry out their responsibilities. For example, the CISO is responsible for ensuring the security of sensitive information and protecting the company from potential cyber threats. Without buy-in and support from upper management, the CISO may struggle to allocate the necessary resources, implement security measures, or enforce security policies. Additionally, a lack of buy-in from upper management can make it difficult for the CISO to effectively communicate the importance of security and educate other employees on best practices. This was one of the previously cited reasons for why CISOs depart from organizations.

If a CISO is unable to get buy-in from the board of directors on security initiatives and budget, they can try the following strategies:

1. **Risk:** Demonstrate the risks and costs of not investing in security: The CISO should provide clear, concise, and data-driven information about the potential risks, costs, and impact of cyber threats on the business. This will help the board understand the importance of security initiatives and budgets.

2. **Alignment:** Align security initiatives with business goals: The CISO should present security initiatives and budgets in the context of the company's overall goals and objectives, demonstrating how they will help the company achieve its strategic objectives.

3. **Support:** The CISO can also reach out to other stakeholders in the company, such as department heads, to gather support for security initiatives. This can help build a coalition that can make a more compelling case to the board.

4. **Collaborate:** The CISO can also collaborate with other departments, such as finance, to find creative solutions for funding security initiatives. For example, the CISO could work with the finance department to identify cost savings or cost-neutral initiatives.

5. **Alternatives:** If the board is unwilling to allocate funds for security initiatives, the CISO can explore alternative funding sources, such as grants or partnerships with other organizations.

Ultimately, as a CISO, you must continue making a compelling case for security initiatives and budgets, demonstrating their value and importance to the company. With persistence and the right approach, it may be possible to overcome resistance and secure the necessary support and resources.

CREATE A TEAM

A CISO needs to create a trusted team to carry out their responsibilities and effectively meet their goals. A team can provide support, resources, and expertise and help the CISO navigate the organization and overcome any challenges they may encounter. Therefore, the CISO should make a concerted effort to build a diverse team that includes internal and external resources and cultivate strong relationships with team members.

A great way to build those relationships is by involving team members in meetings to brainstorm or validate your ideas. Additionally, you need to remove their concerns about getting replaced and get them on your side. With open communication, the CISO can build a sense of ownership and engagement among team members and help overcome any concerns about technology or their competencies. By doing so, the CISO can build a strong, collaborative team that will help you inch closer to your goals.

SOW YOUR SEEDS

To be successful in your long-term initiatives, you need to sow the seeds of your ideas with the stakeholders. This allows them to be mentally prepared for projects and budgets before you ask for their approval. You can achieve this in several ways:

1. **Building awareness:** Develop a clear understanding of the problem you are trying to solve and build awareness of the solution among stakeholders. This can include creating presentations or informational materials that explain the solution and its benefits.

2. **Building a coalition:** Network with others in the organization who have a similar interest in the solution and can support your efforts. This may include seeking out allies in the IT department or other business units with a stake in the solution's success. Reaching out to vendors or industry experts who have experience in similar solutions can help your cause.

3. **Piloting:** Consider piloting the solution in a limited scope before full implementation. This allows you to demonstrate the solution's benefits and gain stakeholders' buy-in.

4. **Gathering data:** Gather data on the solution's potential impact and conduct a cost-benefit analysis. This data can help you build a business case for the solution and provide stakeholders with the information they need to make informed decisions.

5. **Communicating regularly:** Regular communication with stakeholders can help build momentum and buy-in for the solution. This may include workshops, presentations, or other communications that build momentum and buy-in for the solution.

If presented right, planting these ideas in the minds of decision-makers and your peers early on can reduce the chances of resistance and influence their decisions into considering its adoption.

ENDORSEMENTS

You didn't make it here by endorsing products or companies. You made it because of your skills, determination, and hard work.

Products and solutions change all the time. Their message changes, ownership changes, and prices go from free to paid. Additionally, acquisitions by some companies can alter your opinions, shifting your attention towards alternatives. Whatever the case, you should be careful before publicly endorsing a product or company, as the internet never forgets. One wrong decision can come back and haunt you years later and make people question your judgment.

For example, if you endorse a technology product like a password manager, it could increase visibility and credibility for the product and yourself. However, if the product doesn't live up to its promises or experiences security or other issues, your endorsement could reflect poorly on your judgment and credibility.

Instead, if you endorse a company's values, like the right to privacy, it could demonstrate your commitment to those values and align you with the company's mission. On the other hand, if the company's actions no longer align with its stated values, like being acquired by a marketing company that begins to sell user data, it could put you in a bad spot again.

The potential consequences of endorsements can vary widely depending on the context. So, always take your time in doing your research when supporting a cause, product, or company.

The Blame Game

You might wonder if CISOs are to blame when there's a security breach. CISOs are human and have many challenges in their role. It's not fair to place all the blame on the CISO if a security breach occurs, as they cannot operate without buy-in from stakeholders and operate within certain limits. With the complex technology and increasing risks, a CISO does not have a magic wand to fix all security holes or prevent attacks. Unfortunately, CISOs have been taking the blame for breaches. This mindset is wrong and needs to change.

The culture in organizations also needs a shift to be more proactive and introduce security at the design phase. Security is everybody's responsibility, and it's time for employees in the enterprise to know that they play a big role in creating a "Security First Culture". It takes a collective team to solve the security problem. Unfortunately, CISOs sometimes enter an enterprise with false promises, unrealistic goals, and a flapping cape that backfires. As part of a CISOs influence, they are there to empower, educate, and channel security through different teams.

CISOs can find themselves in a difficult situation while navigating the challenges of budget, limited resources, or internal conflicts. The situation can worsen with a breach. What can we do to avoid being in a tough spot? There are a couple of guidelines we can present that are applicable at different stages to minimize the damage when an incident happens.

Pre-Breach

1. **Set expectations:** As mentioned in the first part of this chapter, setting realistic expectations will bring key stakeholders on the same page and better help them understand your situation when dealing with security incidents.

2. **Get everyone on your side:** Educating your peers on your roles and responsibilities will go a long way. Creating those valuable relationships within the organization will give you the support you need when stressed and under the gun.

3. **Due Diligence:** Keeping the stakeholders aware of your achievements will help them know that you are doing what you promised. If a breach still happens during your building efforts, you cannot be blamed, as you had a plan and were on track.

Post-Breach

1. **Respond quickly and effectively:** Implement the incident response plan, contain the breach, and mitigate any harm to the organization and its assets.

2. **Analysis:** Analyze what happened, where we are now, and how to get back to normalcy. An Incident Response team should be on standby to assist with the analysis. At this point, your incident response plan document, and tabletop exercises will come in handy. It will allow you to focus on a speedy resolution rather than going into panic mode.

3. **Transparency:** The best thing you can do after thoroughly analyzing the situation is to be transparent about the incident. If you've done your due diligence up to this point, you should not be afraid of any consequences. It's important for the stakeholders to be informed about the scope of the breach, including details such as how the adversaries gained access, what measures could have been taken to prevent it, and the steps being taken to restore normalcy. When the company serves clients, the clients also have a right to know. Some companies may choose not to let their clients or the public know about a breach. The story will eventually leak from an employee or the hackers will let everyone know by posting the details online. This can end up ruining a company's reputation. Before a breach is made public by hackers or media, you have the first opportunity to present your statements in alignment with management and public affairs committee hoping for some reputational damage control. People will sympathize after the anger subsides. Public trust may get shaken up initially, but people will remember how you handled the situation in the long term.

4. **Lessons Learned:** Once the dust settles, you should have a lessons-learned session with the affected teams. This should not be the time for finger-pointing. Instead, conduct a post-incident review, identify what went wrong, and make a list of remediation steps to prevent similar incidents from happening again.

The due diligence and thoroughness you put into the process will protect your reputation in adverse situations.

How to Stay

CISO Turnover

A CISO's success in a company is determined by their commitment to the company's well-being. The average tenure of a CISO is only 18-24 months, but those who stay longer often leave a lasting impact. It's important to consider what will be remembered about one's role as a CISO after they leave the company. Did they make a significant impact on the company's security and did they create a positive perception of security within the organization? These small contributions can lead to bigger and long-lasting rewards. It's also crucial to continually work on improving one's strengths and address weaknesses to ensure growth in the role.

Beating The Average

When you align yourself with the company's vision, values, and objectives, you get support from the business owners. Once you have stakeholder support, you are motivated to see your goals achieved. Here are some things you can focus on to stay longer in your position and not become the average.

1. **Making an impact:** A CISO should focus on positively impacting the organization, such as implementing new security measures that improve overall security posture or successfully responding to security incidents. A CISOs success will motivate them to do more.

2. **Professional growth:** Staying at a company for extended periods can lead to professional growth and career advancement opportunities. CISOs can continuously learn and develop new skills, which can help them take on new challenges and responsibilities.

3. **Foster relationships:** Building strong relationships with key stakeholders, such as the board of directors, C-suite, and other executives, can help create a supportive work environment and increase job satisfaction.

4. **Alignment with organizational goals:** The CISO should align their goals with those of the organization so they feel invested in its success and motivated to stay for the long term.

5. **Work-life balance:** Finding a good work-life balance can help reduce stress and increase job satisfaction, making it easier to stay long-term. The company will usually be very accommodating if you communicate your particular needs.

6. **Embrace change:** The security landscape is constantly evolving, and a flexible mindset open to change and innovation can help the CISO stay relevant and effective.

Takeaway

Wow, You Made It! There is so much to think about as a CISO. Your ability to communicate security controls and requirements, internally and externally, to your peers, clients, vendors, and shareholders will be crucial to your success.

Treat everyone like a customer. Your professionalism and due diligence will help you earn the respect of your peers and stakeholders and better equip you to translate security needs into actionable plans for the organization.

22. PREDICTIONS

The only thing constant is change

With technology constantly evolving, what was once considered cutting-edge can quickly become outdated. The security landscape is no exception; new job roles are created as new threats emerge and companies adjust their strategies to keep up. Yet, despite its maturity, the Chief Information Security Officer (CISO) role still has room to grow and evolve. In this chapter, we will explore predictions expected to shape the future of the CISO role and provide insights on how to stay ahead of the curve.

REPORTING STRUCTURE

Most CISOs report to either the CTO or CIO if the company's strategy is technology focused. If the organization prioritizes information security, the CISO will usually report to the CEO or some combination of the board of directors. The CISO has a unique role with a lot of responsibility and accountability yet is restricted in terms of authority to make critical decisions. If we are to make decisive decisions and have a chance to defend against witty attackers, we must empower the CISO.

The entire cycle of assessing risk, convincing stakeholders, devising solutions, approving budgets, investing in solutions, and securing the organization takes too long. When a security control finally goes into place, it may become ineffective as newer and better options become available. This has always been the struggle with IT, and security is dealt with similarly, even though IT and cybersecurity have different goals. While the two departments should work closely, their processes should be separate.

Consider a scenario where a CISO reports to a CIO. In this reporting structure, the CIO's main responsibility is to ensure the efficient functioning of the organization's systems, while the CISO is responsible for ensuring the safety and security of those systems. However, this creates a conflict of interest, as the CIO may prioritize system efficiency over security, while the CISO may prioritize security over efficiency. Additionally, the CIO may not fully understand the security risks involved in a decision and may veto a decision made by the CISO. As a result, it's recommended that the CISO should report directly to the CEO or the Board of Directors, ensuring that security decisions are made independently and with the organization's best interests in mind.

Steve Jobs said, "It doesn't make sense to hire smart people and tell them what to do. We hire smart people, so they can tell us what to do." A CISO is hired by the company to tell them how to secure their organization from cyber threats.

I see progressive companies empowering CISOs with the same authority as CEOs, CIOs, or COOs as they realize that a CISO is also part of the business process. This empowerment will be more prominent with entrepreneurs who are not afraid to adopt unconventional management styles and be proactive in risk mitigation. A CISO will eventually be at par with any other C-level executive position. Some companies are testing the waters with CISOs as part of the board; This is where they belong as they need to be a part of the corporate strategy when discussing risk.

Free Reign

For decades, security leadership has been very conventional. Old-school methods are no longer working. We are losing the battles with our adversaries. Hackers often have no qualifications, yet we focus on technical skills, certifications, and university degrees for our security teams. Our focus must shift away from slow, obsolete, and expensive credentials for defending ourselves. We need to look at it from a hacker's perspective. Breaking these boundaries of unconventional methods work, and more entrepreneurs are adopting a free-reign CISO structure led by progressive leaders.

As the new generation of security leaders rises, we see a shift in their approach. They are less micromanaged and given the autonomy to achieve results the way they deem most effective. This approach allows for more innovative and nimble decision-making, and the ability to explore new and effective methods for defending against cyber threats. New threats require new ways of thinking. For example, we see companies that "hack back," explore and monitor the dark web, investigate using private cyber threat intelligence firms as their first option instead of relying on the government or law enforcement agencies, contact peer groups for advice, and generally take responsible actions and remediation steps in their own hands.

RESPONSIBILITIES

A CISO currently has a lot of responsibilities. A quarter of this book talks about the various skills and duties that fall under the realm of any CISO. As we modernize this role, some of these responsibilities will shift, and new ones will need to be added. Some examples of a CISO's changing responsibilities include the following:

1. **Third-Party Security:** As organizations increasingly rely on third-party vendors, the need for security oversight and management becomes more pressing. To preempt supply chain attacks, the CISO may assume responsibility for ensuring the security of these partnerships.

2. **Employee Awareness:** In order to keep pace with the changing threat landscape, employees must stay up to date on best practices for information security. There can be no justification for failing to prioritize security. It may fall to CISOs to spearhead efforts aimed at improving employee awareness and proficiency in security matters.

3. **Staying ahead of the curve:** The technology landscape is in a state of constant flux, and solutions that were popular yesterday may quickly become outdated. For CISOs, it is crucial to keep abreast of the latest technological advancements, including Cloud technology, Artificial Intelligence, and beyond. To remain ahead of the curve and meet the challenges of innovation, CISOs must stay current on industry trends, participate in forums and discussions, and continuously seek out new information and insights.

4. **Risk Landscape:** The need for effective risk management will only increase as organizations become more digital. As a result, CISOs are expected to play a more strategic role in mitigating and managing risks to the organization. The CISO will need to collaborate with multiple lines of defense and intake risk management activities to make proper decisions for the company. The CISO cannot be siloed and must have a proactive approach across domains to managing risk with fellow collaborators.

Some responsibilities become less relevant as new technologies and approaches are developed. For example, as automation becomes more widespread, some manual tasks, such as security incident response, pentesting, and vulnerability management, may become automated. This could reduce the need for a CISO to be heavily involved in these tasks, freeing time for more strategic initiatives. Additionally, as artificial intelligence and machine learning become more advanced, they may play a more significant role in threat detection and response areas. This could shift the focus of the CISO's responsibilities away from low-level technical tasks and towards more strategic initiatives such as risk management and security planning.

Ultimately, the future role of the CISO will depend on the evolving threat landscape and the development of new technologies. Therefore, the CISO must be proactive in staying current and adapting their responsibilities as needed to ensure the ongoing effectiveness of the organization's security efforts.

SIMPLE DECOYS

Artificial Intelligence (AI) and Machine Learning (ML) in security products have become popular approaches for many organizations looking to improve their security posture. However, despite their usefulness in automating many security tasks, these technologies have limitations and can be easily bypassed by determined attackers.

For example, attackers have been able to evade AI and ML-based security controls by using zero-day exploits or developing novel attack techniques that are not yet known to the security community. In addition, they will often use social engineering attacks that exploit human vulnerabilities to bypass security protocols.

To address these limitations, modern CISOs are adopting a hacker's mindset and using similar tactics to defend their organizations. They recognize the value of simple yet effective security solutions that can level the playing field and make it more difficult and expensive for attackers to carry out successful attacks. These may include tactics such as reducing the attack surface by minimizing the number of entry points into an organization's systems and networks or placing decoys within the many layers of defenses that make it difficult for attackers to move laterally within the environment. The goal is to make it expensive for the hacker in terms of time, expertise, and resources.

Most breaches today are a result of a lapse in basic security practices. As a result, CISOs are focusing on basic security best practices, such as regularly updating software, implementing strong passwords with multifactor authentication, and restricting access to sensitive information.

By taking these simple steps, modern CISOs can reduce the attack surface and make it more challenging for attackers to succeed. This can help ensure their organizations are better protected against the ever-evolving threat landscape.

The following sections discuss some unconventional methods security teams are starting to use that will become mainstream soon.

Security Through Obscurity

Security through obscurity is generally considered to be a weak form of security. Obscurity refers to the practice of relying on secrecy or hiding information to protect a system or network, rather than implementing strong security measures such as encryption or access controls. Obscurity can sometimes provide a layer of security, but it is not a reliable or sustainable security strategy on its own. Attackers can often use various methods, such as social engineering or reconnaissance, to uncover obscured information and gain unauthorized access to a system. Therefore, relying solely on obscurity as a security measure can leave a system vulnerable to attacks.

On the other hand, security through obscurity still has some advantages. For example, it's common practice in web security to hide a website's resources, especially the login page. This prevents an attacker from trying brute force attacks with stolen credentials on the login page. For example, most internet websites run on WordPress, the most popular Content Management System (CMS). Its default admin login page is: www.example.com/wp-admin

Hackers run scripts on the internet that go through millions of websites to look for that wp-admin Universal Resource Identifier (URI) and try a common list of usernames and passwords until they get a hit. However, they can't initiate this attack if they're unable to find the login page. This concept is known as security through obscurity. For example, one could set the login page to: www.example.com/MyHiddenLoginPage007. This adds another layer of security just through hiding and misdirection.

It is important to note that a website and all its resources need to be downloaded in the browser to display a website. So, it's not always possible to hide code. At the same time, security professionals take obfuscation techniques to the next level by obscuring all sorts of things. For example, putting misinformation in code comments, error pages that leak false information, dummy email addresses hidden in code for bots and scraping tools to pick up, obfuscated code that is not used anywhere, and DNS entries that reveal information that misdirects hackers. All this is to waste a hacker's time with minimum effort from our side.

Honeypots

Honeypots are decoy systems or networks set up specifically to distract and lure attackers away from critical systems and data. They are designed to mimic a target environment, such as a Windows or SQL server, and are configured to appear as vulnerable systems or services attractive to attackers. When an attacker targets a honeypot, security teams can observe the attacker's actions and gain valuable intelligence about the attacker's tactics, techniques, and procedures (TTPs).

We've known about honeypots for a while now. Lately, I've seen them on clients' networks during penetration tests. Honeypots waste an attacker's time, giving them false hopes while alerting the SOC team and providing them with more time to get rid of the threat. Moreover, they help contain attacks. If an attacker targets a honeypot, security teams can isolate the attacker and prevent the attack from spreading to other systems and networks.

Honeypots can be a valuable tool for security teams looking to gain a deeper understanding of attacker behavior and improve their overall security posture. However, it's essential to deploy and manage honeypots carefully, as they can also attract malicious actors and expose sensitive information if not properly secured.

While honeypots are not a new technique, they will become mainstream with the availability of freely accessible open-source software (FOSS), combined with one-click deployments and easy tutorials. I won't be surprised if popular security frameworks include them in their next revision.

Canaries

Hackers are getting smarter at evading detection tools by MDR or SOC providers. Canaries are like tripwires in a network. Hackers will go straight for the data. Like honeypots, canaries present an opportunity to provide some bait to hackers but also get notified of their presence in real-time. For example, suppose someone opens an Excel document with the name passwords.xlsx that contains a canary. In that case, it will trigger an email alert to the administrator notifying them that someone has accessed that file.

Companies are now beginning to take this very simple technology approach for better alerting. Canaries can be inserted in databases, web URLs, files, executables, or folder paths. Additionally, they can be fake user accounts or decoy data. These get triggered with an unauthorized scan or directory traversal during the reconnaissance phase of a hacker. Catching them early in the attack phase gives us a better chance of deterring the attack.

Canaries are a proactive way for security teams to detect potential breaches and take action before sensitive information or systems are affected. They can also be used to detect when an attacker is attempting to bypass security controls, providing an early warning system to the security team. Overall, canaries are an effective tool in a modern security team's arsenal and can help enhance an organization's overall security posture.

There are a few companies and open-source projects that offer canary services. Something as simple and effective as canaries should be part of every organization, small or large. You will see more of these techniques either offered as services or baked into products.

Fighting Fakes with Fakes

Social engineering is a preferred tactic among hackers when targeting individuals. They often use professional networking sites such as LinkedIn to gather current user information. By creating fictitious profiles, complete with AI-generated images, hackers engage employees in conversation, manipulating them to extract confidential data. One effective defense is to create a phony LinkedIn profile for a fictional employee within the company. This decoy profile not only thwarts hackers' attempts by engaging them in meaningless conversations, but it also serves as a phishing trap that automatically flags any emails containing suspicious links or money transfer requests. Security teams are immediately notified of the phishing attempt, and the phishing domains are blocked. Moreover, this strategy can serve as an instructive moment for other users, highlighting the importance of remaining vigilant when dealing with unknown contacts.

The potential impact of this could be significant. It's worth noting that hackers often invest a significant amount of time in scouring social media platforms to gather information about a company long before they launch an attack. Stopping them at this early stage can be a highly effective way to thwart their efforts. To mislead attackers, some companies have resorted to posting bogus job descriptions that include requirements for experience in non-existent products or technologies. As a next step, artificial intelligence technologies could be deployed to automate communication with fake profiles, thereby engaging the attacker in a never-ending loop.

As defenders become more creative in their use of decoys, we can expect to see an increase in the use of obfuscation techniques to add an additional layer of protection to networks and systems, making it more difficult for attackers to carry out successful attacks.

PRIVACY

What isn't stored cannot be breached.

Privacy and security go hand in hand. They complement each other. The less data you store, the fewer chances of anyone stealing it. Data privacy will become an integral part of a CISO's responsibilities. While a Chief Privacy Officer (CPO) or a Director of Privacy will have their role and place in specific organizations, there is plenty of overlap with the security practice. As if the CISO already didn't have enough responsibilities, privacy will need to be rolled up under a CISO to create better synergy for data protection.

With the rise of data breaches and cybercrime, more and more regulations around data privacy are being implemented across the fabric of organizations, like GDPR in Europe and CCPA in California, to name a few. Therefore, a security professional must have a good handle on the details and how to incorporate them into the security practice.

Privacy protection can be broadly categorized into two domains:

1. **Personal Data Privacy:** This domain involves protecting the privacy of personal information, also known as Personally Identifiable Information (PII), such as names, addresses, social security numbers, health records, and financial information. This requires following data protection regulations such as GDPR or HIPAA, and implementing appropriate security measures to prevent unauthorized access, use, or disclosure of personal data.

2. **Corporate Privacy Policies:** This domain ensures the privacy of an organization's sensitive information is protected, such as trade secrets, financial data, and confidential communications. This information requires strong security measures, such as access controls, encryption, and monitoring of sensitive data, as well as establishing and enforcing corporate privacy policies that govern how sensitive information is collected, stored, and used.

Some reasonable privacy practices that can be implemented for securing an organization include:

1. **Data Minimization:** Collecting and storing only the minimum amount necessary for a specific purpose reduces the amount of data vulnerable to breach or misuse. For example, a company should not collect and store sensitive information, such as social security numbers, unless it is essential for the business process. Even for client verification purposes, such as date of birth, the software could store a hash of the information, which is a cryptographic equivalent, instead of the actual data. This approach would confirm the accuracy of the date of birth without retaining the actual information.

2. **Strong Security Measures:** Encryption, access controls, and other security measures can help protect sensitive data from unauthorized access and misuse. For example, a healthcare organization could encrypt patient data when stored and only allow authorized personnel to access it through secure, encrypted channels.

3. **Privacy by Design:** Implementing privacy protections at every stage of the data processing lifecycle can help ensure that sensitive data is protected from the outset. For example, a financial services company could implement privacy by design principles by conducting privacy impact assessments before launching new products or services and regularly auditing their data practices to identify and address any privacy risks.

4. **Transparent Data Practices:** Being transparent about the data collected, how it is used, and who has access to it can help build trust with customers and partners and reduce the risk of data breaches and cyberattacks. For example, a tech company could provide clear and concise privacy policies that explain how customer data is used and protected and regularly communicate updates to these policies to customers.

Zero-knowledge providers are a great example of companies that respect privacy. These companies don't store any data about you that they don't need in order to provide you with the service. They purge their logs frequently and implement end-to-end encryption so even they cannot see the contents. When breached or accessed by internal employees, they see nothing useful, just anonymized metadata required for functionality. Furthermore, their business model is transparent. They don't sell your data to be abused by third-parties. You will often see such companies produce open-source applications so that their code can be publicly audited.

A CISO will require skills encompassing data transparency, public audits, privacy laws, data collection, and optout procedures.

CISO-as-a-Service

The quickest way for organizations to hire a CISO is through a service that rents or leases a CISO. This is also known as a Virtual CISO or vCISO. As the demand for CISOs increases exponentially, the ratio of vCISOs also increases significantly as compared to traditional full-time CISOs. Smaller and mid-sized companies are also looking towards similar security advisory services primarily due to cost and flexibility.

A vCISO is known for their ability to get quickly and effectively started on the job. Since they often work with multiple clients, they are always fully engaged and responsive to the unique requirements of different organizations. Unlike a permanent employee, they do not have any personal interest in the company, and they are solely focused on delivering results. As a result, they are able to provide unbiased and objective judgments without being influenced by internal politics or biases. These qualities make vCISOs particularly appealing to the next generation of leaders and companies, as they provide an accelerated approach to handling security risks, despite facing many of the same challenges as traditional CISOs.

Takeaway

As time passes, the roles and duties of a CISO can undergo alterations, and it is our duty to identify trends and stay informed on how organizations are handling their security stance under the guidance of a CISO. This chapter covers some predictions regarding the evolving role of a CISO. It's noteworthy that the responsibilities will keep transforming and adjusting in response to emerging challenges.

23. CONCLUSION

Drop by drop creates a river

This book has comprehensively covered various aspects of cybersecurity leadership to offer a well-rounded approach. It is always beneficial to periodically revisit your overall goals and objectives, review the bigger picture, and reflect on why you began this journey and where you ultimately hope to end.

Breaking down the daunting task of becoming a CISO into smaller, manageable pieces is key. By focusing on one aspect of the role at a time, improving one skill after another, and understanding the various elements involved, you can gradually gain a deeper understanding of the role.

There is no one-size-fits-all solution; many paths lead to the position of CISO, and there are various types to choose from. However, the journey becomes easier with a positive attitude and the support of a strong network. This structured approach also benefits existing CISOs, allowing them to realign and become stronger leaders, paving the way for future generations.

WHAT'S NEXT?

At the beginning of the book, we noted that a CISO sits at the apex of the cybersecurity hierarchy. The CISO is responsible for overseeing the organization's information security efforts and steering it towards a state of stability and predictable outcomes. So, where do you go from here?

You can't be a CISO forever. The job has stress, burnout and is usually short-lived. CISOs may choose to pursue careers in related fields, using their experience as their most valuable asset. The following are some ideas for a great career transition.

Stability

The journey of most CISOs typically involves advancing from one CISO role to another, which may repeat several times. They often move laterally to other CISO positions. Ultimately, many CISOs aspire to settle into a role on the board of directors, which offers greater stability than the fast-paced and high-stress nature of the CISO role. Some may pursue board positions at startups as co-founders or advisors, seeking a change of pace and a move away from the constant pressure of the CISO role. With a demanding job, taking steps towards a balanced and sustainable career path is essential.

Educator

Many former CISOs choose to transition into the role of an educator, leveraging their expertise and experience to share their knowledge with others in the field. They may take on roles as instructors, trainers, or speakers, providing training and education on cybersecurity, risk management, and information security. This allows them to continue making a difference in the industry while reducing the stress and demands associated with being a CISO.

By sharing their expertise and experience with others, they are helping to shape the industry's future and advance the knowledge and skills of those who follow in their footsteps.

Prepare The Next Generation (CISO-ng)

A leader's role is ongoing, constantly evolving, and requires effort and attention. As a CISO, you are responsible for guiding your organization toward stability and predictable outcomes in terms of cybersecurity. However, at some point, you will need to hand over the reins to a successor and transition into a different role. This can be challenging and uncertain, especially if you are one of the many CISOs with a relatively short tenure in their role.

As more CISOs reach the end of their careers or move into less hands-on positions, the need for skilled and experienced leaders in the field of cybersecurity becomes increasingly critical. This is why leaders need to start thinking about the future and preparing the next generation of CISOs early in their careers. In addition, by sharing your knowledge and experience with others, you can help to build the capacity of the next generation of leaders and ensure that your organization continues to be well-protected against the threat of cyberattacks.

In the last five to seven years of their careers, some CISOs transition into great mentors, sharing their expertise with others and helping to guide the next generation of leaders. By taking on a mentorship role, they can continue to contribute to the development of the cybersecurity field and positively impact the future of their organization and the industry as a whole. Whether through formal or informal mentorship programs, speaking engagements, or other initiatives, former CISOs can play a vital role in shaping the future of the cybersecurity field and ensuring that it continues to grow and evolve in a positive direction.

No matter what path you choose for yourself, remember the struggles you went through and try to remove the thorns from the path of those that will walk in your footsteps.

INDEX

Artificial Intelligence, 224
Attitude, 105
Auditor, 12
Breaches, 47
Budget, 31, 200
Burnout, 138
Buzzwords, 158
Canaries, 226
Cancel Culture, 209
CCPA, 51, 227
Certifications
    CEH, 144, 192
    CISSP, 54, 192, 195
CFO, 20, 30, 57, 200
CFP, 94, 186
CIS Controls, 53
CISO Mixers, 201
Communication, 83
Conflict Resolution, 204
CTF, 101
Cyber Insurance, 33, 57
Cyber Resiliency, 37
Defense-In-Depth, 49, 98
Deputy CISO, 78

Echo Chamber, 152
Emotional Intelligence, 91
Entry Level, 144
Ethnic Bias, 150
Fines, 51
Frameworks, 52
Gatekeepers, 65, 136
GDPR, 51, 227
Hiring, 17, 96
Honeypots, 225
Imposter Syndrome, 117, 125
Influence, 59
Job Description, 195
Kill Chain, 99
Layoffs, 180
Leadership, 88
LinkedIn, 110, 186
Mentorship, 68, 111, 145
Negotiation, 174
Networking, 109
NIST, 51
Non-Profits, 31
Overconfidence, 132
Pentest, 56

Policy Documentation, 16
Privacy, 227
Professional Jealousies, 116, 149
Project Management, 79
Public Speaking, 94, 185
Recognition, 148, 200
Regulators, 61
Remote Work, 168
Reporting Structure, 221
Resignations, 203
Risk Analysis, 27
Risk Assessment, 55
Salary, 173
Security Awareness, 14, 24
Security Culture, 17
Shift Left, 42
S-SDLC, 56
Strategy & Tactics, 61
Swag, 35
Toxicity, 90, 105
vCISO, 22, 76, 229
Vendors, 34, 158
Wasta, 112
Writing, 93

www.PhantomCISO.com

Printed in Great Britain
by Amazon